IMAGES of America

PIKE COUNTY

On the cover: **LUMBER DAYS.** Lumbering was a huge part of Pike County's early days. This was a common scene in most townships and boroughs where sawmills and timber yards provided lumber for the immediate and outlying areas. The early daredevils of the county floated the lumber down the often dangerous and unpredictable Delaware River to points as far as Trenton and Philadelphia. (Courtesy of Pike County Historical Society.)

IMAGES
of America

PIKE COUNTY

Lori Strelecki

ARCADIA
PUBLISHING

ISBN 978-0-7385-6562-0

Published by Arcadia Publishing
Charleston SC, Chicago IL, Portsmouth NH, San Francisco CA

Printed in the United States of America

Library of Congress Control Number: 2009924685

For all general information contact Arcadia Publishing at:
Telephone 843-853-2070
Fax 843-853-0044
E-mail sales@arcadiapublishing.com
For customer service and orders:
Toll-Free 1-888-313-2665

Visit us on the Internet at www.arcadiapublishing.com

Contents

ACKNOWLEDGMENTS

The main source of the images included in this publication, aside from where noted, are from the fabulous archives of the Pike County Historical Society.

The society has been a major photographic contributor to other Arcadia publications, pertaining to Pike County and the surrounding areas, by other authors. The history of Pike County is colorful, diverse, and interesting. The people who make up its history are equally engaging. Although the Pike Historical Society is the official historical society of the county, it is merely a hub for the gathering and preserving of the history that encompasses the entire county. It is with much thanks that I acknowledge the Bushkill Historical Society, the Dingmans Ferry Delaware Township Historical Society, and our county historian George Fluhr for their willingness to help with this publication. It is also vital to thank all the people who have carefully documented our county's history in the past, and those who continue the documentation through present day, in particular, Charles Quilici, Mim Carpenter, Roxanne Scott, Lynn Heller, Noel McCullough, and Danielle Schneider.

It is their love of history that keeps it alive and well in old Pike, and their stewardship that keeps the records safe and sound within the walls of our respective societies.

INTRODUCTION

When Pike County was established in 1814, it consisted of just five townships. Today's Pike County is home to 13 boroughs and townships, each of which boasts their own beauty and identity. While each one of these townships and boroughs have played an interesting and intricate part in the county's rich history, there have been several publications over the years that have detailed the events and places that make up the whole county. This publication is geared to highlight some of the most interesting and quirky occurrences, even those that may be slightly controversial, in an attempt to bring to light the personality and color that make Pike County of note. The chronological history has not been a consideration, as I do not dub myself a historian; there are many others, both past and present, that are better qualified to do such, and I thank them for their hard work. This book will, hopefully, give the reader a more intimate look at the people places and events that shaped the county.

Pike County is a publication that started out with much ambition and sought to cover all of the county's history through images. In setting out to complete the project, I realized how much information we had on some townships, and how little on others. While the photograph collection of the Pike County Historical Society is quite vast, it primarily depicts Milford, Dingmans Ferry, Lehman Township, Milford Township, and Shohola. Although there certainly are enough pictures to fill this book from those places, I humbly apologize for the lack of depiction of the rest of the county. I plan on initiating a drive to collect photographs from the areas in which we are lacking in the near future so I can sleep better at night knowing each township and borough is equally represented within the archives of the county museum.

That said, it is my intention to tell a story, through photographs, of the people, places, and events that formed Pike County's interesting history. I am not a historian, in the sense that I do not so much dwell on dates and names, but focus on the feeling of an era, an event, or a place. History is of interest to me for its ability to remind us that things were not always as they are now, and for the value of knowing about the things that happened before our time. Because of this, we can gauge the change in so many aspects of today's society.

So please enjoy your trip through Pike County in days past. It is not all hearts and flowers, for in each life a little rain must fall.

One

The County

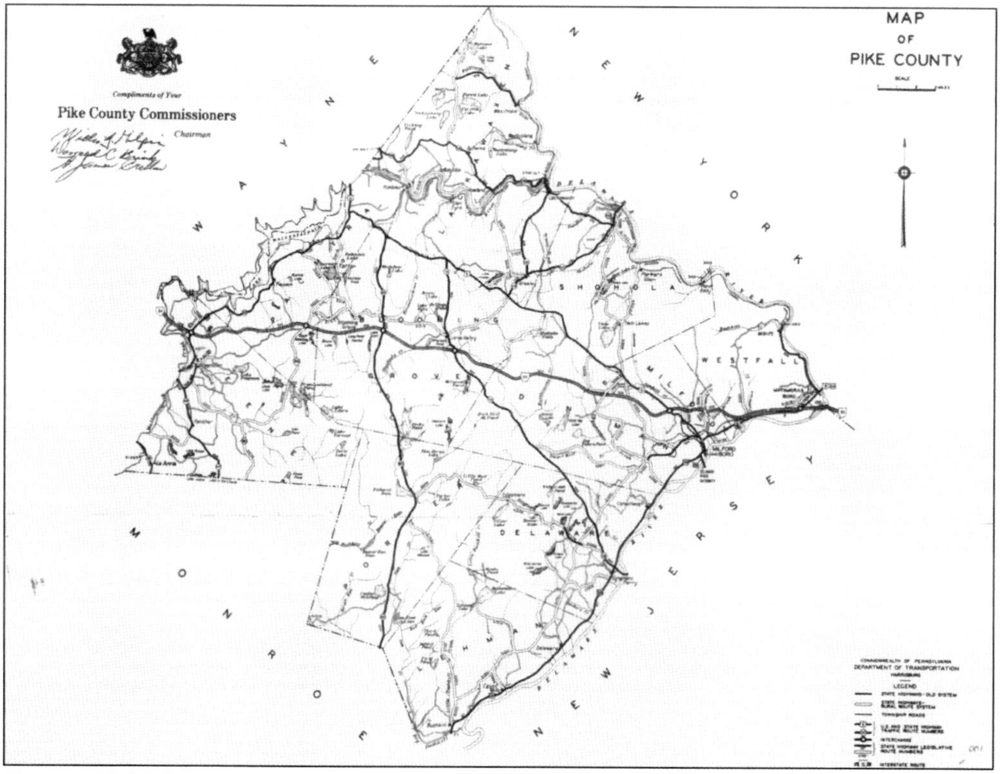

ORIGINS. Pike County separated from Wayne County on March 26, 1814. It then was comprised of the townships of Middle Smithfield, Delaware, Upper Smithfield, Lackawaxen, and Palmyra. Lehman Township was added in 1829, Dingman Township and Milford joined the ranks of Pike in 1832, Greene and Westfall in 1839, Blooming Grove in 1850, Porter Township in 1851, and Shohola in 1852. Matamoras and Milford Boros came about later in time. The names Smithfield and Middle Smithfield fell by the wayside, leaving the 13 townships and boroughs that make up current-day Pike County.

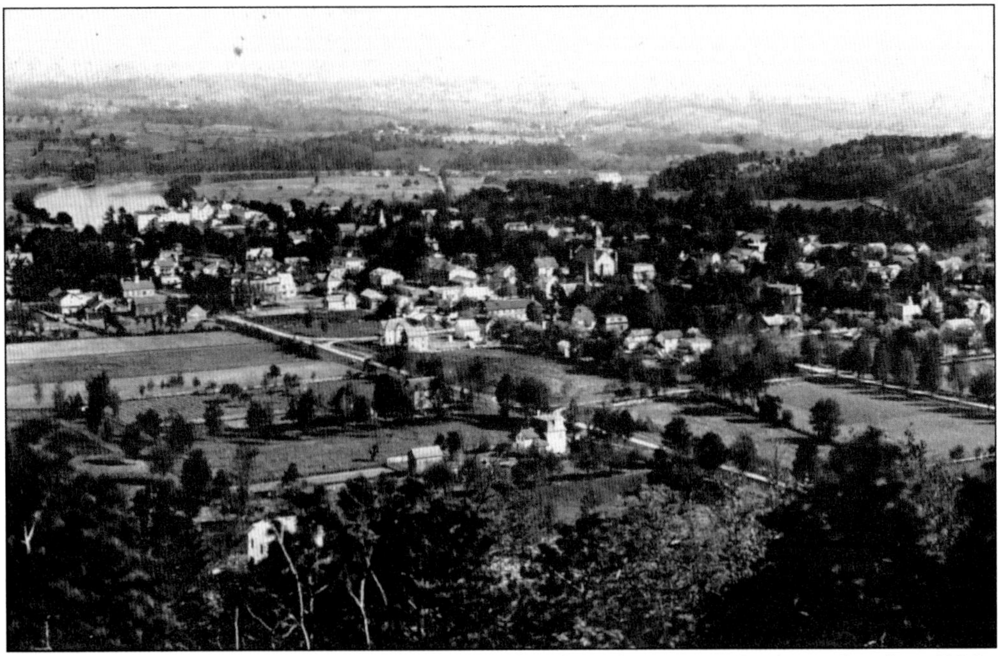

MILFORD. Milford Township and Borough is worthy of much coverage. In the mid- to late 1800s, it emerged as a favorite locale for city folks seeking refuge. Its small-town charm and ability to cater to tourists made it a popular destination, both past and present. This view of the town, taken from what is known as "the knob," allows for the viewer to understand the beautiful surrounding areas, filled with mountains, streams, rivers, and waterfalls—all just a short distance from the village.

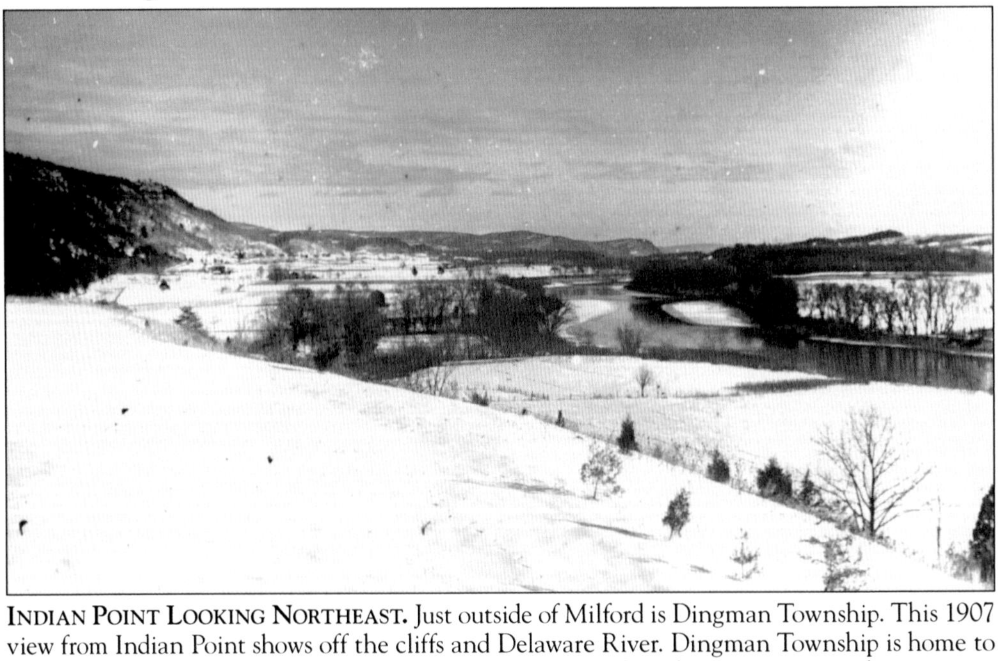

INDIAN POINT LOOKING NORTHEAST. Just outside of Milford is Dingman Township. This 1907 view from Indian Point shows off the cliffs and Delaware River. Dingman Township is home to many significant places in Pike County's history, including the Silver Spring House home to one of the oldest brewery's in Pennsylvania and the Beaver Lake Camp for Boys.

Upper Glen, Bushkill, Lehman Township. Bushkill, in Lehman Township, is known for farms and waterfalls. Bushkill Falls are a popular tourist attraction in season. Other places of note include resorts such as Tamiment, and the once-popular retreat for garment workers from New York City known as Unity House.

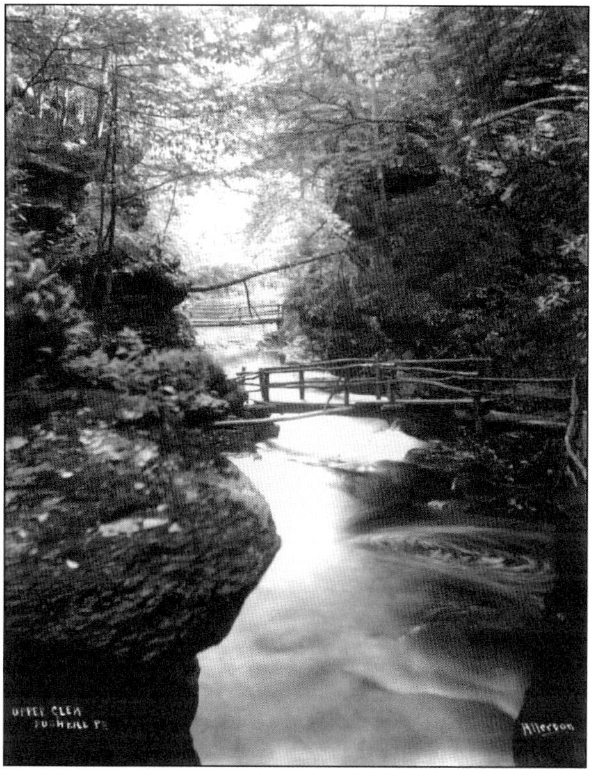

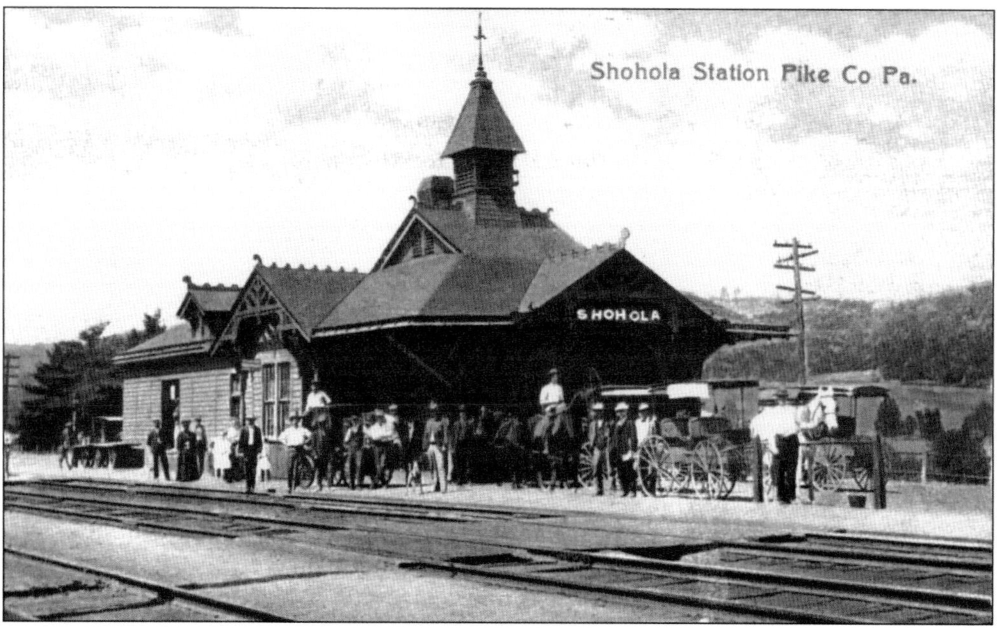

Shohola Railroad Station. Shohola's history is quite diverse and interesting. A popular retreat from the city life, it was accessible by way of the Erie Railroad. During the Civil War, a train carrying prisoners of war wrecked near the Shohola station, and the many wounded were taken to a local inn and tavern that was transformed into a makeshift hospital to treat the injured men. The dead were simply buried along the tracks.

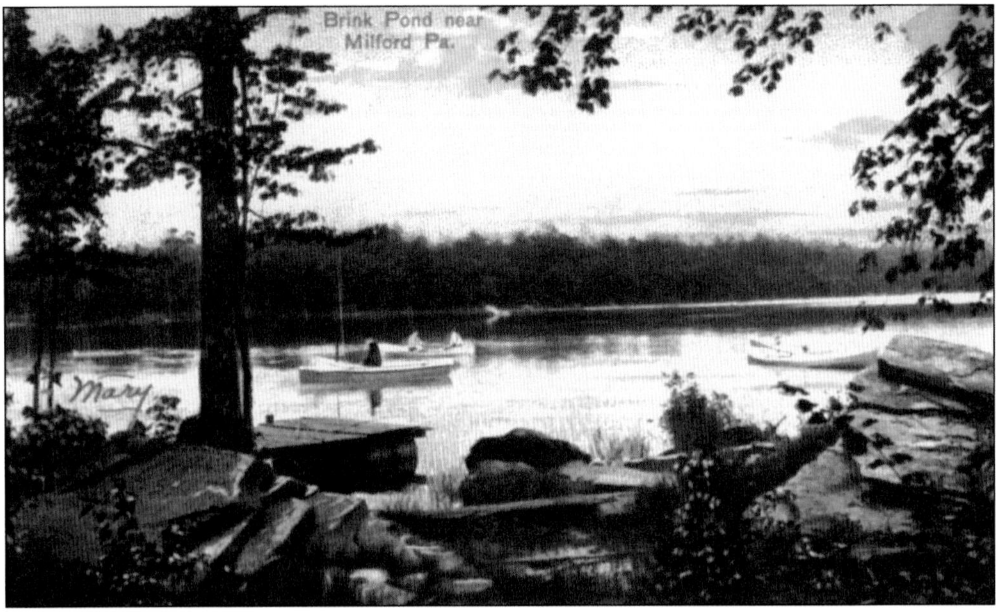

TWIN LAKES/BRINK POND, SHOHOLA. Although located in Shohola, an area known as Twin Lakes has become an entity in and of itself. The little and big lakes that make up this beautiful area were once called Brinks Pond. An inn called the Watson House was a popular tourist destination, and an early account recalls a story of a movie being filmed in the area that called for a bear to be involved in a scene. Watson himself agreed to row the bear across the lake to the Watson House. The bear did not take too kindly to the trip and took a few swats at Watson. Both the bear and Watson recovered from the experience.

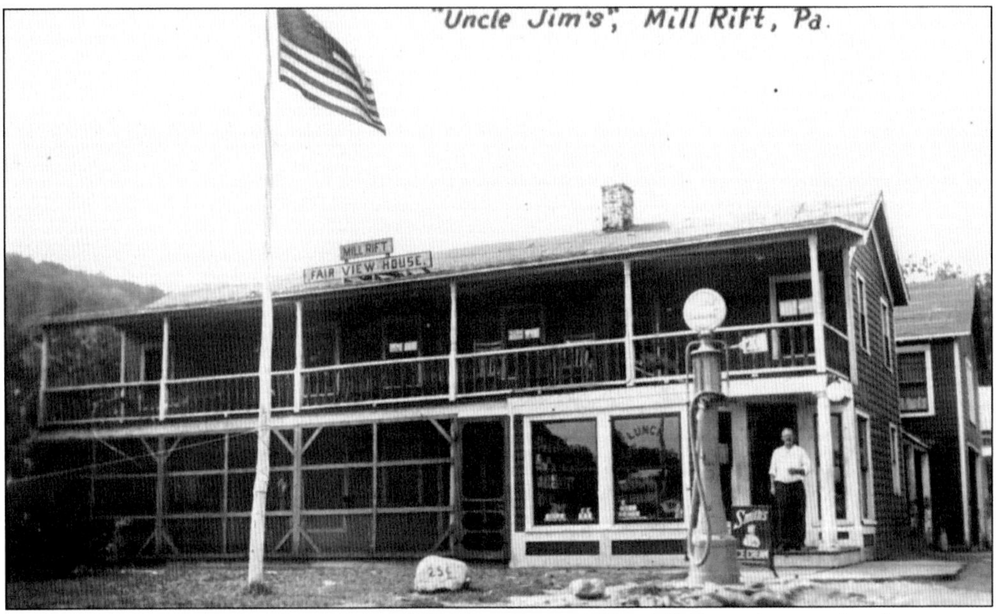

"UNCLE JIM'S" MILL RIFT, 1930. Mill Rift, a part of Westfall Township, is the destination after a winding, picturesque drive along the Pennsylvania side of the Delaware River. The town consists of little more than an inn and a post office but was once a popular stop for raftsmen in the days of the lumber industry.

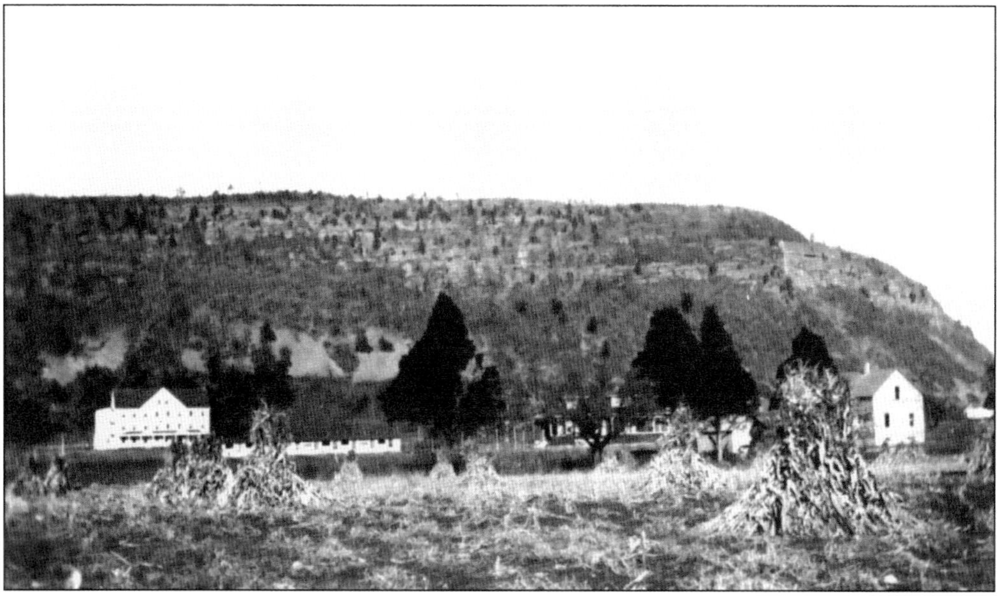

MATAMORAS MOUNTAIN. Matamoras Borough was incorporated in 1905, and it joined Milford Borough as one of the two boroughs in Pike County. Early settlers in the area found the access to the Delaware River both a curse and a blessing. Native American attacks put the Dutch farmers ill at ease, and they often only farmed the Pennsylvania side of the river, while living in New York or New Jersey. Today the area is primarily residential with the cliffs and bluffs along the Delaware River allowing spectacular views.

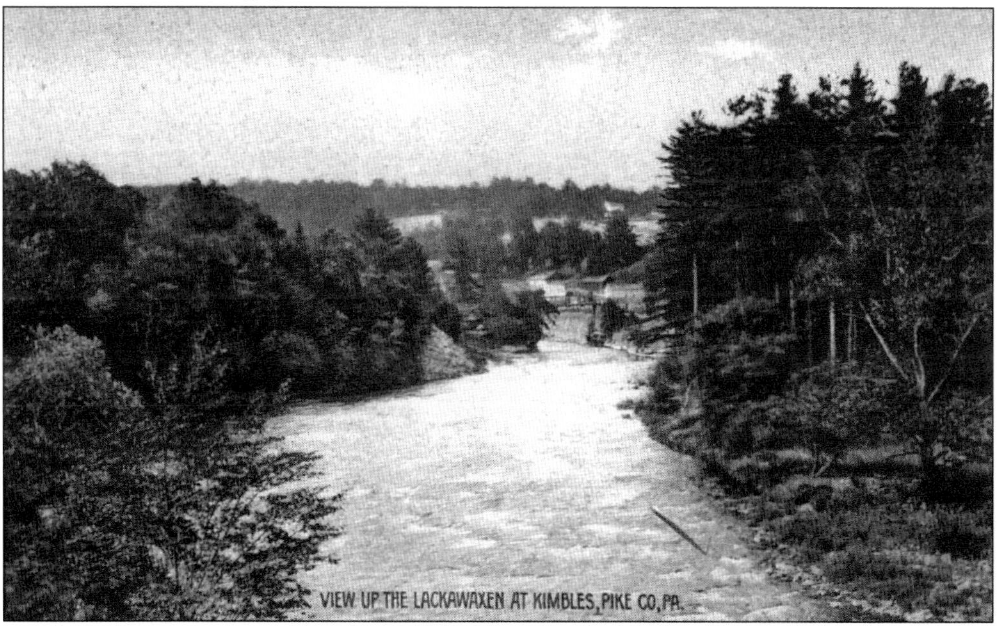

LACKAWAXEN RIVER AT KIMBLES. Lackawaxen Township was named for the Lackawaxen River, which meets the mighty Delaware River and provided early rafters and loggers with a byway to the Delaware. Smaller rafts called colts were used to navigate the wild flowing river, and the word *Lackawaxen* is Native American for "swift waters." At one time, 28 locks on the Delaware and Hudson Canal were located in Lackawaxen.

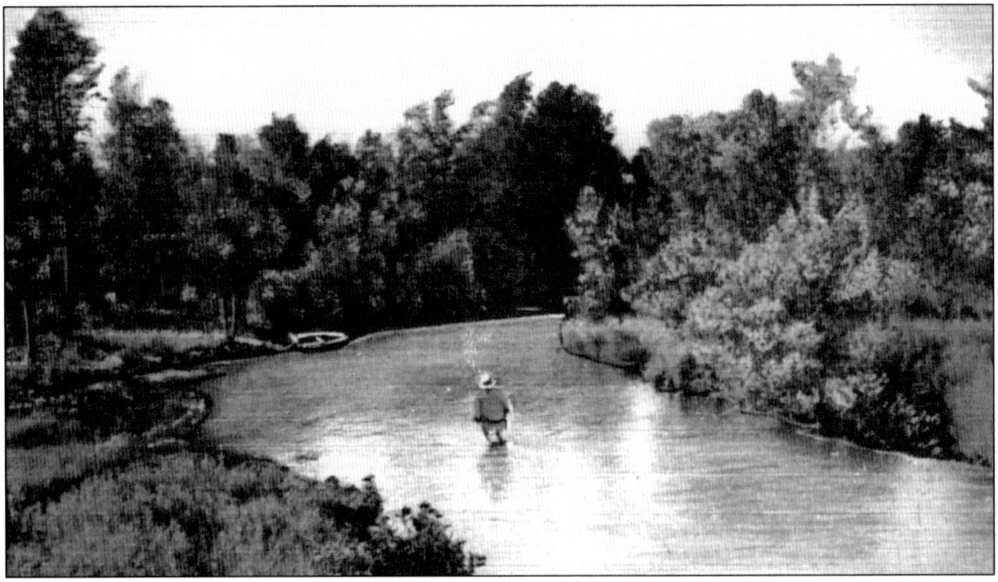

PROMISED LAND LAKE, GREENE TOWNSHIP. Trees and bees are what Greene is noted for. Dense evergreen and hardwood forests make up a majority of the township. There were no honey bees in America during Native American times, as the Europeans brought them over. They were known as "the white man's fly" according to the original settlers in Pike, the Lenape Indians. Greene's blossoms were a favorite of bees, and their attraction to the area was taken advantage of by beekeepers.

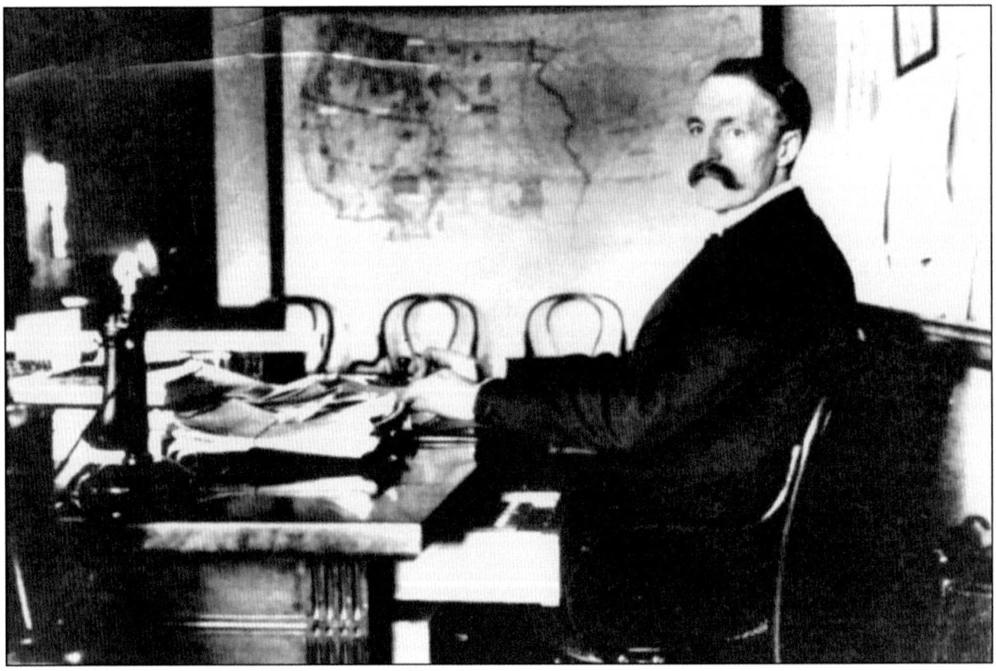

GIFFORD PINCHOT IN PORTER TOWNSHIP. In 1921, Gifford Pinchot, then commissioner of forestry, created Delaware State Forest by comprising all of the state forest's reserve holdings in both Pike and neighboring Monroe County. That allows for about 60 percent of Porter to be within state forest boundaries. Washington Irving visited the area and nearby Honesdale in 1842.

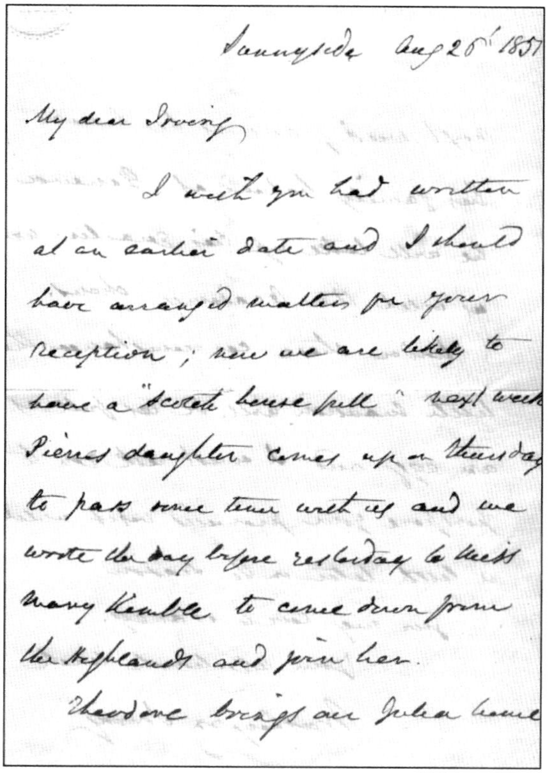

Sunnyside Aug 26th 1857

My dear Irving,

I wish you had written at an earlier date and I should have arranged matters for your reception; now we are likely to have a "Scotch house full" next week. Pierre's daughter comes up on Thursday to pass some time with us and we wrote the day before yesterday to Miss Mary Kemble to come down from the Highlands and join her.

Theodore brings on Julia home

LETTER FROM WASHINGTON IRVING. Pictured here is a letter from Washington Irving, who visited Pike County.

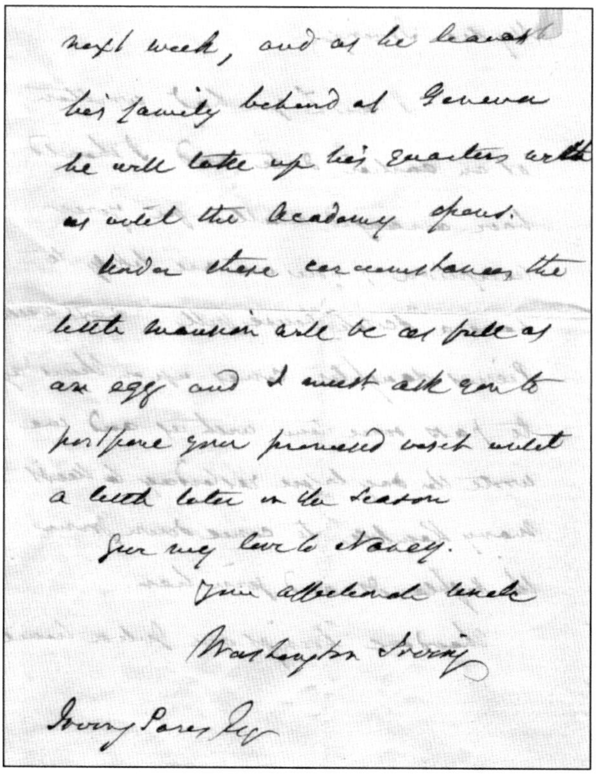

next week, and as he leaves his family behind at Geneva he will take up his quarters with us until the Academy opens.

Under these circumstances the little mansion will be as full as an egg and I must ask you to postpone your promised visit until a little later in the season.

Give my love to Nancy.

Your affectionate uncle

Washington Irving

Irving Paris Esq

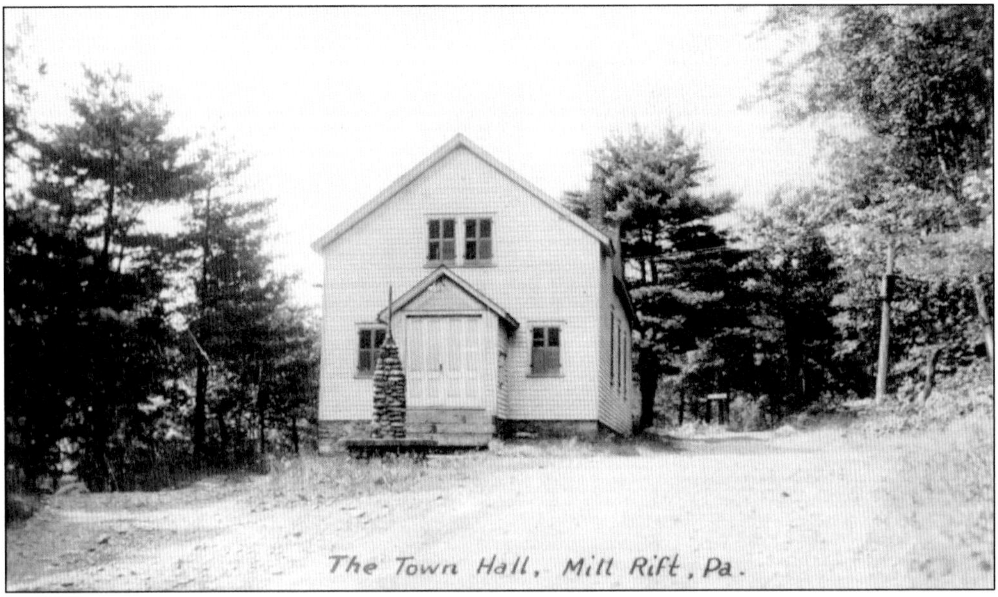

TOWN HALL OF MILL RIFT. A Part of Westfall Township, Mill Rift erected a town hall in 1905. The Mill Rift Literary Association funded the project.

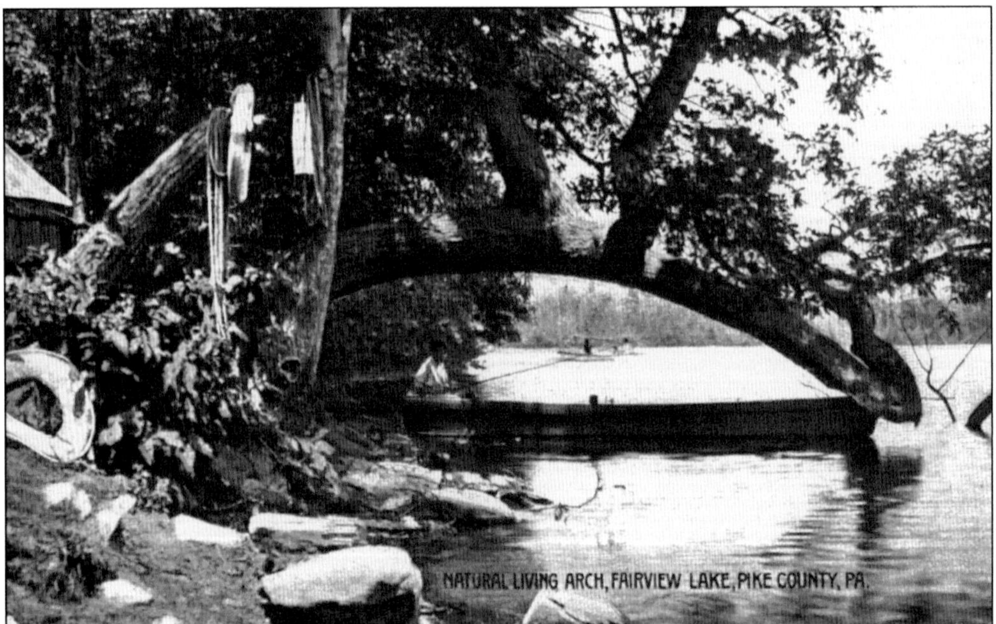

FAIRVIEW LAKE, PALMYRA TOWNSHIP. Palmyra Township is one of the oldest in both Wayne and Pike Counties. Both counties share the name Palmyra for this area. It originated in Wayne, but joined Pike in 1814. Fairview Lake is a natural lake noted for a variety of fish.

Two

WHERE TO STAY

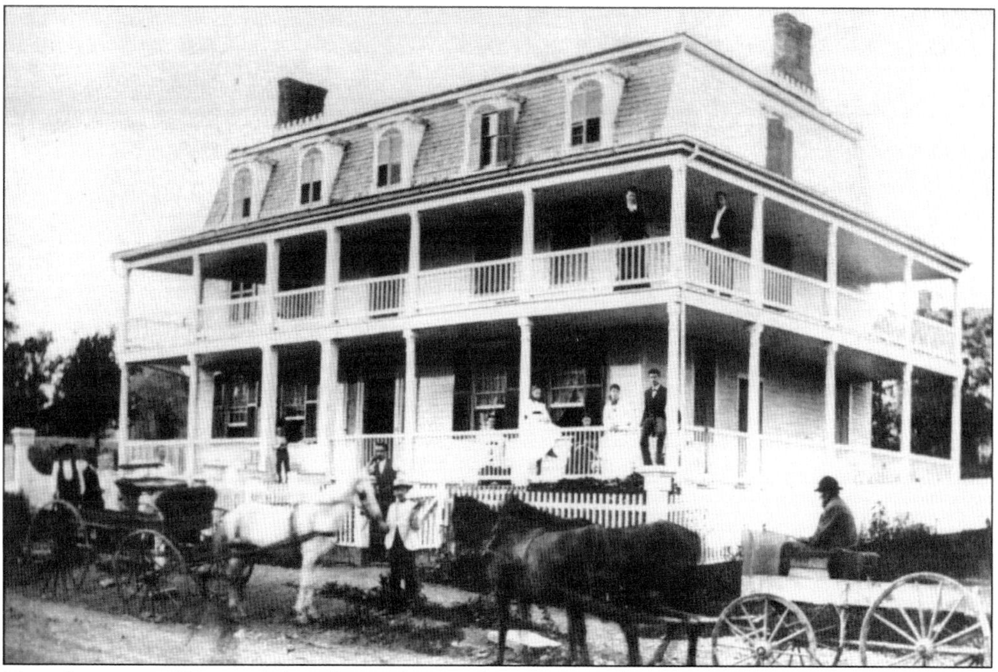

THE JARDON HOUSE. Pike County's popularity as a destination increased through the mid- to late 1800s. Early inns and boardinghouses that once catered to raftsmen and lumbermen expanded their hospitalities to visitors of all kinds. Attracted by fresh air, mountains, streams, and fabulous waterfalls, many city folk chose to recreate among Pike's flora, fauna, and fluviarchy. The Jardon House could house 30 guests, and the rates in the mid-1930s were $3 per day and $12–$15 per week. F. X. Jardon, the proprietor, described the place as "centrally located and offering French cuisine."

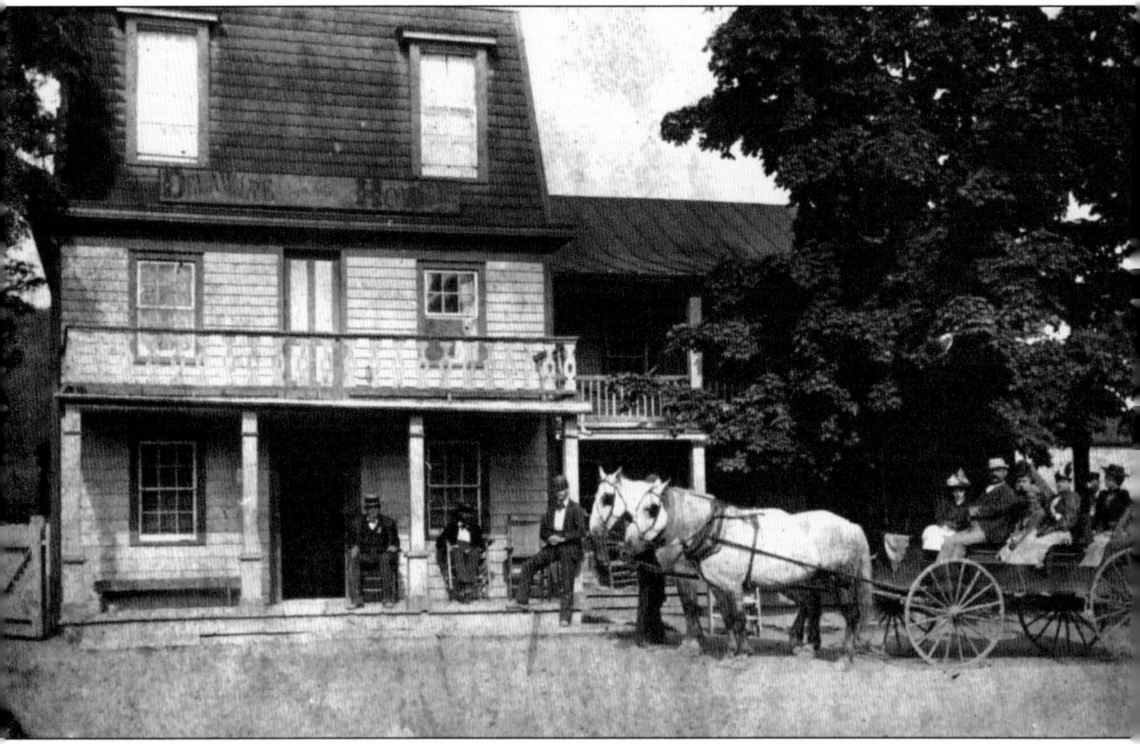

THE DELAWARE HOUSE, DINGMANS FERRY. The Delaware House opened in 1866. It was known to be the center of much of the town's activity. Early owner John Lattimore was charged with selling liquor without a license and to minors. The inn changed hands in 1870, and its reputation was cleaned up by new owner Randall Van Gordon. The Delaware House was a favorite stopover for cyclists in the 1890s. In 1902, it could accommodate 20 guests, and the rates were $7 a week or $1.25 a day.

DELAWARE HOUSE ADVERTISEMENT, 1866. In its early days, the Delaware House's front porch saw many a poker game and meeting of "malcontents." In the 1870s, the Delaware House hosted cycling clubs such as the Scranton Bicycle Club, Brooklyn Bicycle Club, and the Wissahickon Wheelmen of Germantown.

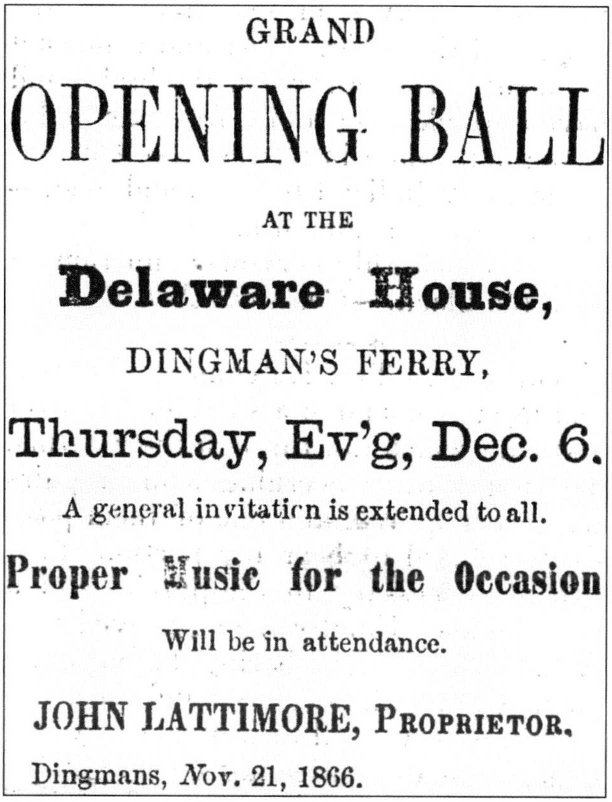
GRAND

OPENING BALL

AT THE

Delaware House,

DINGMAN'S FERRY,

Thursday, Ev'g, Dec. 6.

A general invitation is extended to all.

Proper Music for the Occasion

Will be in attendance.

JOHN LATTIMORE, PROPRIETOR.

Dingmans, *Nov.* 21, 1866.

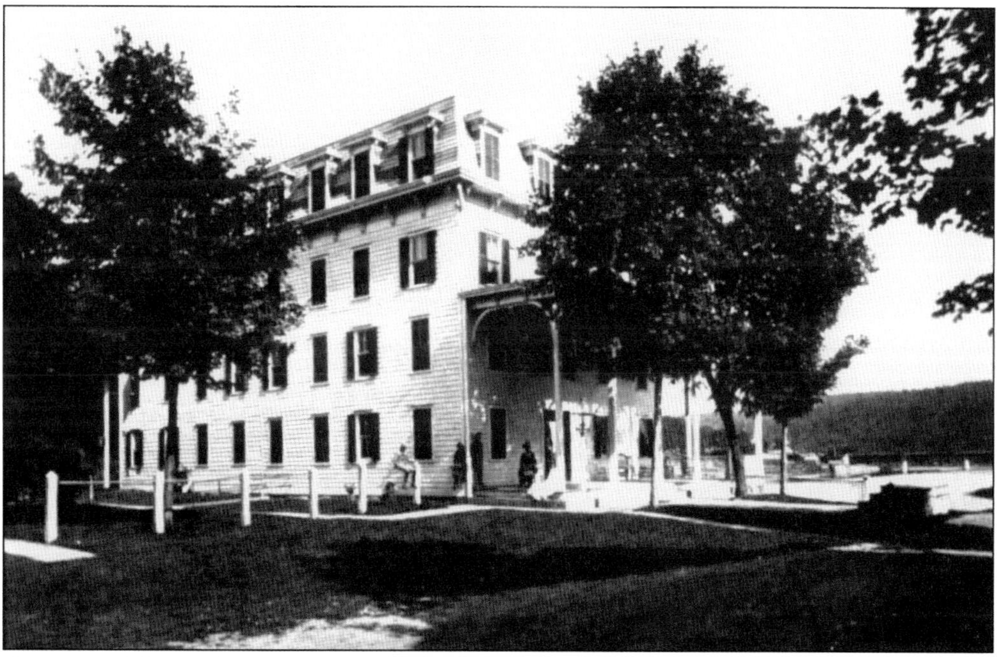

DELAWARE HOUSE, LACKAWAXEN. Not to be confused with the other Delaware House, this one, located in Lackawaxen, was named for the river, while the previously mentioned was named for the township.

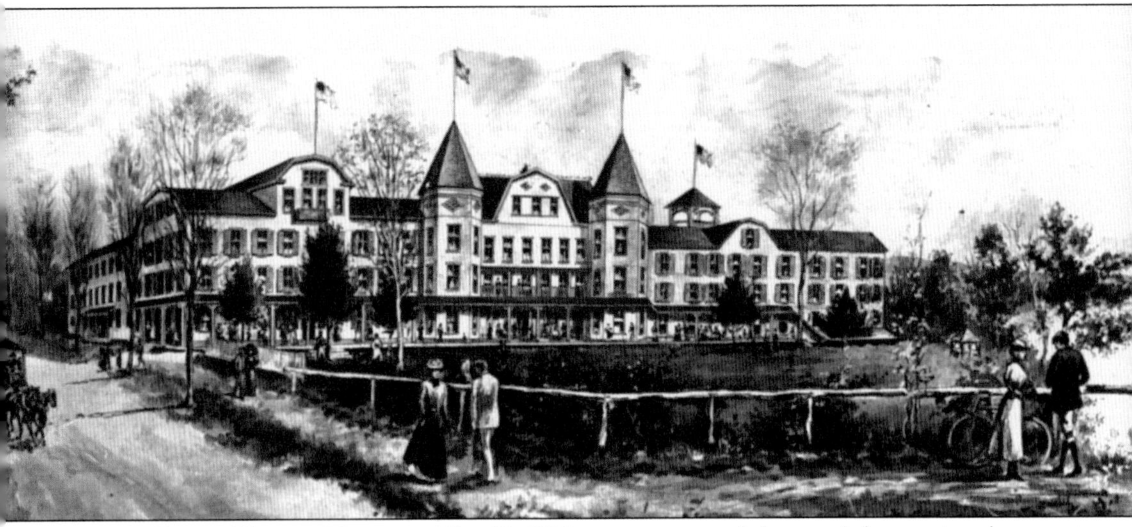

THE BLUFF HOUSE, MILFORD. The Bluff House was one of the area's largest inns/resorts; it could accommodate 350 people. P. N. Bournique was the proprietor, and rates in the 1930s were $3 per day and $15 per week. The Bluff House offered boating, bathing, fishing, and lawn tennis, as well as music and dancing, bowling, and billiards.

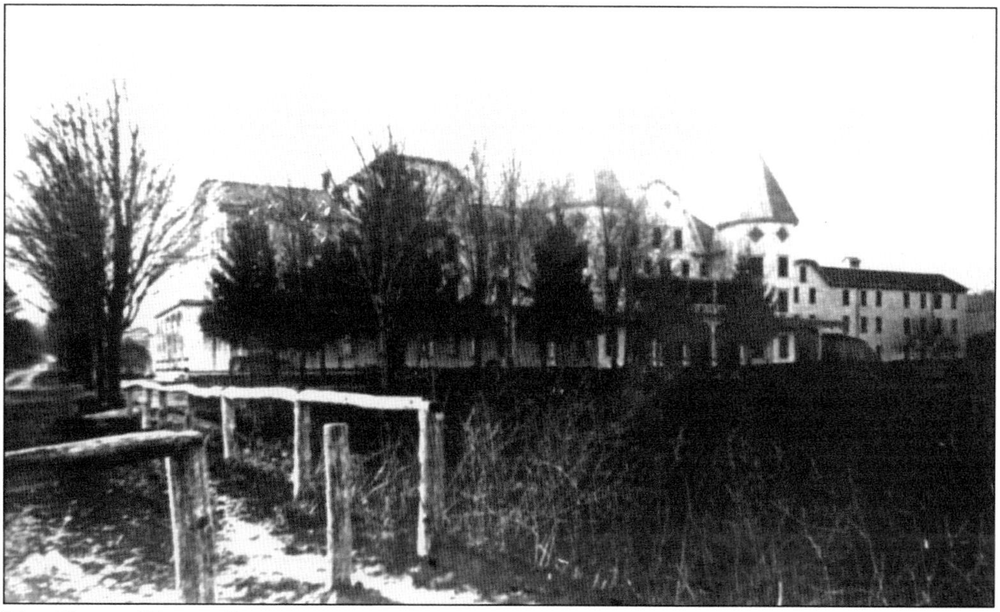

THE BLUFF HOUSE BOAT LANDING AND BATHING BEACH. The boat landing and bathing beach along the Delaware River made the Bluff House a popular spot for tourists. It was built in 1876 by H. G. Wells and situated overlooking the Delaware River.

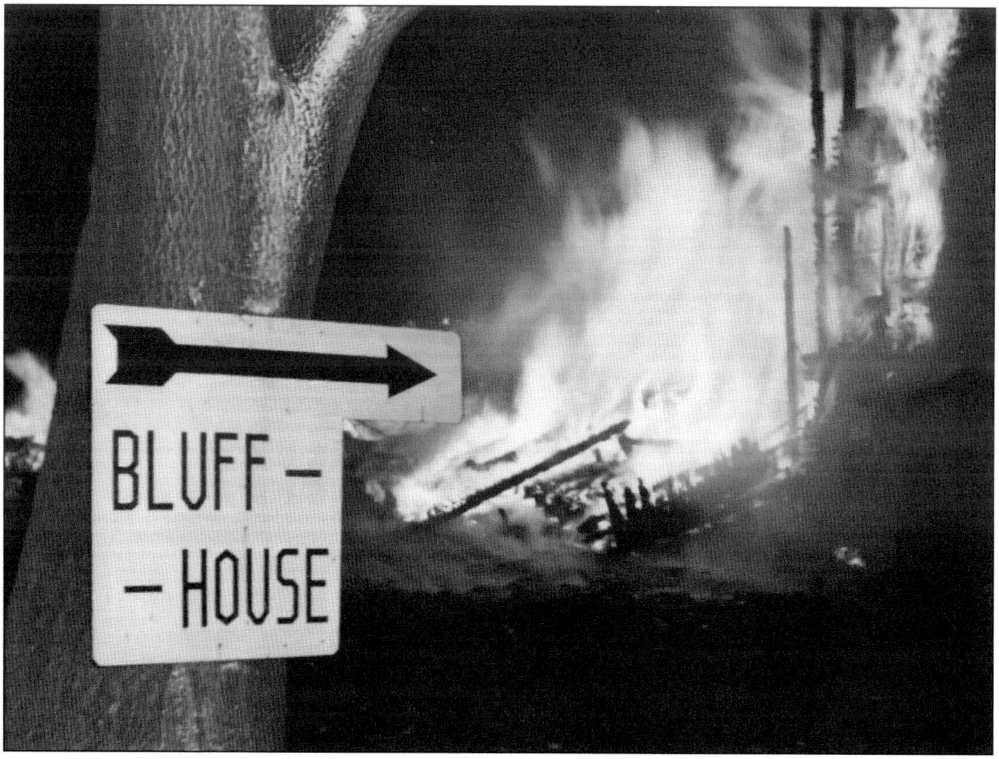

BLUFF HOUSE FIRE. The Bluff House burned down in 1947. It is said that if the wind had been blowing in the opposite direction that night, the village of Milford would have been lost to fire as well.

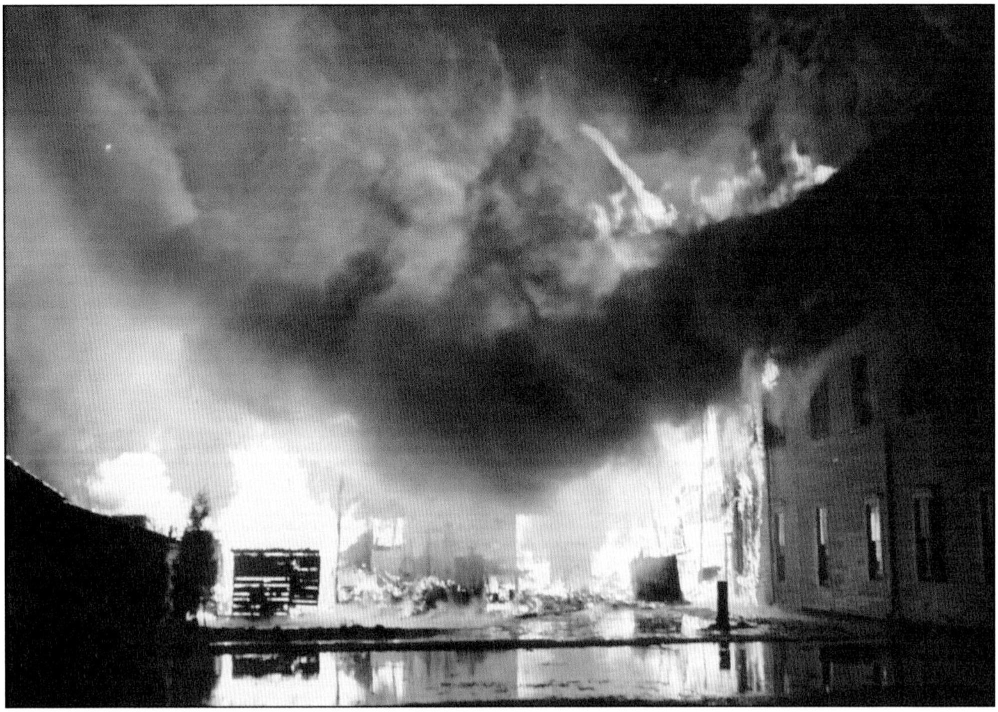

Bluff House Fire, February 1947. While under renovation, in the cold of February 1947, the hotel burned to the ground. The fire lit up the sky for miles, and gale force winds carried sparks across the river into New Jersey.

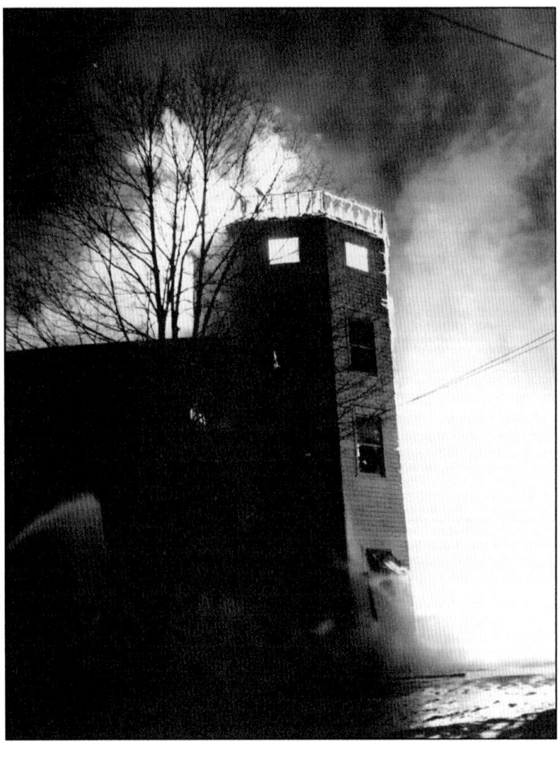

Bluff House Remains. After the devastating fire, the grand inn was never rebuilt.

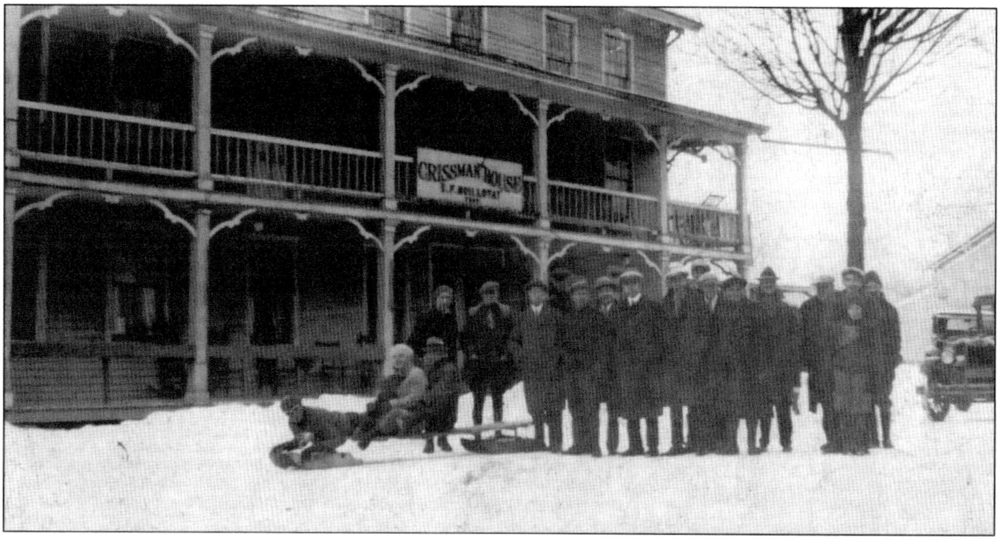

THE CRISSMAN HOUSE, MILFORD. During the mid-1930s, the Crissman House could accommodate 60 guests with rates from $2 to $2.50 per day and $10 to $14 per week. Built in 1825 by Timothy Condee, it was originally called the Pike County House. It was one of the first Pike County hotels to be open year-round. It was renamed the Crissman House in 1853 when Cyrus Crissman purchased it.

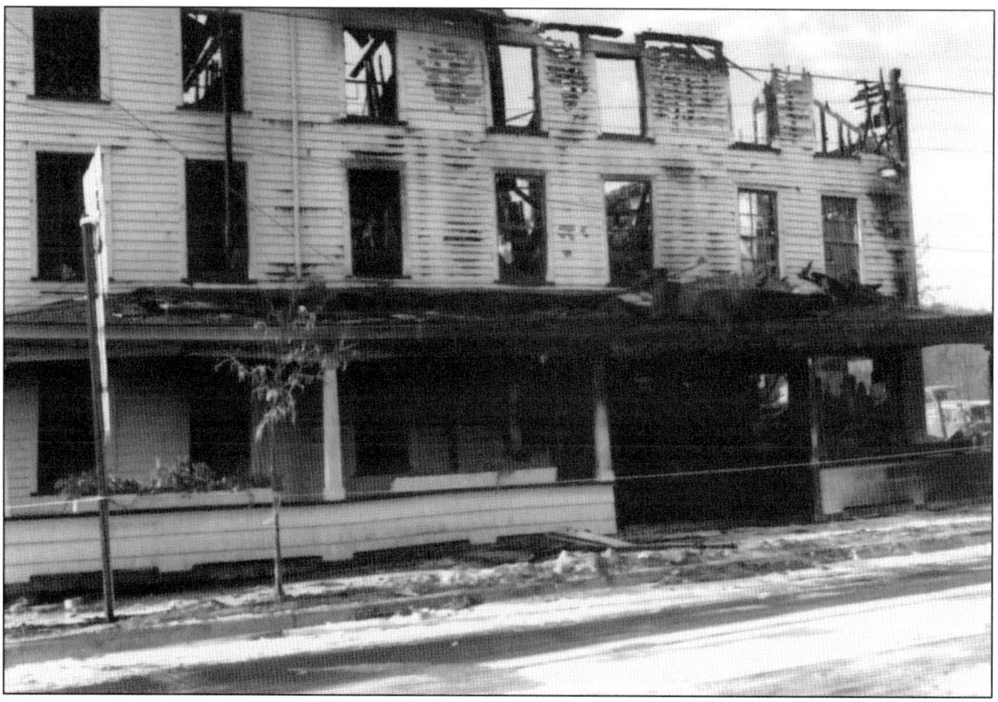

CRISSMAN HOUSE DESTROYED BY FIRE. On Sunday evening, February 7, 1960, the Crissman House caught fire. Once again the winds of winter took their toll, making it a difficult battle for the firefighters. Nearby homes and businesses were in danger as sparks, embers, and fragments threatened to spread the fire. A space heater caused the blaze.

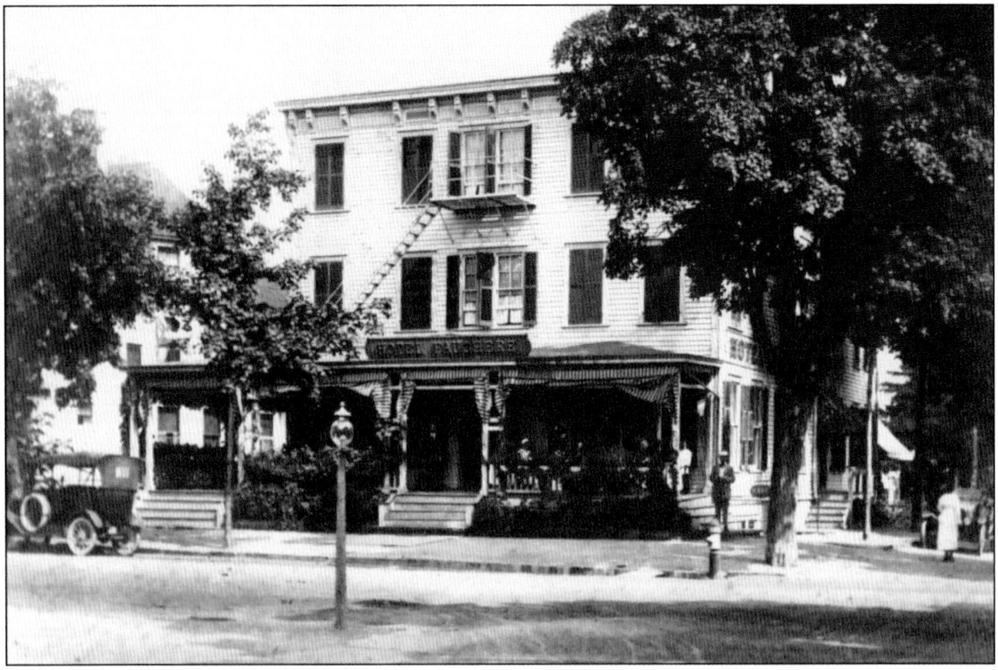

The Hotel Fauchere. Louis Fauchere came to Milford in the mid-1860s and established the Hotel Fauchere. Its "established 1857" may refer to the time when a relative of Fauchere's owned the building, and it was called the French Inn. Fauchere was an innovator and renowned chef credited with signature dishes of chicken marango and lobster Newburgh. He is also credited with bringing the first billiards table to Milford, something that is non-existent in the borough today.

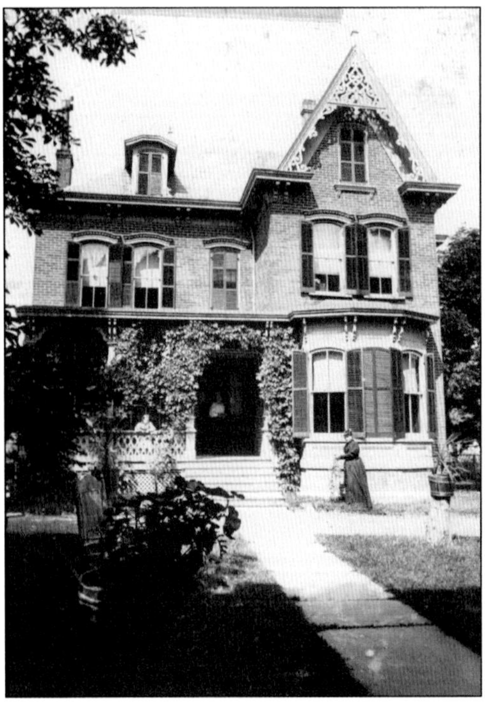

Brick Cottage at Hotel Fauchere. In the mid-1930s when Warren Chol was the manager of the Hotel Fauchere, capacity was 75 people and the rates were $3.50–$5 per day. Advertised as having "private baths en suite" and French cuisine, it was centrally located with "Auto Parties" being their specialty.

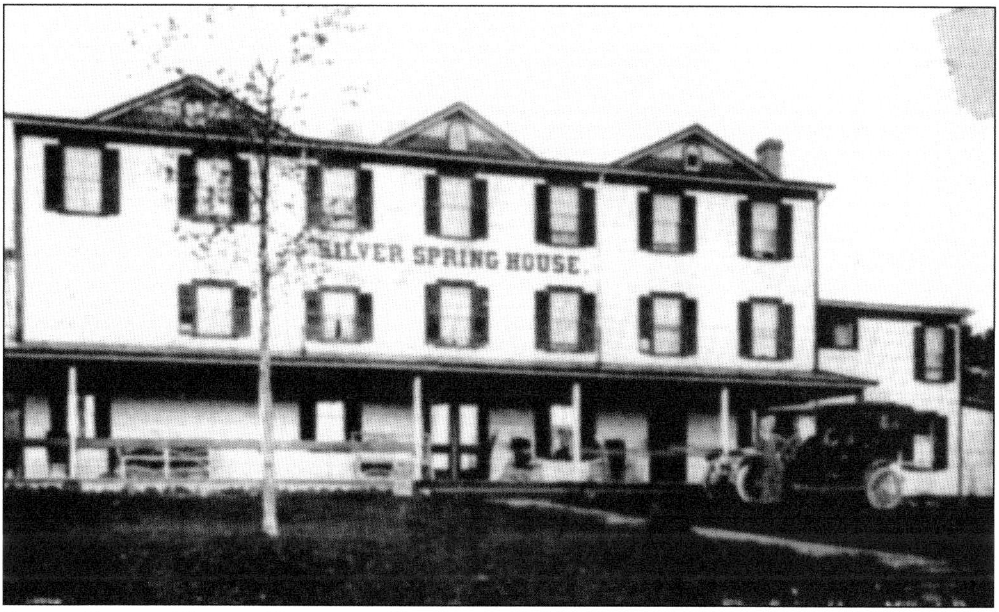

SILVER SPRING HOUSE, DINGMAN TOWNSHIP. Milford's popularity as a summer resort town only made it possible for nearby areas to reap the benefits of the tourist trade. The Silver Spring House was started in the mid-1890s as a 40-room summer boardinghouse by Eugene O. Boillotat. It was built on the site of an abandoned brewery.

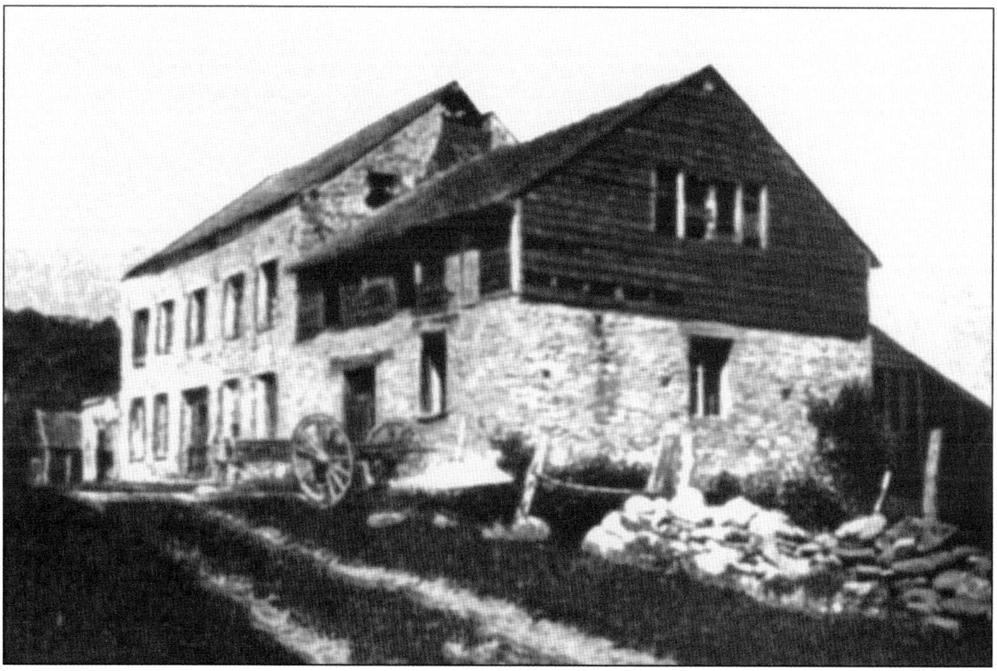

SILVER SPRING HOUSE BREWERY. The Silver Springs Brewery was built in 1840 by Remy Loreaux, a Frenchman. He purchased a parcel of land with an exceptional spring that made it possible to brew good beer. He was indicted around 1864 for maintaining a brewery without a license. Loreaux's beer was famed far and wide. Old timers claimed Loreaux's product "was of the richest quality, having more of the characteristics of ale than of modern lager."

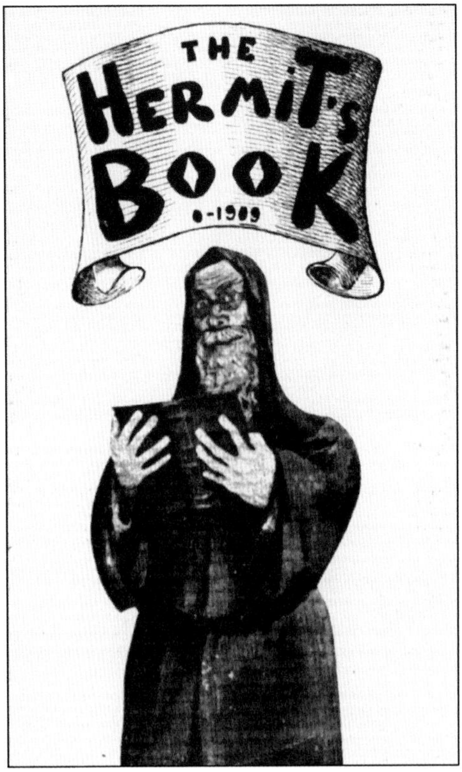

THE HERMIT'S BOOK, 1909. One of the more interesting places to stay in the county was known as the Hermitage. It was conceptualized by Louis Ragot, who also happened to be an excellent sculptor and designer. He felt the need to make a stay at the Hermitage, an experience not soon to be forgotten. He provided guests with a copy of the *Hermit's Book* so they could understand the "Legend of the Hermit," as created by Ragot.

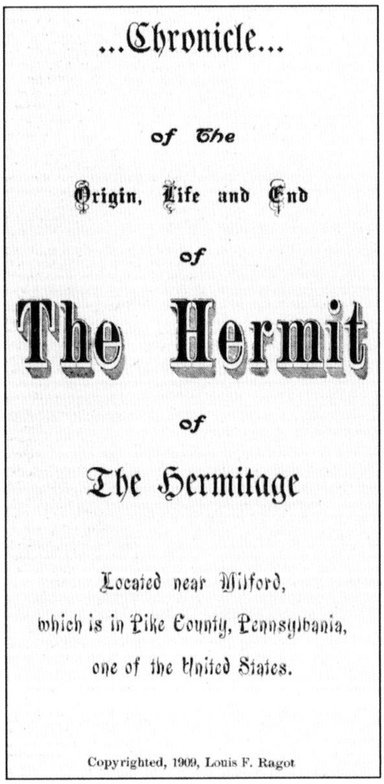
...Chronicle...

of The

Origin, Life and End

of

The Hermit

of

The Hermitage

Located near Milford,

which is in Pike County, Pennsylvania,

one of the United States.

Copyrighted, 1909, Louis F. Ragot

THE HERMIT'S BOOK. Ragot weaves a story including the Goddess Diana and her sister Muses, who came to find virgin forests where their sacredness would be respected.

CHAPTER I.

THE HERMIT'S ANCESTORS AND DESCENDANTS.

To speak only of what we know of as fact, we will go back no further than Adam to trace the Hermit's ancestors.

It is a well-known fact that Adam was solitary, and alone, in the Garden of Eden, like all genuine hermits should be, and that he was the First Hermit that ever lived, until the coming of Eve.

Then to mention only the most celebrated descendants, we have:

Pipion, the first man that ever had the Chicken's Pip on account of not drinking cool in summer.

Porus, one always open to a good drink.

Puggos, who was terribly flat-nosed through drinking at the barrelhead.

Geulehaut, the first inventor of flagons, (because there were many others after him).

Grandgousier, A giant celebrated for his big gullet, father of Gargantua;

Gargantua, a gigantic man. Ruler in Utopia, founder of the Abbey of Theleme, whose motto was "Fay ce que vouldras" (Do what thou wilt).

Pantagruel, the Giant Hermit of the Hermitage, Son of Gargantua and hero of this true story;

Louis F. Ragot, his direct descendant and Museinspiredsymbolicsculptor. Do you understand this fully? Well, drink a Hermit's Sip.

THE HERMIT LEGEND. As the legend tells it, Pantagruel, aka the Hermit, after a period of travel and intense study eventually transforms into his true nature as a hermit.

CONTENTS

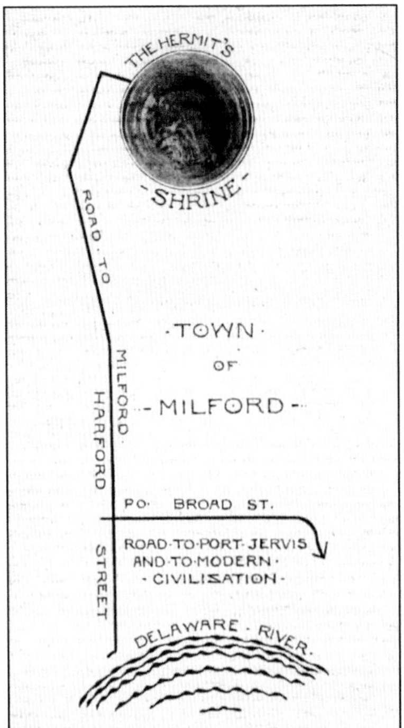

Sketch showing where the Hermit's Shrine is located and the road to Milford, a nice little town that has grown and prospers near to it.

LEGEND'S CONTROVERSY. While some say Louis Ragot borrowed the legend of the Hermit from Francis Rabelais (1494–1553), a French humanist, others claim it was solely the creation of Ragot, with the names Pantagruel and Gargantua the only thing in common.

AUTHOR'S PROLOGUE.

Kind gentlemen and kinder gentlewomen, who willingly apply your minds to the ennobling pastime of reading this great and estimable chronicle of the Giant Hermit of the Hermitage, let me tell you that this is a true story which, like an heirloom of the family, was to be kept secret, but :

So many persons have inquired about that Celebrated Hermit that we feel it our duty to the kind and inquisitive public to publish from the most accurate records, his wonderful linealogy and marvellous experiences, until he came to be famous the world over. All that is printed here is the truth, as it was preserved in the Ragot family, his descendants.

It might be said right now that "Ragot," in French, means "Tittle-tattle," which will vouch for the truth of all that you will find printed here, as everybody may imagine, and to establish my rightful claim to be a Direct Descendant of the Celebrated Giant Hermit, I will add that my name in French, besides "tittle-tattle," also means "short and thick." So you will understand that there is not a better Direct Descending Line than one from a Giant to a short and thick man, as one of my ancestors must evidently have contracted that habit from birth, to have been named Ragot.

With due apology to the Illustrious and Grandific Maitre Rabelais (Francois) "Le Joyeulx Cure de Meudon," Original Historiographer of said Giant Family, to whom I am indebted for the genesis of the Hermit's Chronicle.

LOUIS F. RAGOT.

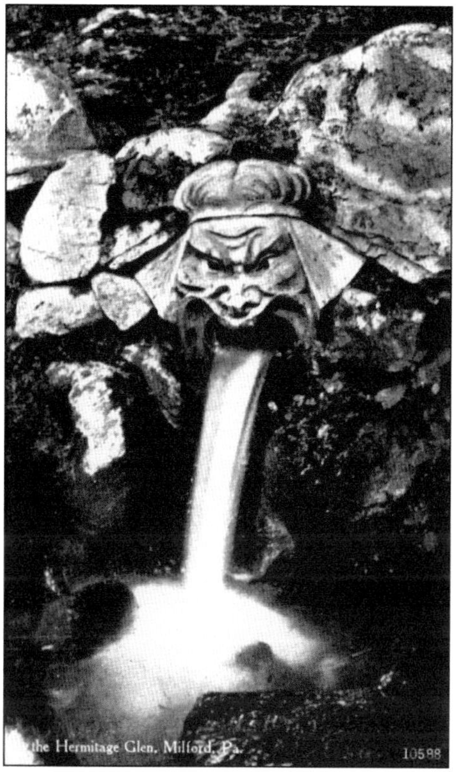

THE HERMIT FOUNTAIN AND SCULPTURES. An imaginative sculptor, Ragot created this fountain, which was located on the Hermitage grounds. Ragot also created a wishing chair to be placed on the grounds, as well as a sundial, which later sold for $7,500. His work was of much interest to collectors.

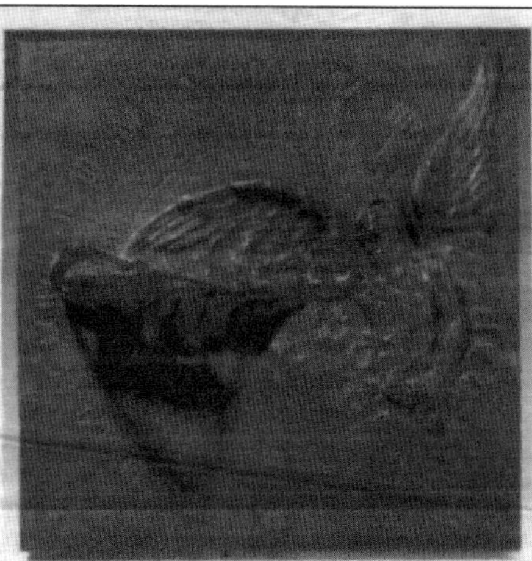

This sundial by Louis Ragot of Milford, Pennsylvania, is signed and dated 1904. The cast figure of a winged Father Time holds an hourglass in his left hand and the scythe in his right hand, which forms the gnomon. It is engraved "LAT 46°31' Copyright 1904 by Louis Ragot" and "Louis Ragot Sc, 1904 Milford, Pa." on the lower right. It sold for $7500 (est. $3000/4000) on the phone.

Maine Antique Digest, June 2008 3-C

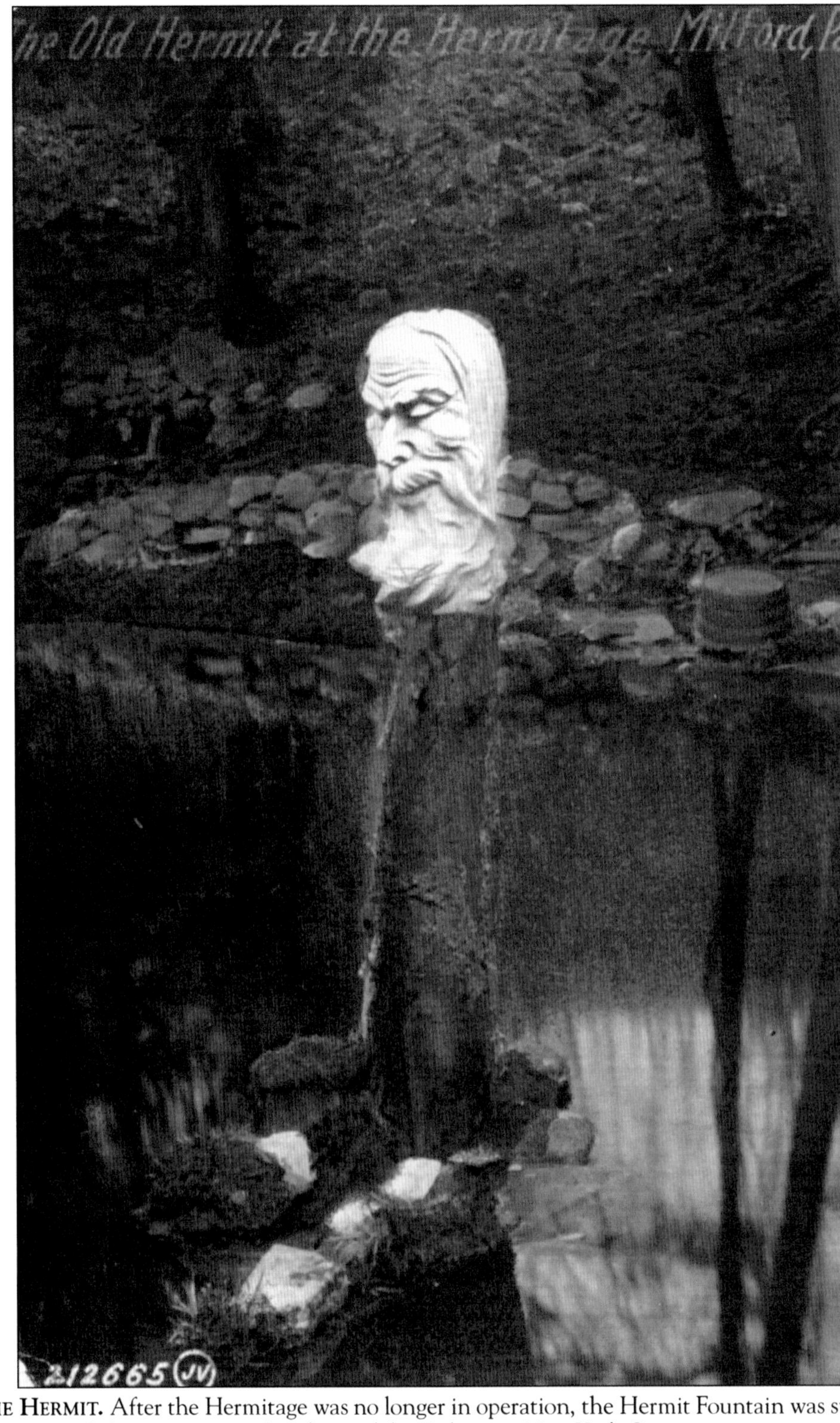

THE HERMIT. After the Hermitage was no longer in operation, the Hermit Fountain was stolen. It is rumored that it once stood in front of the Dakota in New York City.

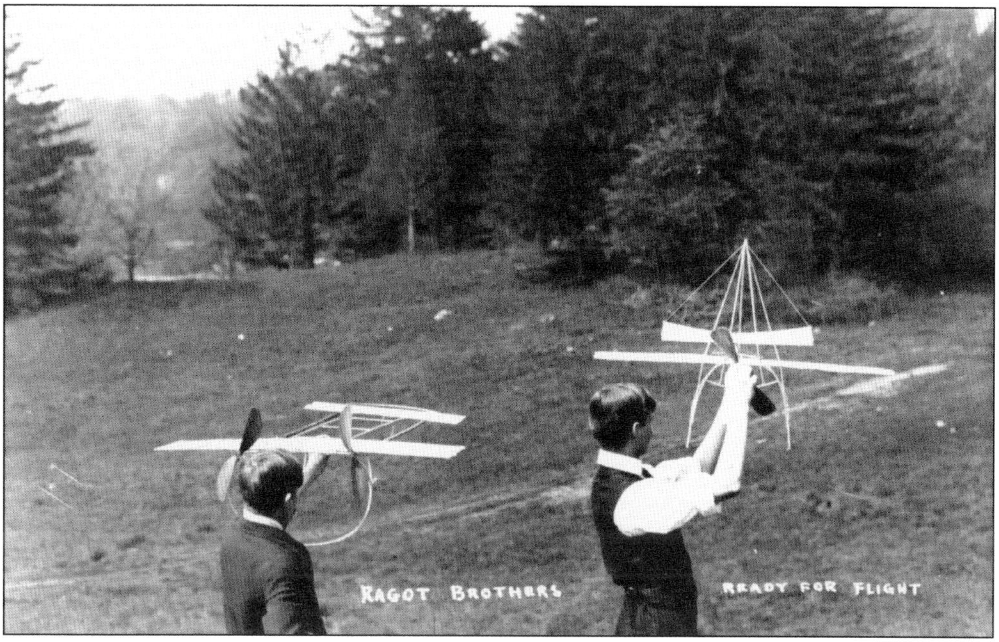

THE RAGOT BROTHERS. The interests of Louis Ragot spanned quite a wide and diverse gap. He and his brother even built an aeroplane. Ragot also designed four ornate bronze mantels and screens for St. John the Divine on Amsterdam Avenue in Harlem, New York, where they can be seen today.

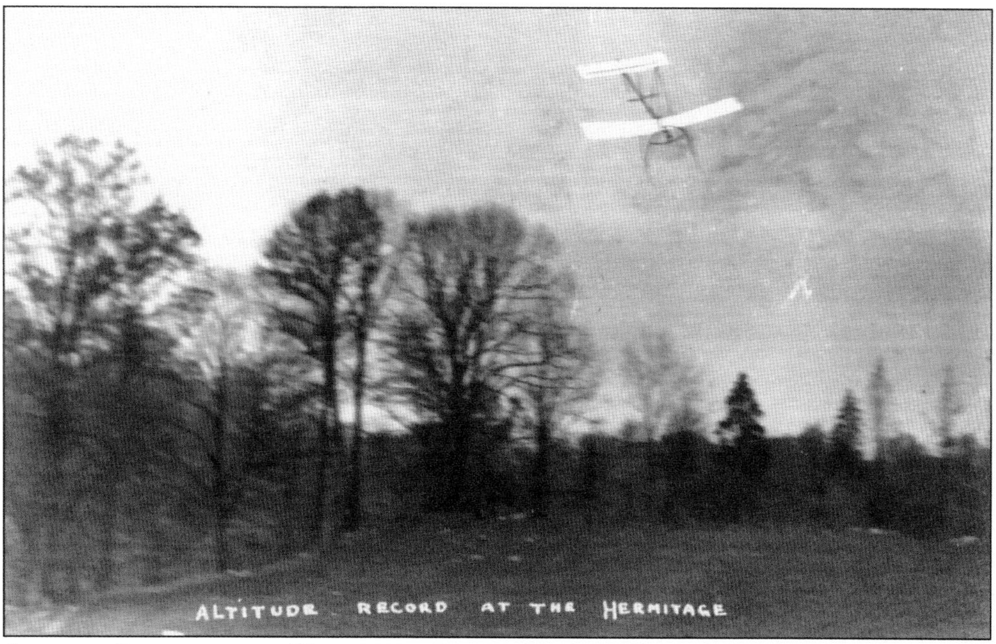

ALTITUDE RECORD AT THE HERMITAGE. Despite their best efforts, the brothers Ragot reportedly never got their plane to fly. In 1922, the rates to stay at the Hermitage were $21 per week and up.

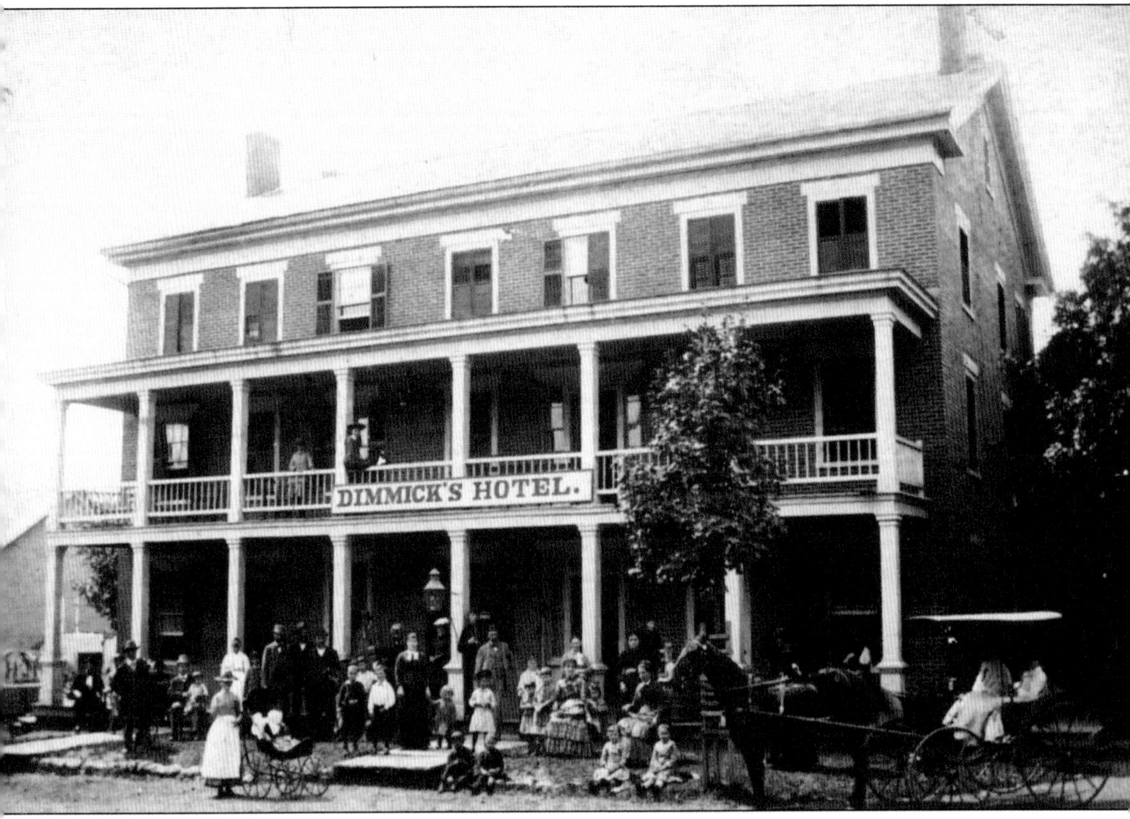

Dimmick's by Hensel. The Dimmick was built in 1828 in Milford by Samuel Dimmick, who had been a soldier in the War of 1812. It burned in 1855 and was rebuilt by Frances Dimmick, his daughter.

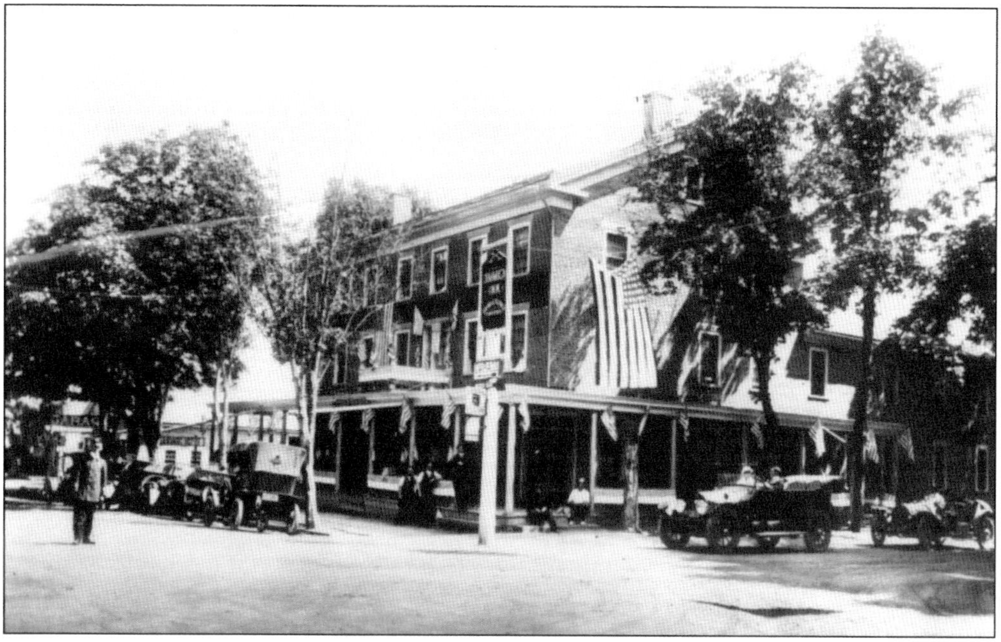

DIMMICK INN, 1918. Ernest Wood appears here directing traffic in 1918. The Dimmick Inn was a favorite stopping place for rafts men in its early days, and it is the oldest inn of Pike still in operation today.

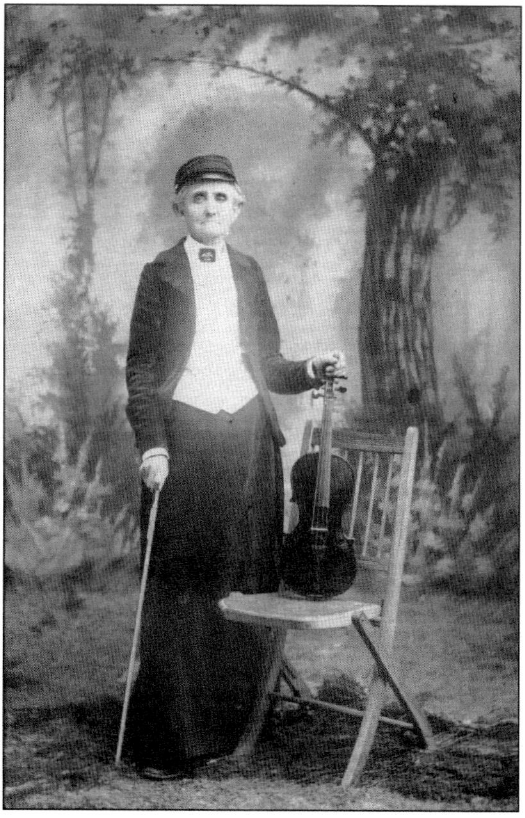

MISS FANNIE DIMMICK. Known as Miss Fan, Fannie Dimmick was touted as "the biggest hearted woman ever born in the Delaware Valley." She was known for wearing men's clothing and was an accomplished horsewoman, as she could ride sidesaddle or astride. She was an excellent markswoman and hunter, fly-fisherwoman, and fiddle player.

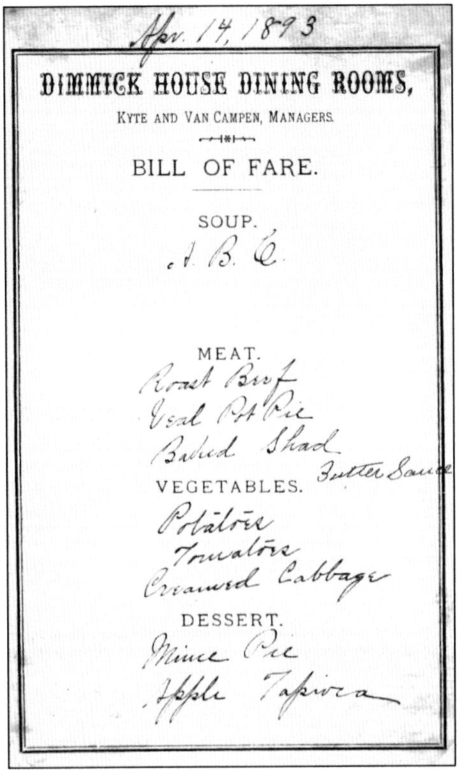

Apr. 14, 1893

DIMMICK HOUSE DINING ROOMS,

KYTE AND VAN CAMPEN, MANAGERS.

BILL OF FARE.

SOUP.

A. B. C.

MEAT.

Roast Beef

Veal Pot Pie

Baked Shad Butter Sauce

VEGETABLES.

Potatoes

Tomatoes

Creamed Cabbage

DESSERT.

Mince Pie

Apple Tapioca

BILL OF FARE. The Delaware River is known for its shad. The Dimmick's menu reflects the local fare. "ABC" soup and apple tapioca were no doubt tasty treats for the weary traveler.

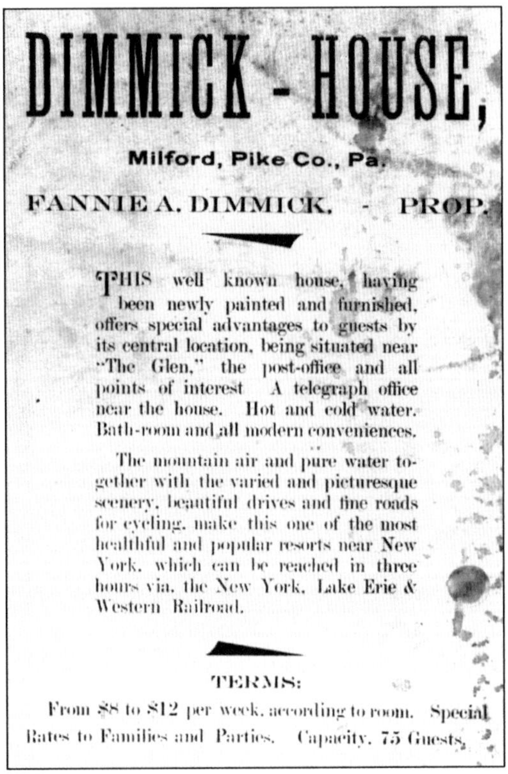

DIMMICK - HOUSE,

Milford, Pike Co., Pa.

FANNIE A. DIMMICK, - PROP.

THIS well known house, having been newly painted and furnished, offers special advantages to guests by its central location, being situated near "The Glen," the post-office and all points of interest A telegraph office near the house. Hot and cold water. Bath-room and all modern conveniences.

The mountain air and pure water together with the varied and picturesque scenery, beautiful drives and fine roads for cycling, make this one of the most healthful and popular resorts near New York, which can be reached in three hours via. the New York, Lake Erie & Western Railroad.

TERMS:

From $8 to $12 per week, according to room. Special Rates to Families and Parties. Capacity, 75 Guests,

RATES AT THE DIMMICK. In the 1930s, the rates at the Dimmick were $2.50–3.50 per day and $15–$18 per week. The Dimmick also boasted a grill room that was open until midnight, private baths in six rooms, dancing, and catering to auto parties.

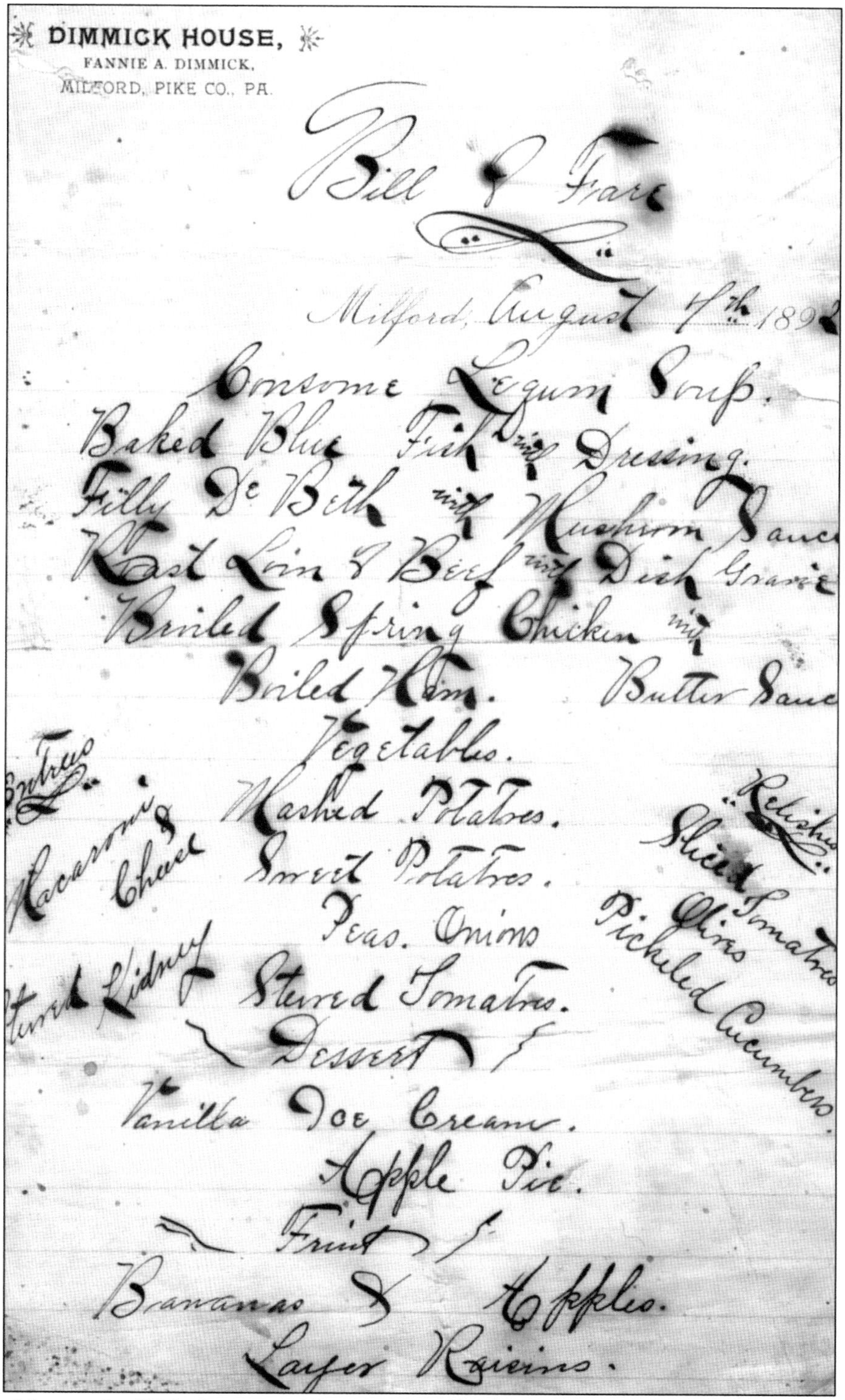
DIMMICK HOUSE,
FANNIE A. DIMMICK,
MILFORD, PIKE CO., PA.

Bill of Fare

Milford, August 7th 1892

Consome Legum Soup.
Baked Blue Fish with Dressing.
Filly De Beth with Mushroom Sauce
Roast Loin of Beef with Dish Gravie
Broiled Spring Chicken with
Boiled Ham. Butter Sauce

Vegetables.
Mashed Potatoes.
Sweet Potatoes.
Peas. Onions
Stewed Tomatoes.

Entrees
Macaroni & Cheese
Stewed Kidney

Relishes
Sliced Tomatoes
Olives
Pickled Cucumbers

Dessert
Vanilla Ice Cream.
Apple Pie.

Fruit
Bananas & Apples.
Layer Raisins.

RARE MEALS. In 1892, diners could enjoy a stuffed kidney. These menus were created and written by Miss Fan, who catered to her guests for 40 years with "genuine charm and unfailing heartiness."

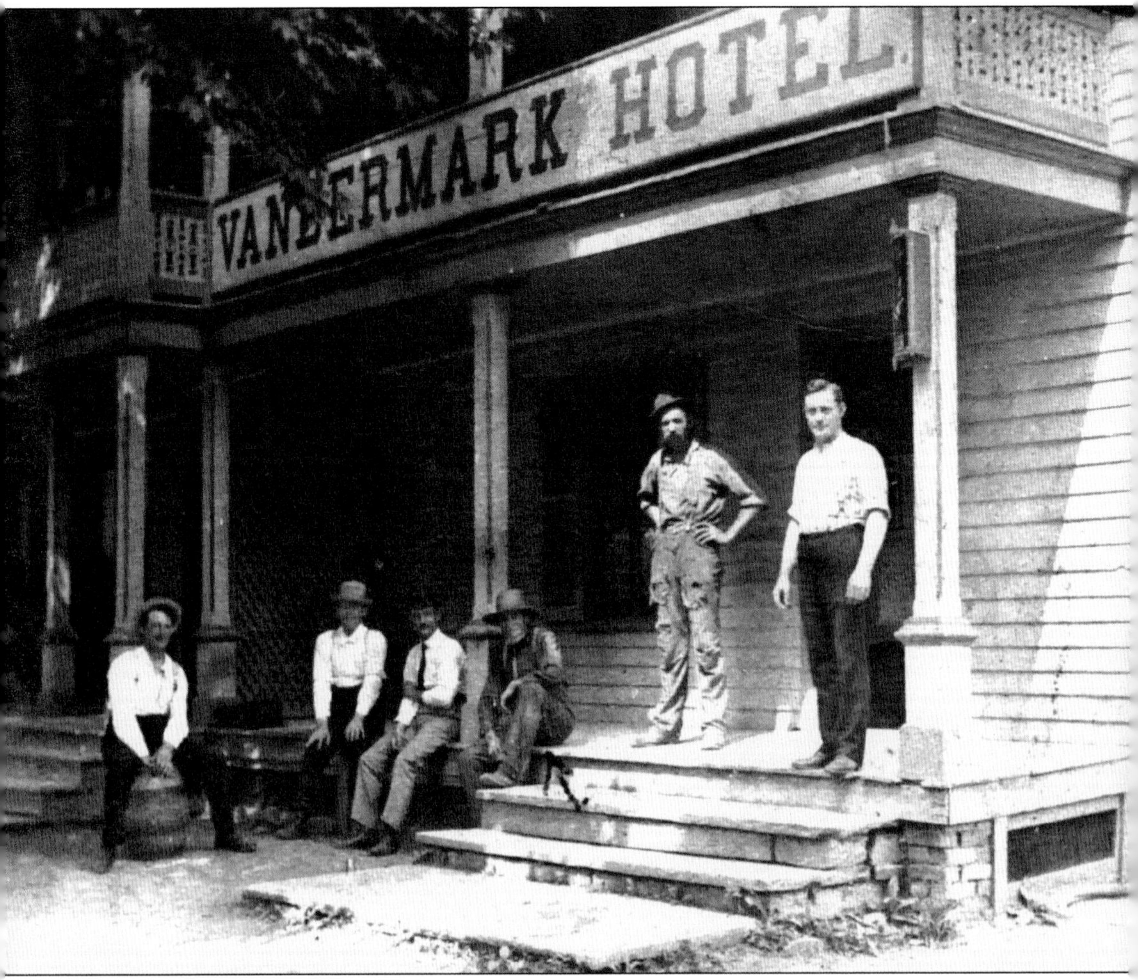

THE VANDERMARK HOTEL. The Vandermark Hotel was built in the 1700s and hosted the first court for Pike and Wayne Counties. This hotel no doubt saw the good, the bad, and the ugly through the years, as the early tavern days of Milford were not as refined as they are now. The hotel was torn down to make way for the Pike County Administration Building in the early 1980s.

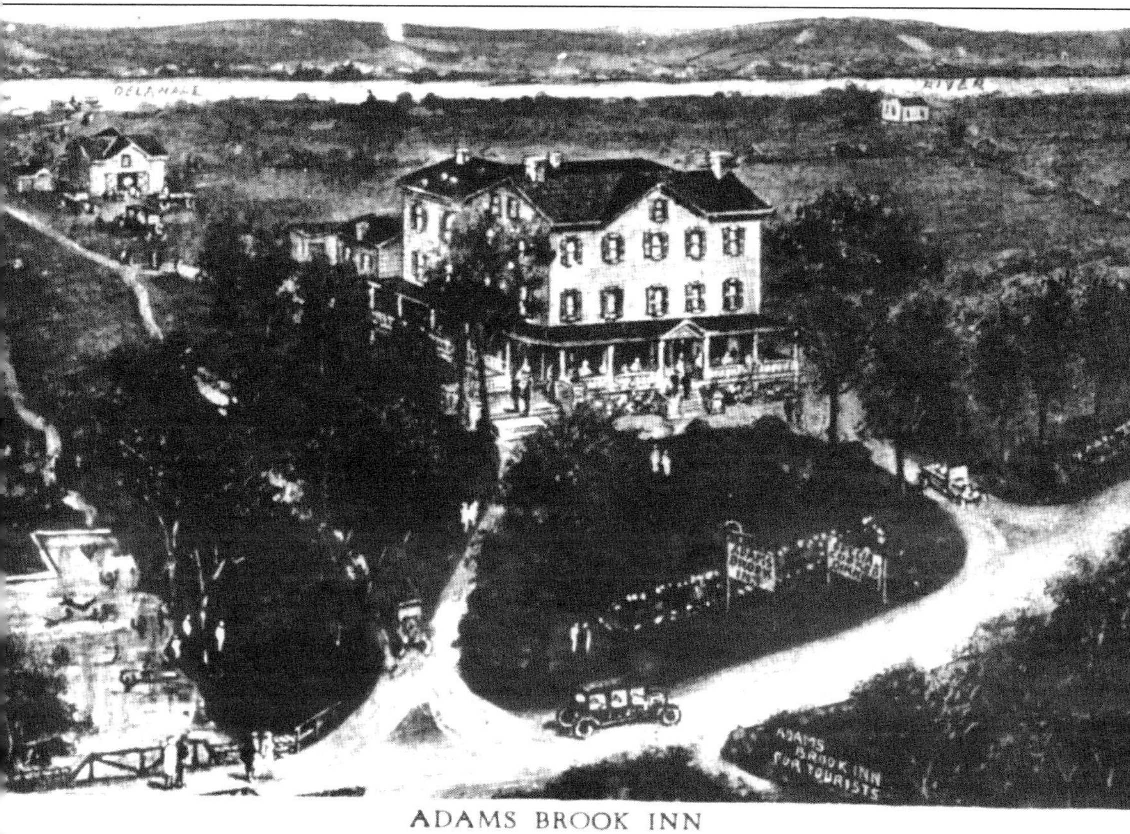

ADAMS BROOK INN. The Adams Brook Inn is seen here as it was built in 1891 by Lafayette Quick. It offered guests a lovely setting on the Adams Brook Creek and Delaware River. The natural landscape of the area includes a grotto and beautiful water falls.

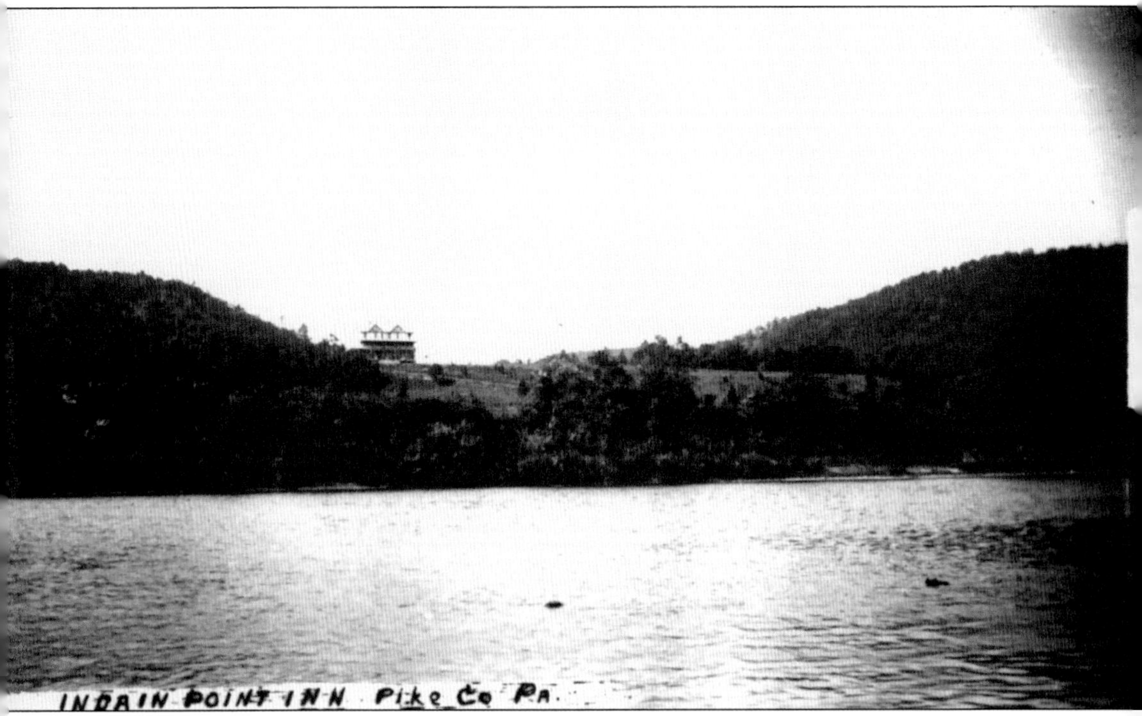

INDIAN POINT INN. Indian Point Inn was located opposite and overlooking Minisink Island. In early times, the land on which the inn was built was known as Pow Wow Hill, and it was a meeting place for Lenape Indians and also a place for the medicine man to contemplate things. The Battle of the Raymondskill took place in the immediate vicinity.

Three

Getting There

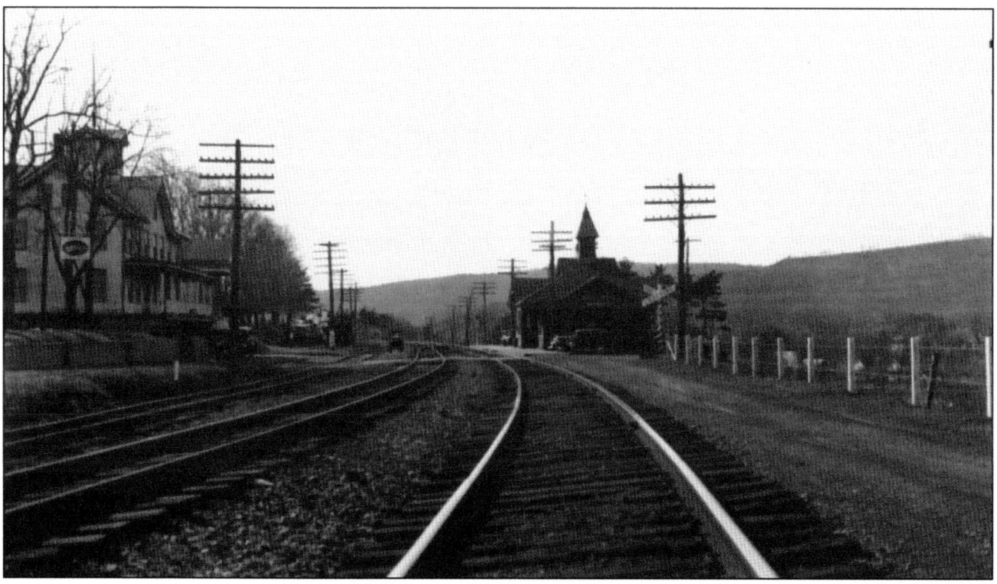

ROHMANS INN, SHOHOLA. Rail travel afforded different locals, previously not easily reached, to become accessible to tourists and trades people alike. Although rail travel allowed for much good in Pike County, it also proved quite disastrous at times, as many accidents have been reported over the years. The worst in Pike's history occurred in 1899 near Lackawaxen. A coal freighter slammed into a train carrying 800 Confederate prisoners en route to Elmira, New York. Rohmans Inn, then known as the Shohola Hotel, served as a makeshift hospital for the wounded and the 75 fatalities. The cause was a drunken dispatcher.

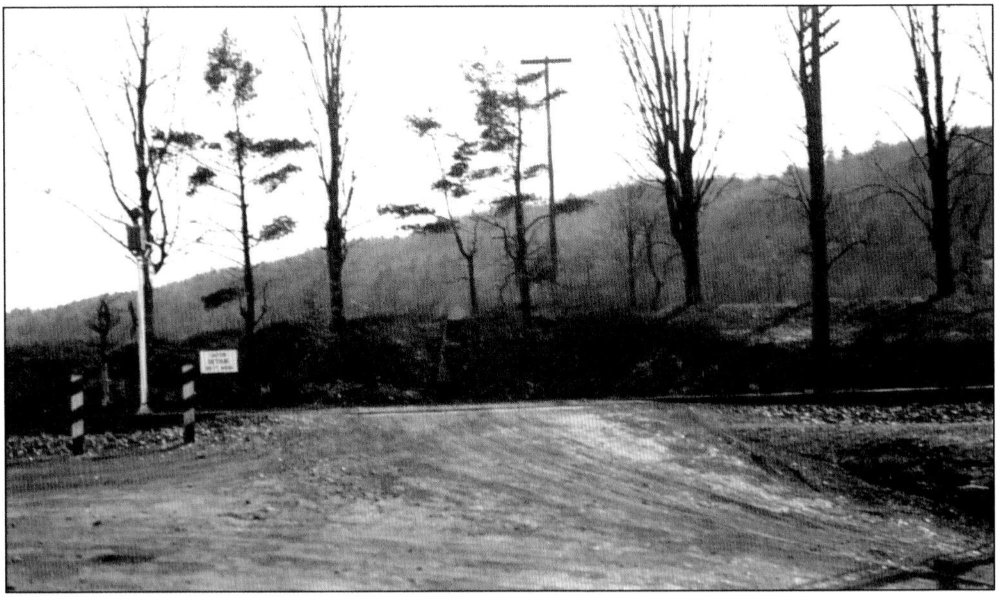

The Erie Railroad, Shohola. The Erie Railroad brought supplies, visitors, and mail into Shohola while taking bluestone and lumber out. It was a four hour trip from New York City to Shohola.

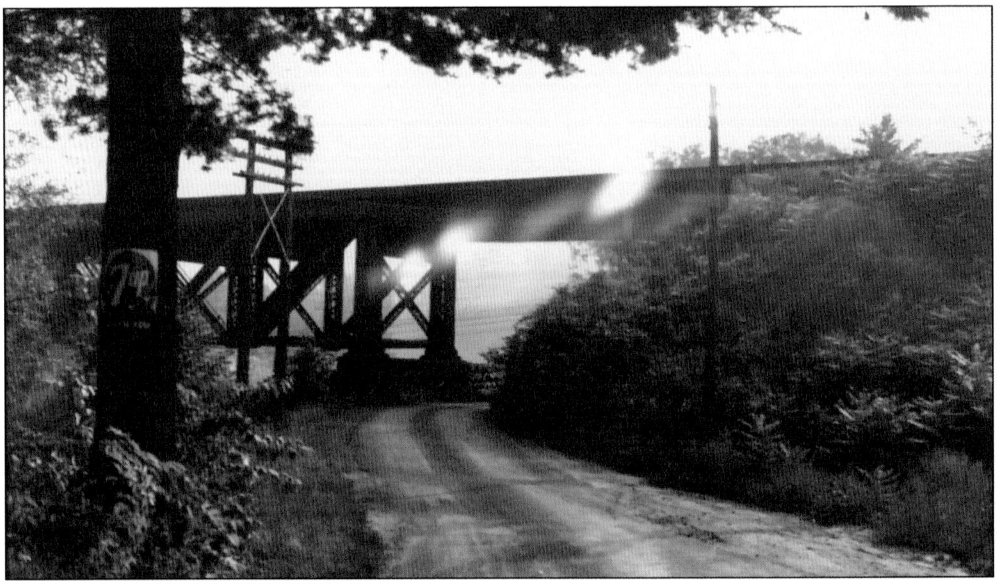

Erie, West of Lackawaxen. In 1848, the "Weary" Erie Railroad made its way to Lackawaxen. By 1898, the Delaware and Hudson Canal was surpassed by the speedier transport provided by trains. Trains also allowed for the transport of bluestone, Lackawaxen's prized export.

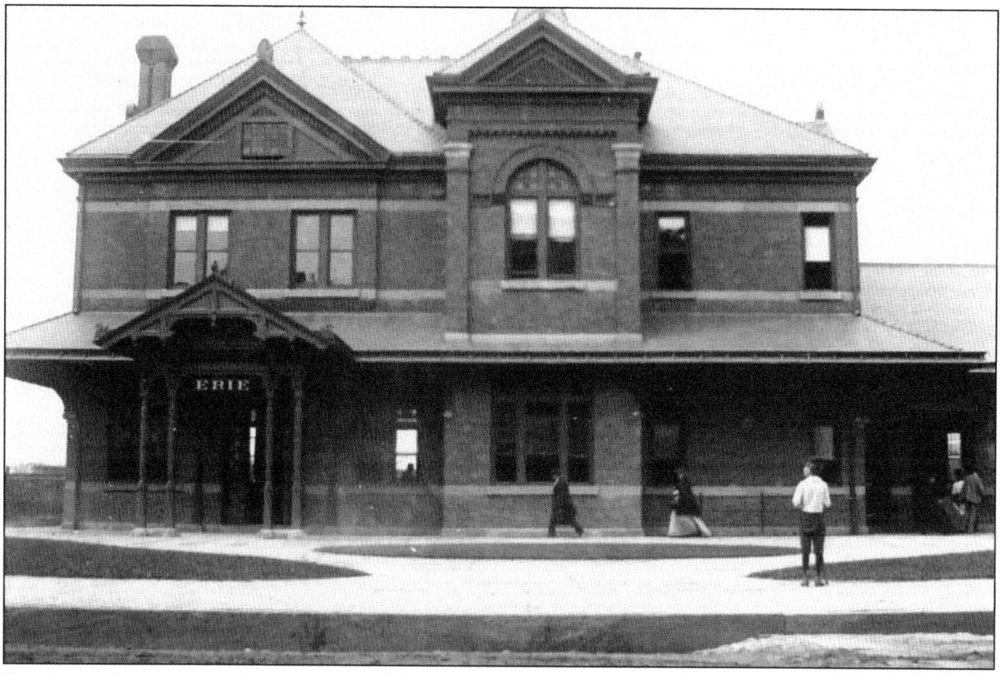

The Erie Railroad, Port Jervis, New York. Though not in Pike County, the rail line that went through Pike near Shohola and Lackawaxen was the Erie. Passengers not bound for these points would get off at Port Jervis and take a coach to their destination.

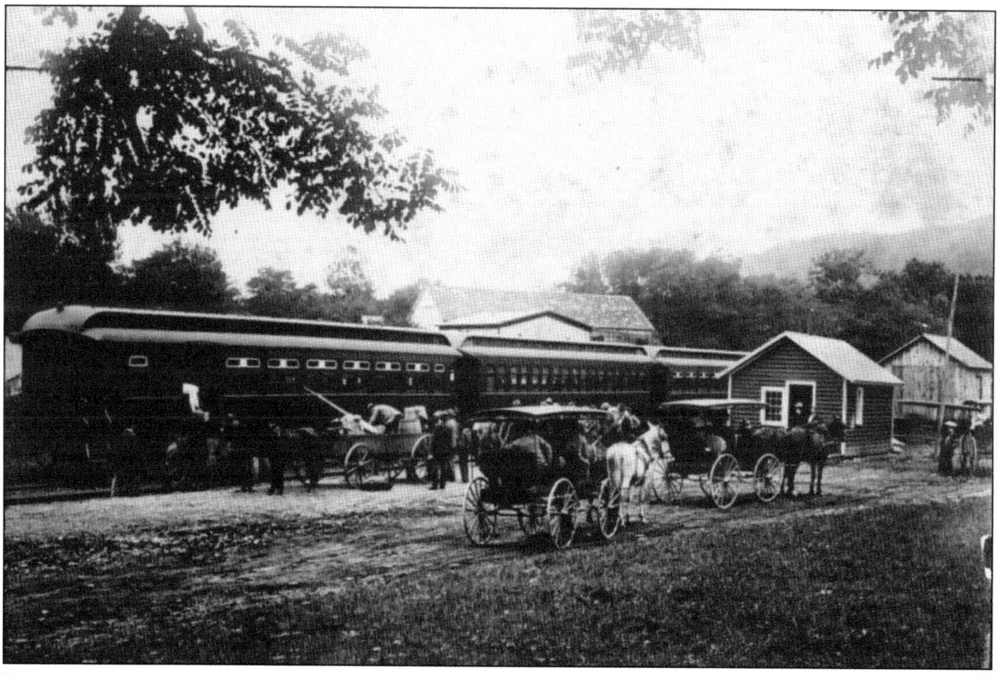

Bushkill Railroad Station, Lehman Township. The Palace Car went where the Delaware Valley Railroad (DVRR) never made it to. Known as the "Little Dinky," it made possible an influx of tourists to the Lehman Township area. Those looking for further transport could hop aboard the Palace Car to destinations along the River Road.

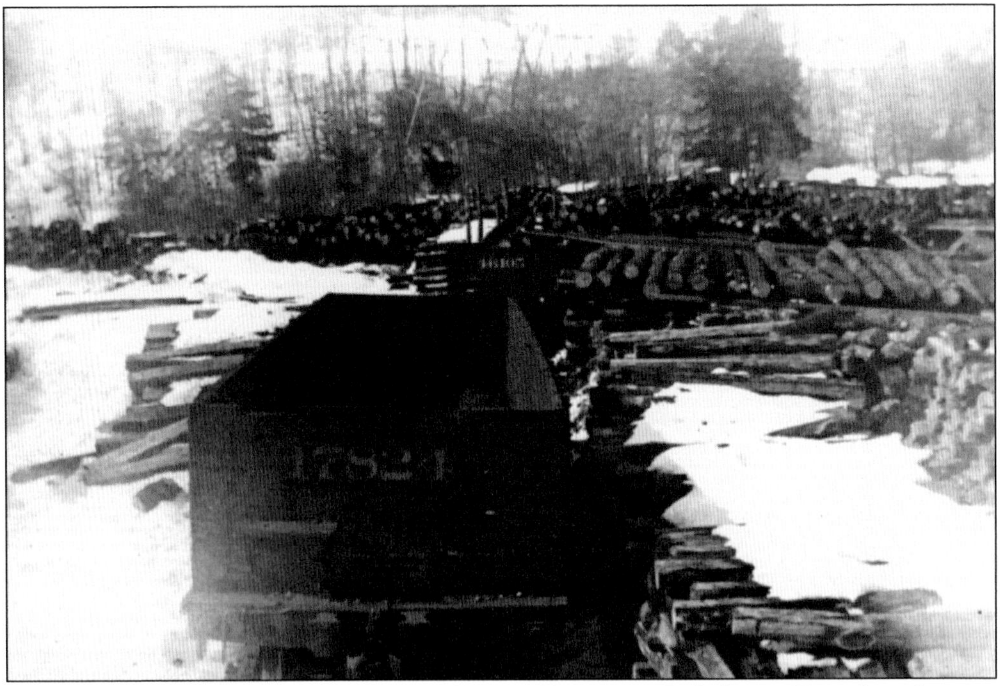

Delaware Valley Railroad Ties and Props, Bushkill. In Lehman Township, the stop at Bushkill was intended to be more than just a means to export railroad ties and mine props. The line originated in Stroudsburg in 1897 and was to provide passenger service all the way to Milford and Matamoras. Bankruptcy limited the length of the line.

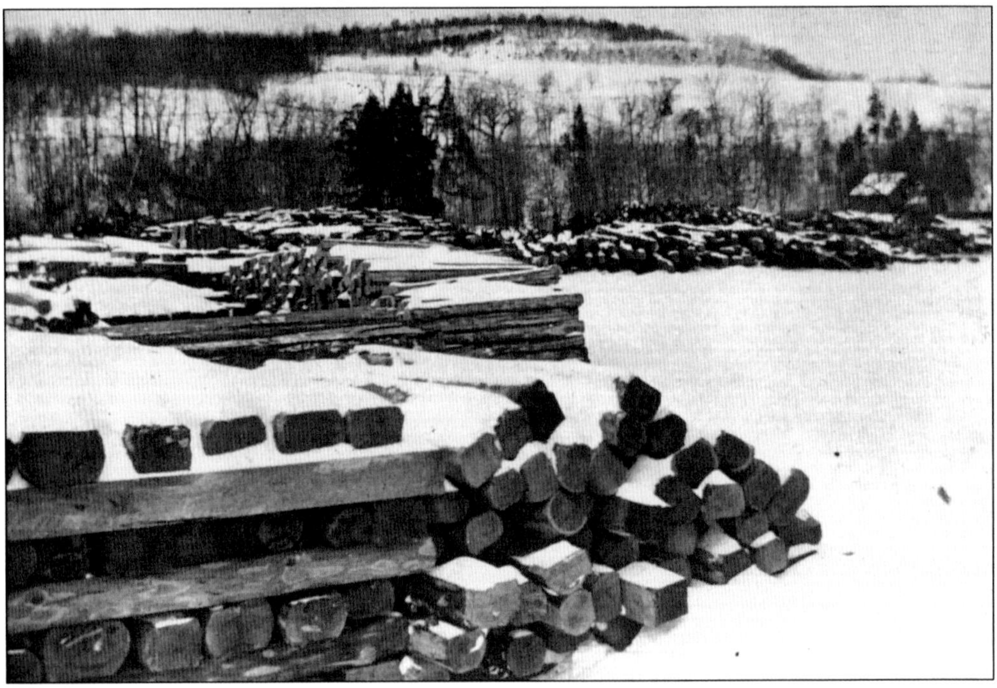

Ties and Props, Bushkill. Lumber no longer needed to be transported by rafts down the unpredictable Delaware River now that freight trains were on the scene.

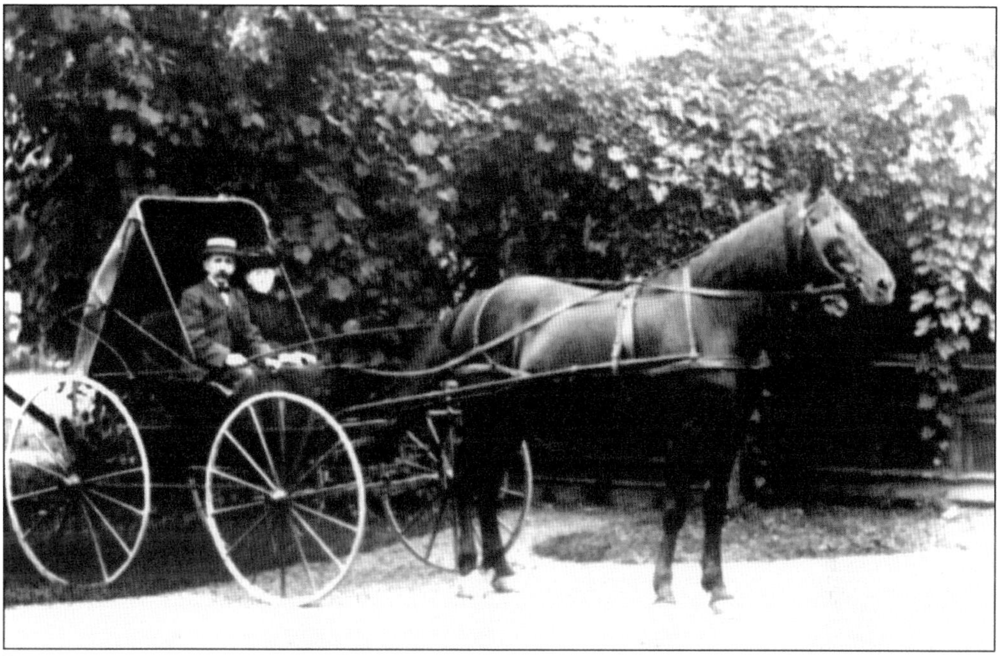

PRIVATE HORSE-DRAWN VEHICLE. Before planes, trains, and automobiles, horse-drawn vehicles were the way to travel through Pike County.

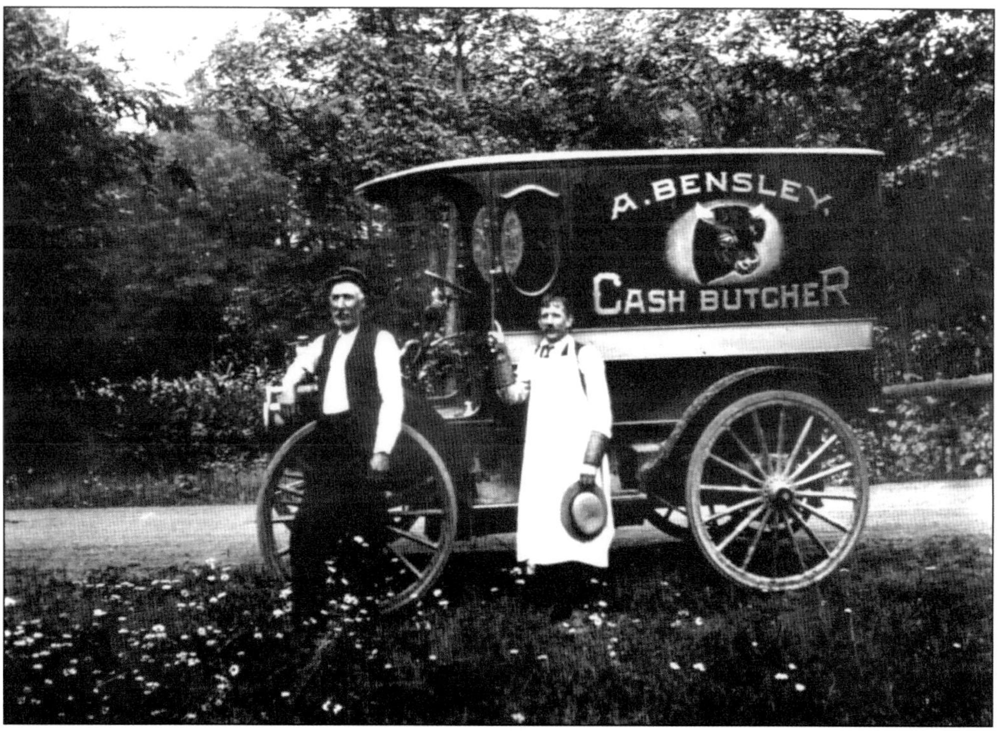

ALPHEUS BENSLEY. Alpheus Bensley (right) owned one of the first self-propelled vehicles in the area. He peddled his wares up and down the old stage roads. Pictured here with John Middaugh, his butcher business served a wide area including parts of New Jersey accessible via ferries.

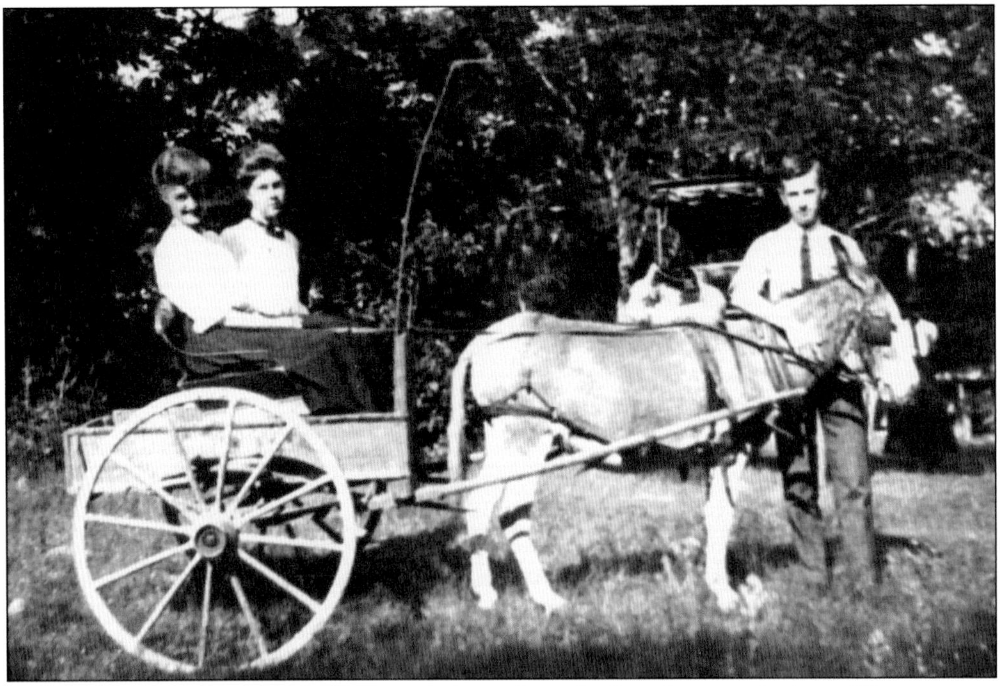

DONKEY CART. If one lacked a horse, a mule might make for a decent substitute. These women are pictured with their spiffy transport outside the Bluff House in Milford in 1903.

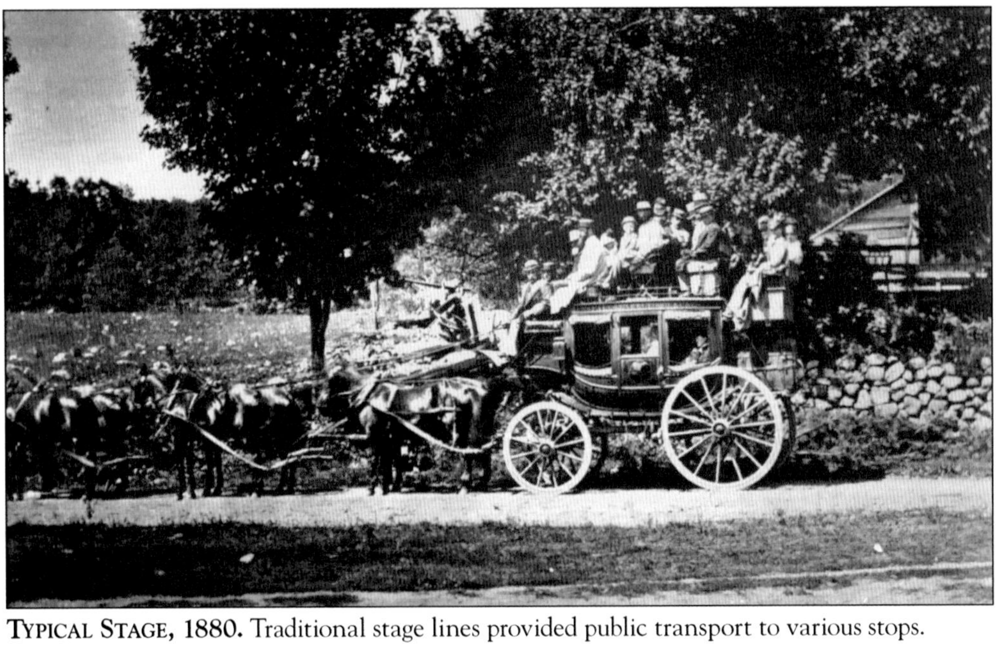

TYPICAL STAGE, 1880. Traditional stage lines provided public transport to various stops.

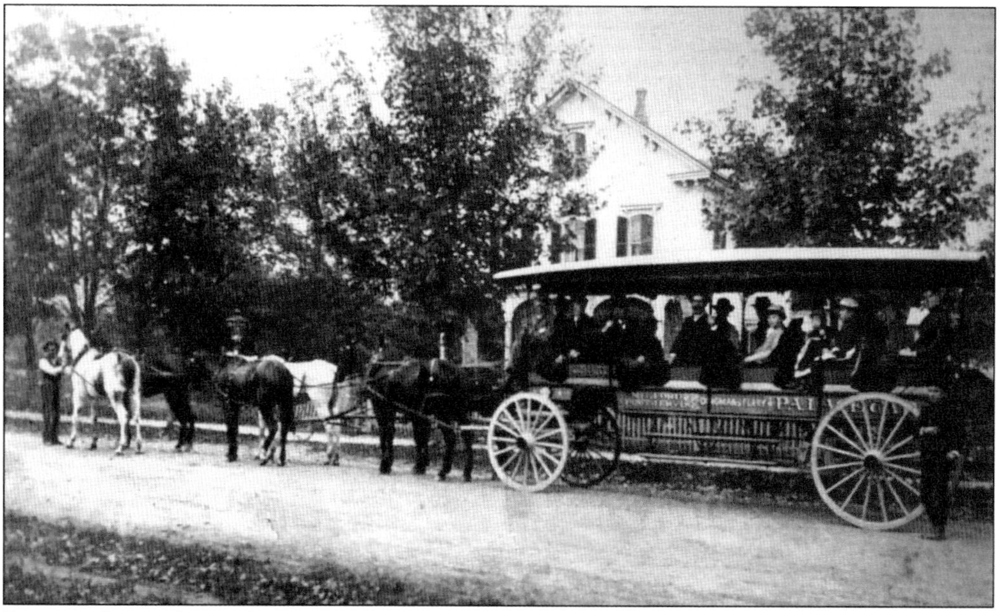

PALACE CAR. The early answer to today's bus, the Palace Car ran passengers from Milford to Stroudsburg.

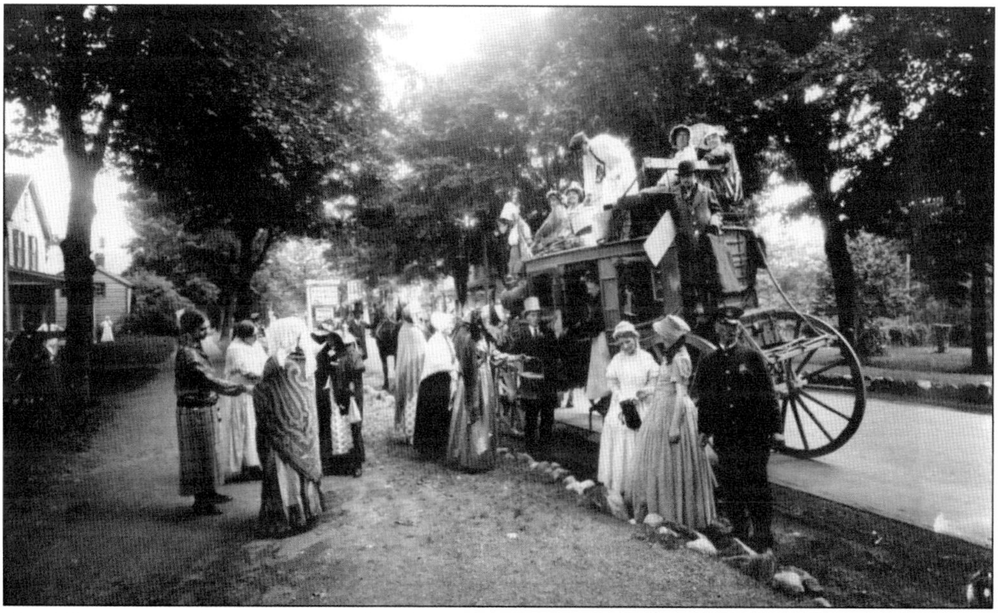

THE HIAWATHA STAGECOACH. The Hiawatha was a familiar sight from 1840 to 1890. This particular model of coach was one of the most luxurious of its time. The Hiawatha first made long distance runs to Honesdale along the Owego Turnpike and later, with the train's arrival to Port Jervis, picked up tourists bound for the village of Milford. The Findlay family ran the local transport business for many years. The Hiawatha could seat around 21 passengers, including the brakeman and the driver, when the bench seats it had were bolted to the top. Stage travel was far from glamorous. The elements, unsavory passengers with body odor and head lice, and a driver's propensity to imbibe all played a part in the overall enjoyment (or lack of) in a trip. Coaches often overturned on the rocky roads of Pike.

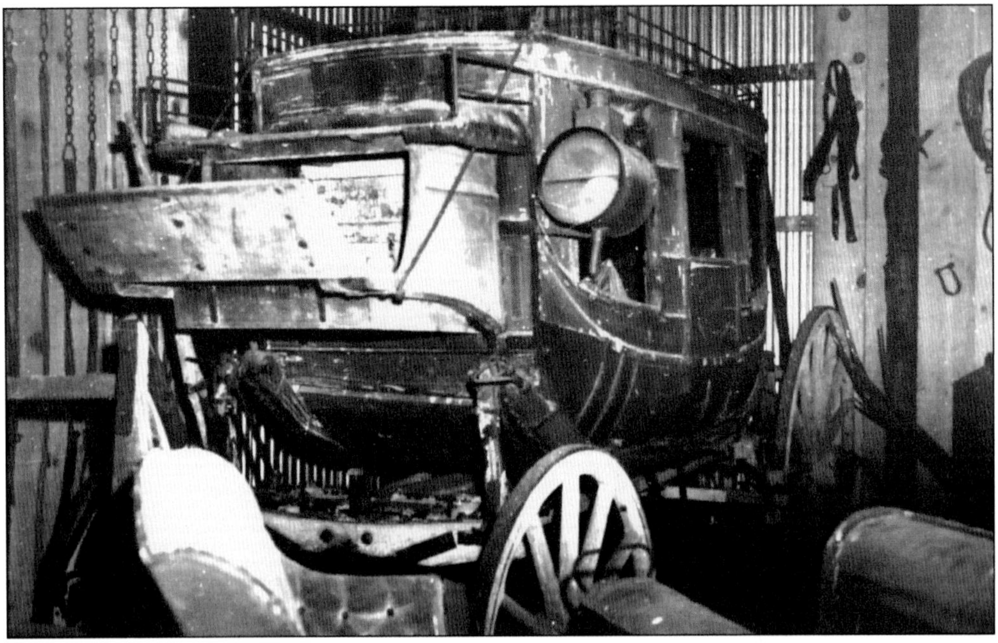

THE HIAWATHA BEFORE. Years of travel made the Hiawatha road weary and worn down. Stored in a barn located at Moon Valley Park in Milford, for many years after its practical use, the Pike County Historical Society lead the campaign to have it restored to its one time splendor.

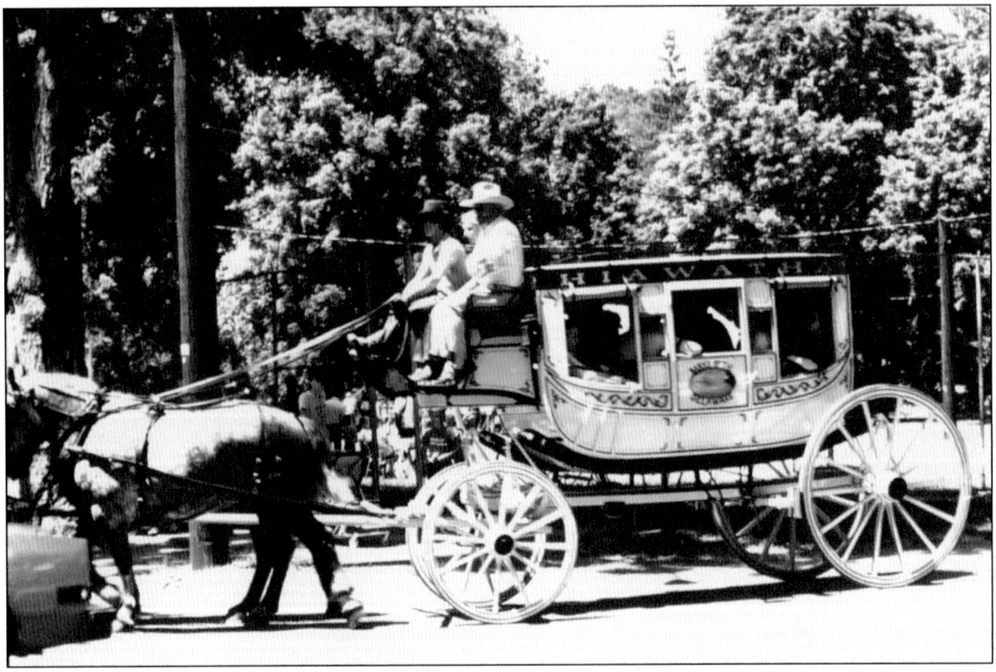

THE HIAWATHA AFTER. Once all "spiffied" up again by an Amish carriage maker outside of Lancaster, the Hiawatha became a part of the permanent collection of the Pike County Historical Society. Some reports say the Hiawatha was in use as early as 1840, however, this model of coach can be traced to the Abbott and Downing Wagon Company of Concord, New Hampshire, as being manufactured in 1850.

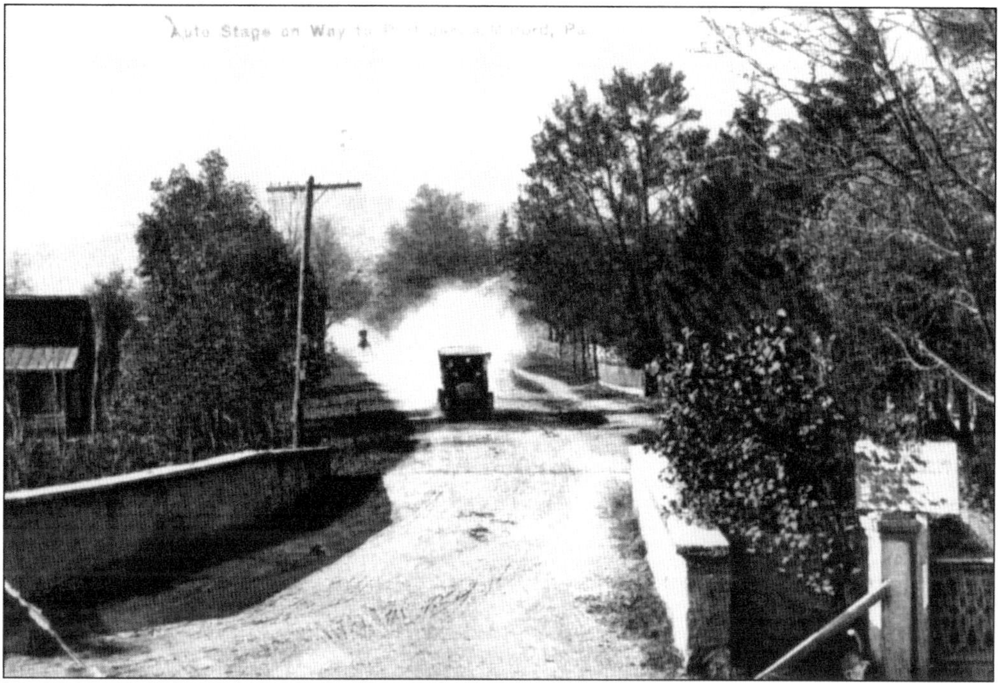

AUTO STAGE. This auto stage ran from Milford to Port Jervis, New York.

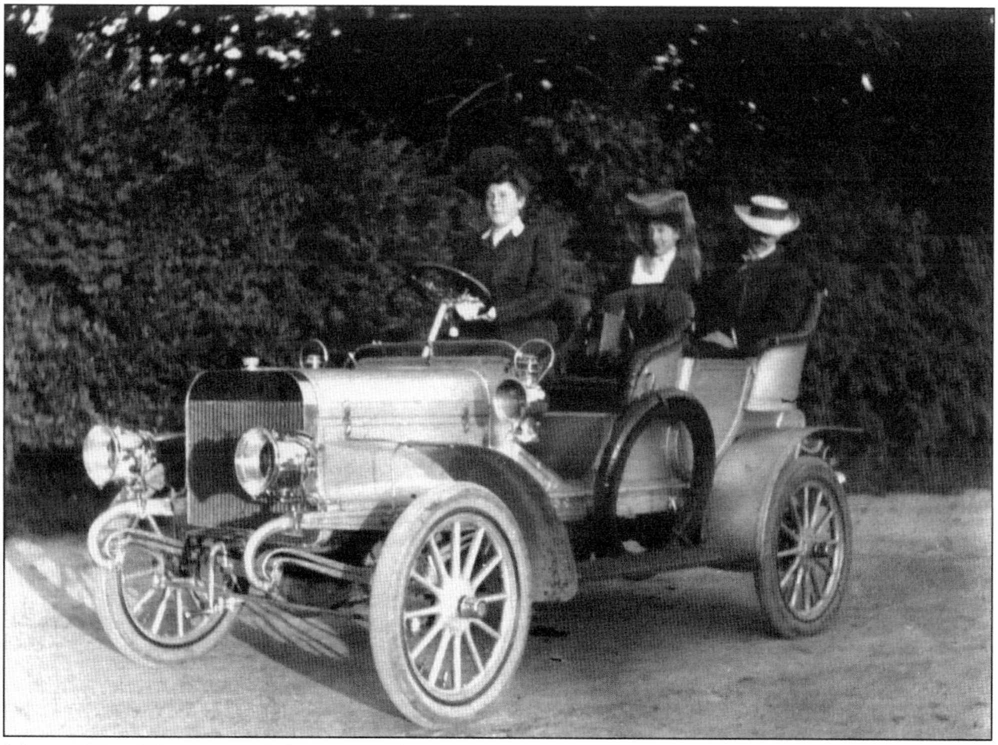

MODEL T 2. The automobile was a welcomed luxury and started an influx of automobile groups to the area on tours. Many inns and hotels catered to the groups. Goggles, aviator caps, and driving gloves were all necessities.

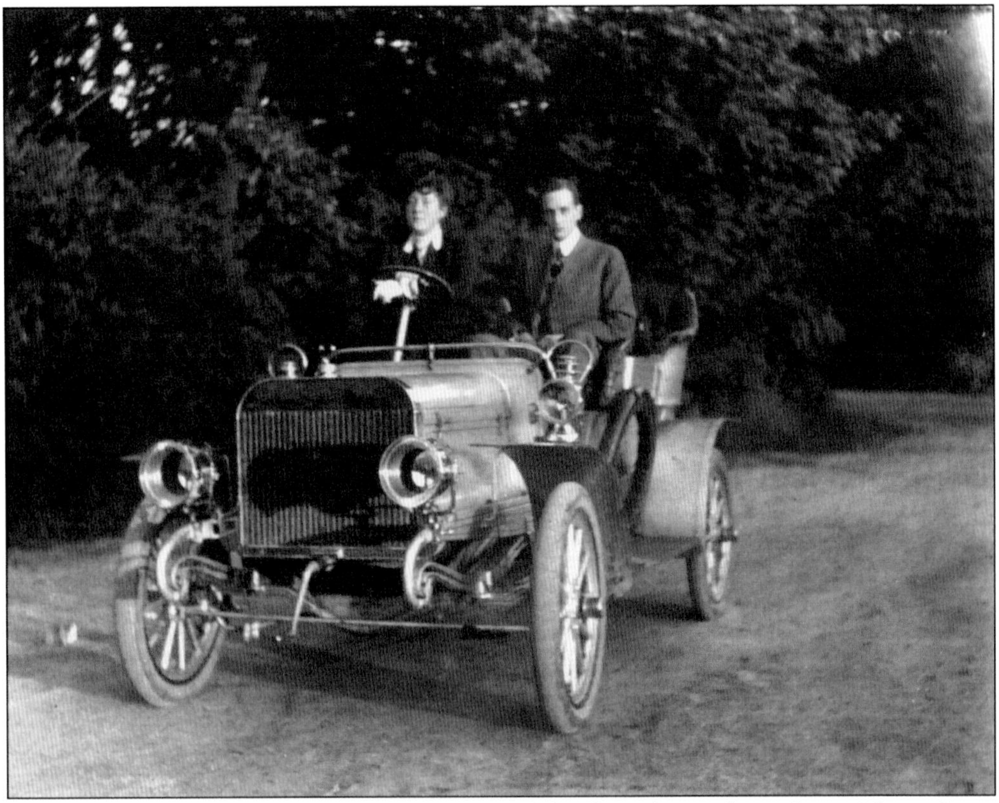

MODEL T. Since the early days of the automobile, there have always been "those damn women drivers."

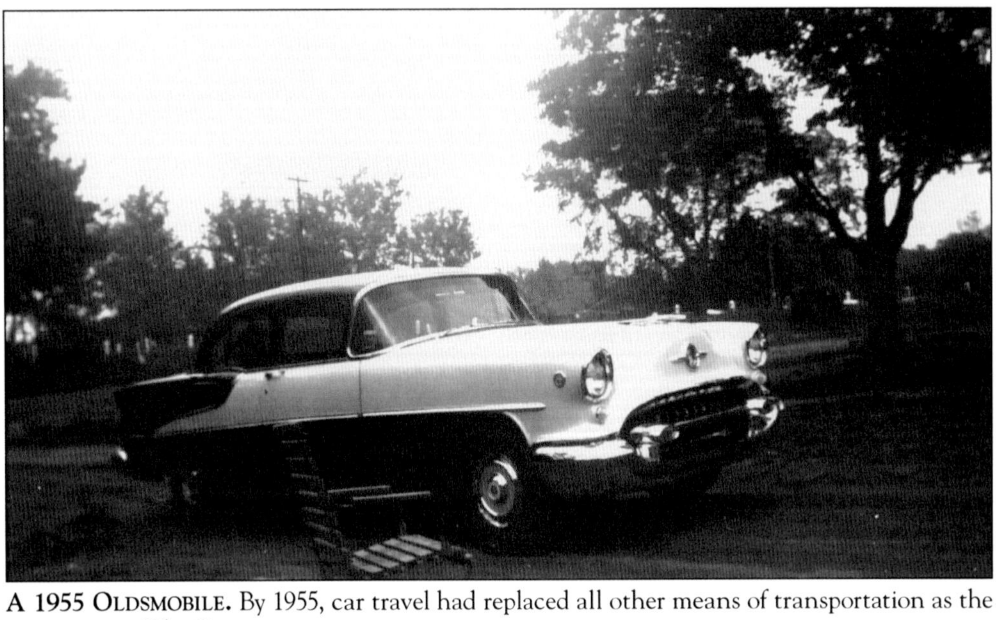

A 1955 OLDSMOBILE. By 1955, car travel had replaced all other means of transportation as the way to get to Pike County.

Four

WATER

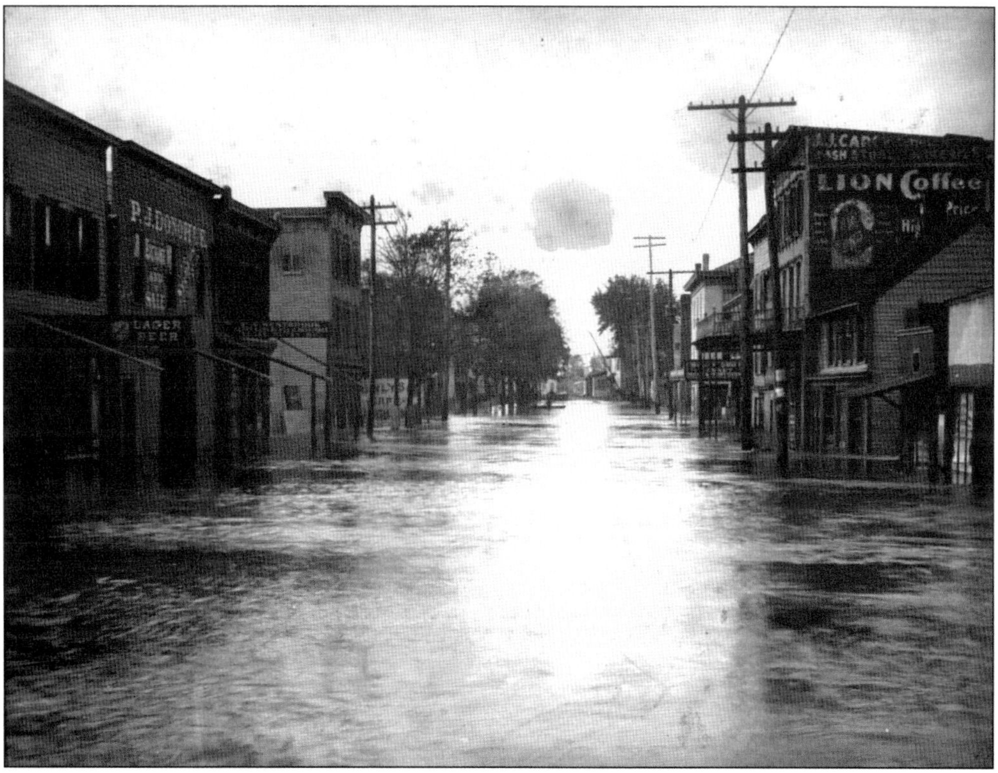

THE 1903 FLOOD. Pike County has experienced the highs and lows of water in all its forms. In October 1903, a flood ravaged Pike County, causing massive destruction and death. Bridges and dwellings were lifted from their foundations and carried into the mighty Delaware to be torn to pieces. John S. Durant was riding his bicycle across the Barrett Bridge when it collapsed and was swept away. He clung to floating debris until onlookers were able to pull him to safety.

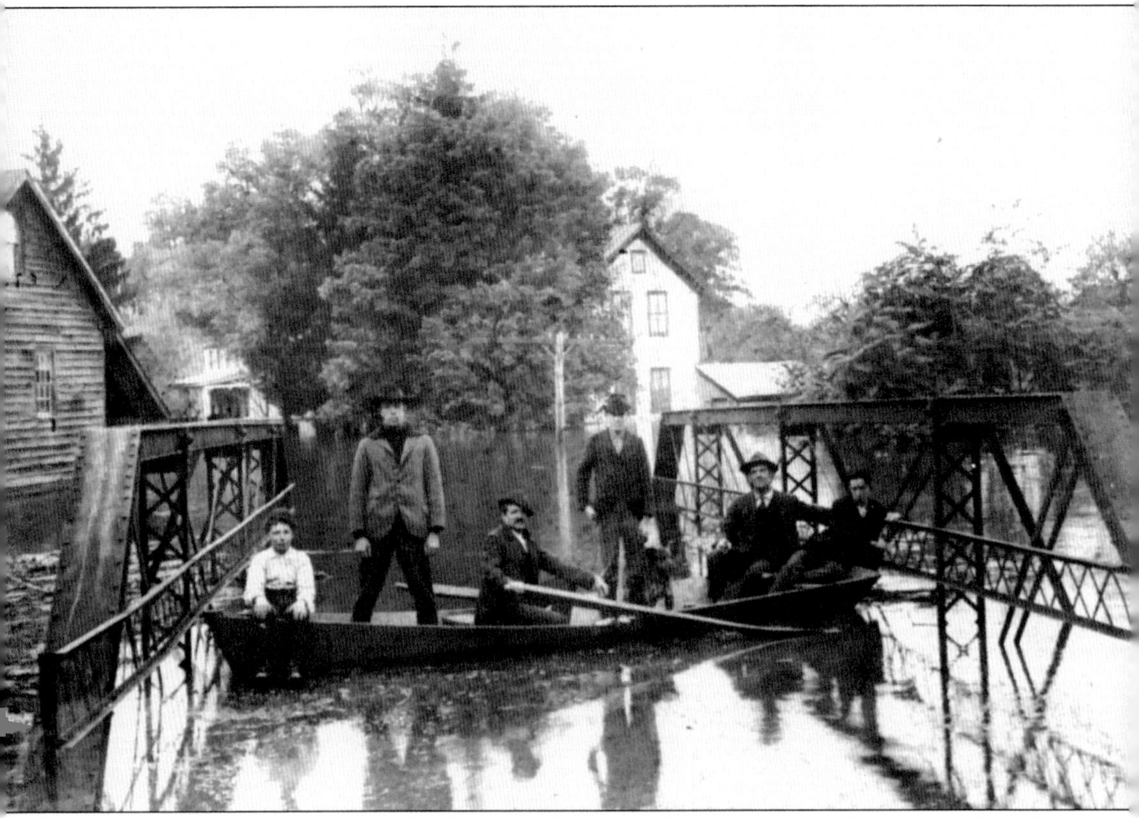

HAROLD BURNET AT METZ ICE HOUSE, MILFORD. Floodwaters caused many to take to boats in order to save themselves and others. Harold Burnet (second from left), certainly considered an interesting Pike County character, was the owner of a lion. In the years following the flood, he had a property that included a swimming pool, which he left unfilled in order to house the animal.

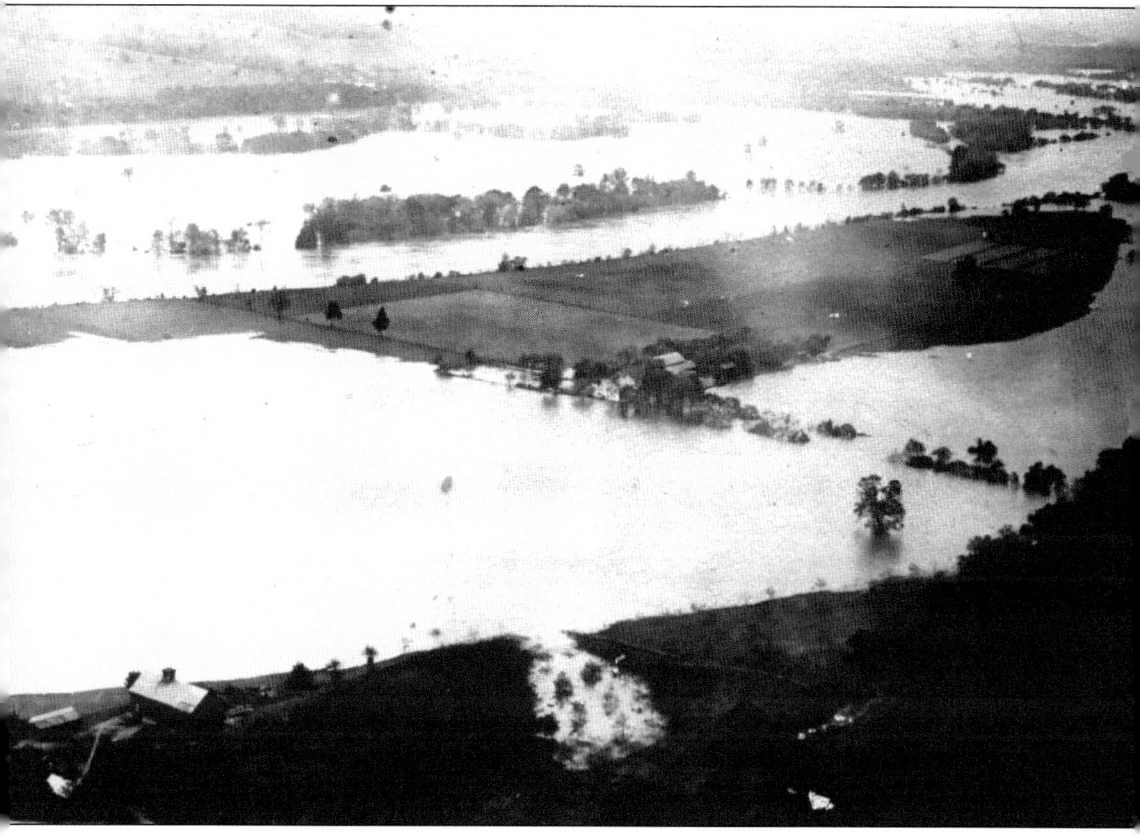

THE 1903 MODEL FARM. This area was farmed as far back as Lenape occupation. The flood ravaged acres upon acres of farmland and the casualties mounted. Among the fatalities, Stanley French, who was found by his brother with his body buried in the sand up to his shoulders with just his head above water. Blood was oozing from his ears, and no water was found in his lungs. It was determined that Stanley was killed by a blow to the head caused by debris and was dead before he went under water.

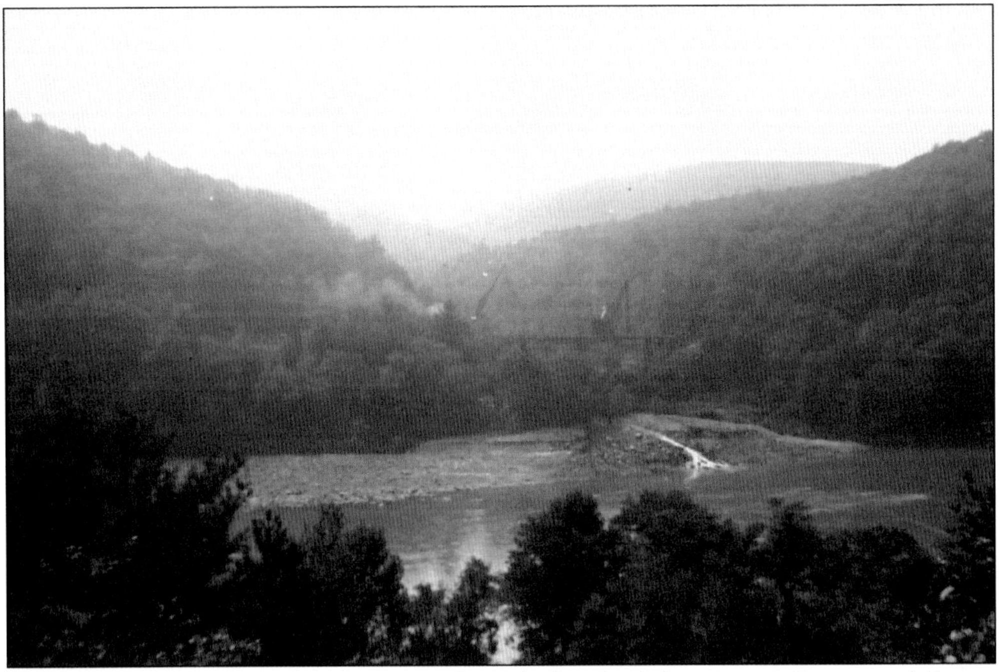

Flood of 1955. The rare combination of two back-to-back hurricanes, Connie and Diana, caused the most devastating flood to ever ravage Pike County.

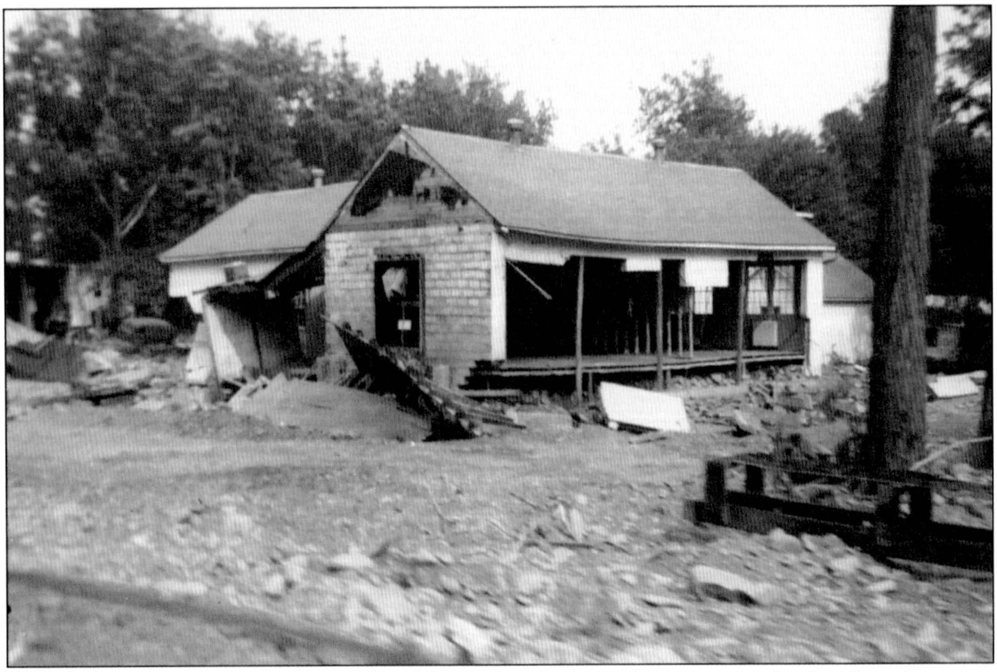

Campers sent Running during the Flood of 1955. In August, at the height of summer camp season, the floodwaters made necessary the evacuation to higher ground of scores of camp kids and counselors. They made their way to the safety of higher ground via human chains. Campers were surrounded by water with no recourse, and supplies had to be brought to them until they could be safely rescued.

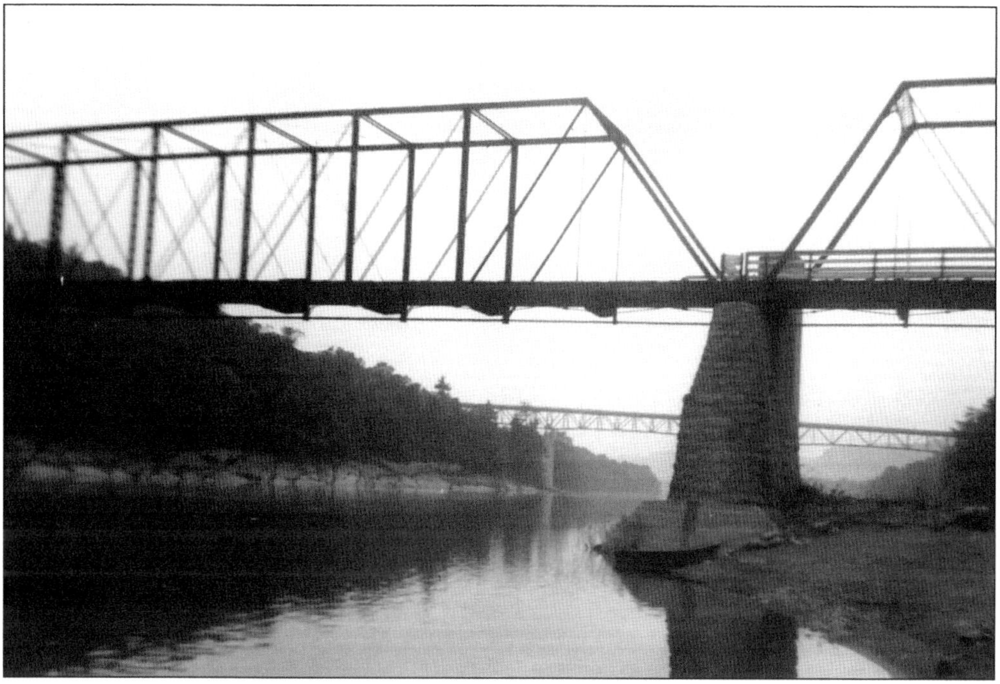

FLOOD'S DESTRUCTION. Bridges and railroad bridges were destroyed and roads disappeared beneath the giant lake created by the flood.

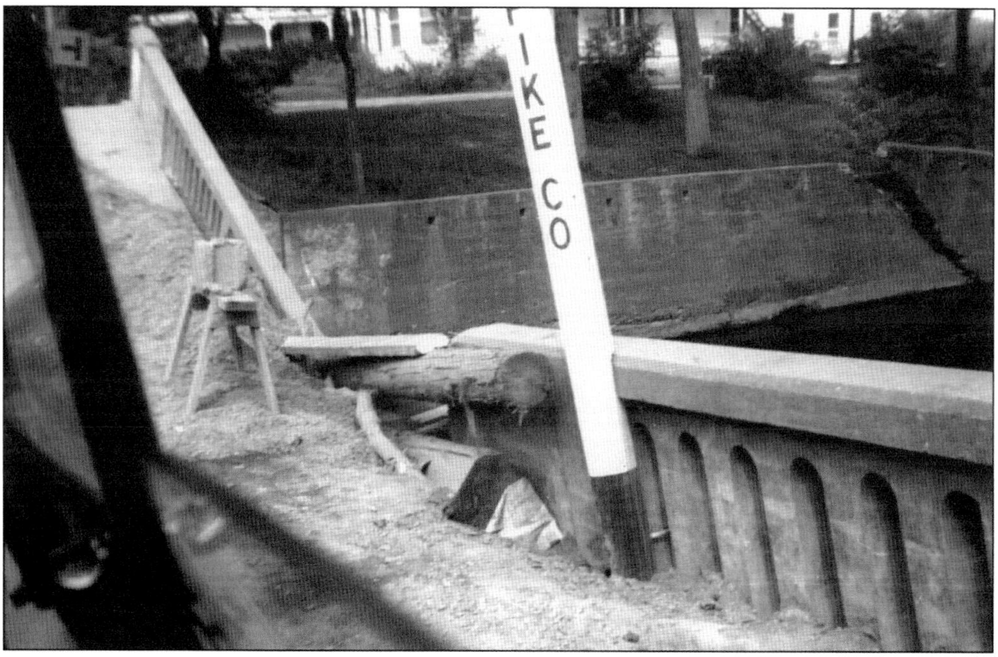

NEED FOR PREVENTION. Scores died, and thousands were made homeless in eastern Pennsylvania and western New Jersey by the hurricane-fed floods. This flood and earlier ones became one of the reasons for the proposed Tocks Island Dam Project sighting flood control as a perk of the project. There is much doubt that anything could have been done to prevent this situation given the back-to-back wallop that the hurricanes produced.

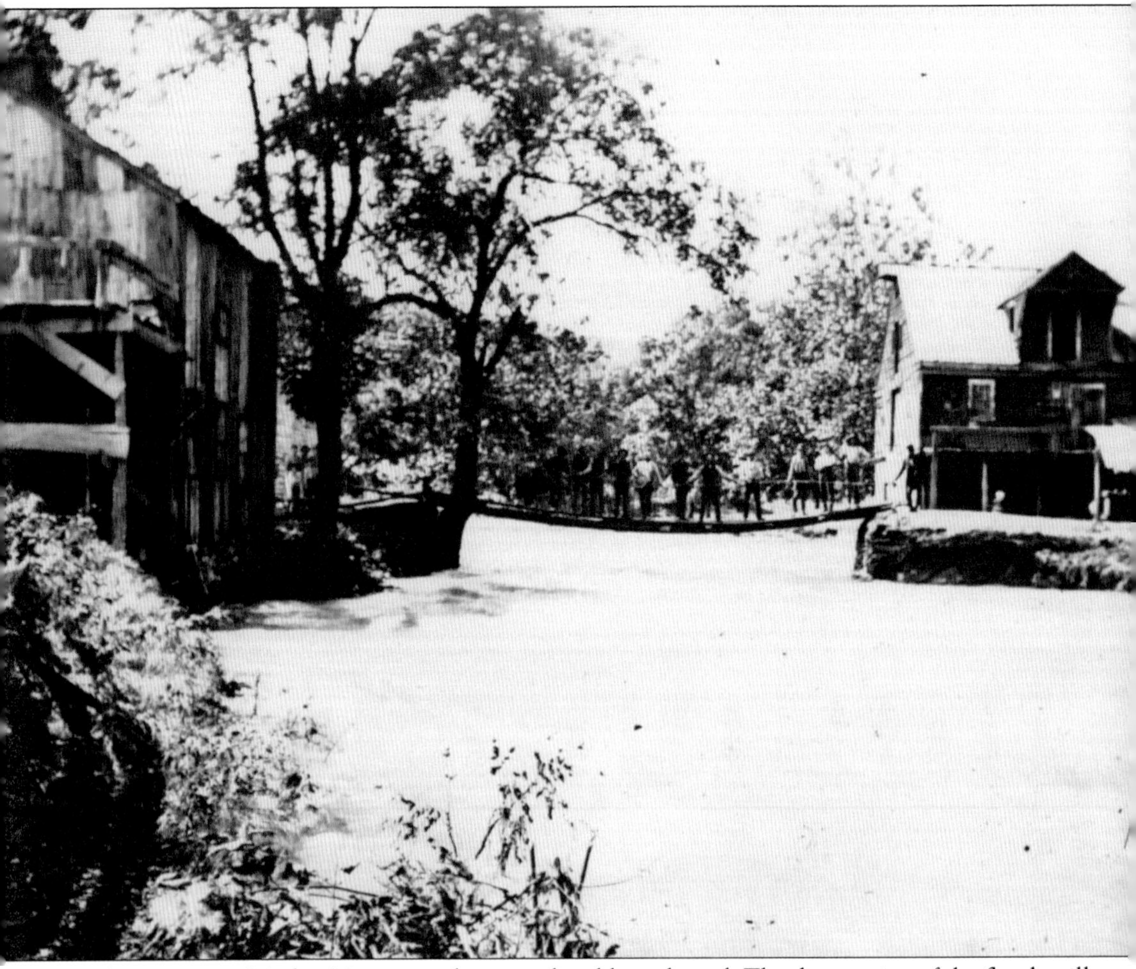

AFTERMATH. Mother Nature can be unpredictable and cruel. The devastation of the floods will not soon be forgotten.

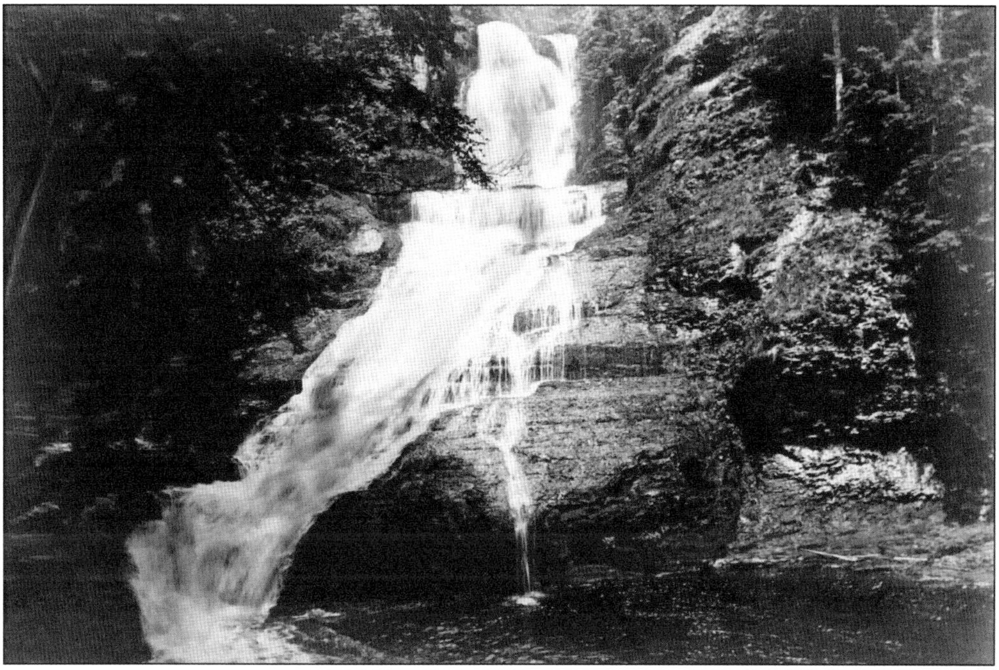

HIGH FALLS, DINGMANS FERRY, 1889. The fluviarchy of Pike County certainly is an additional factor in the Delaware River's water level equation. Run-off from melting snow, rain, and donations from the Delaware River tributaries all make for many uneasy hours for those living along the river.

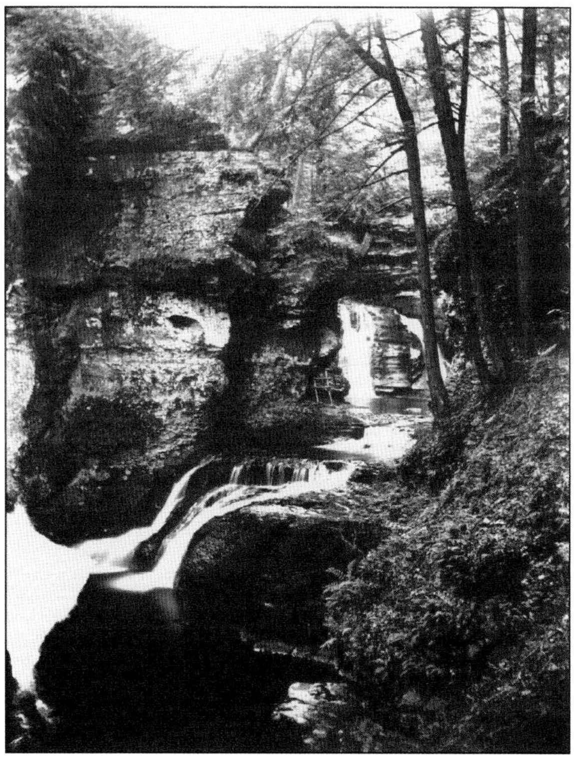

ROCKY GORGE, ADAMS BROOK, DINGMANS FERRY. Rocky Gorge is fed by Adam's Creek and named after the Adams family who resided there in 1861.

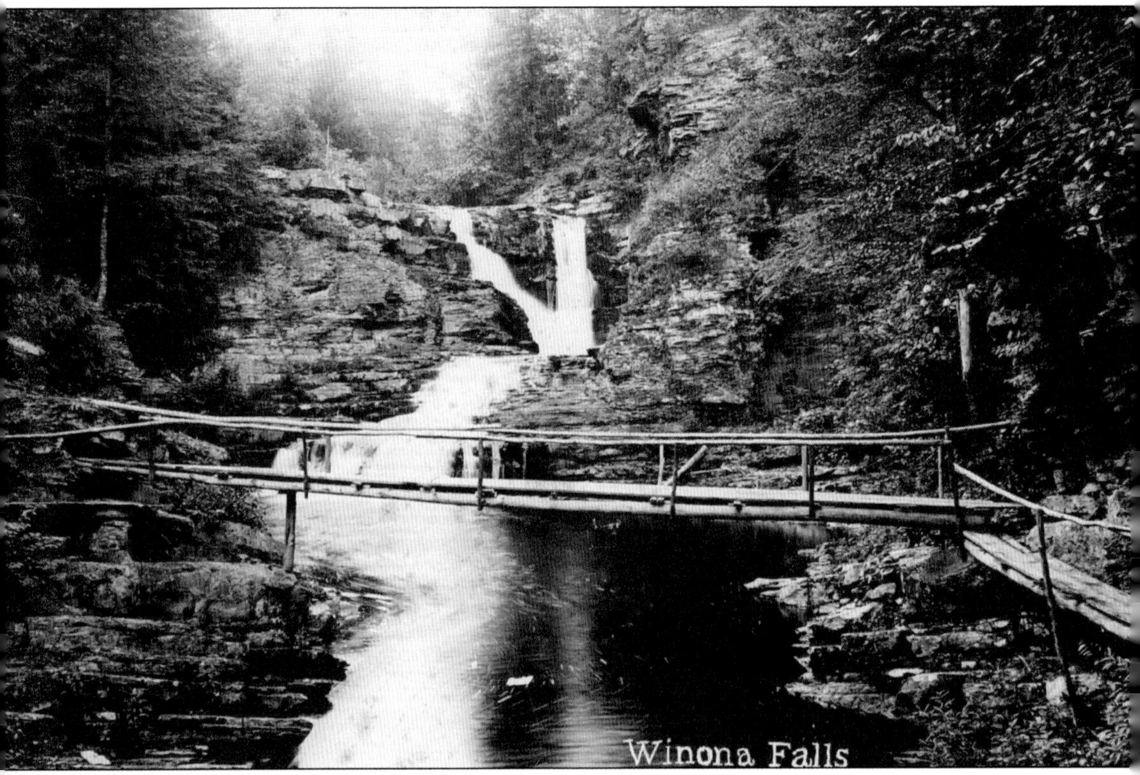

WINONA FALLS, LEHMAN TOWNSHIP. Legend dictates that Native American princess Winona pined over her unrequited love, a white soldier. Not able to live without him, she attempted to take her life by jumping from the top of the falls. In an effort to save her, the soldier also fell to his death.

BUSHKILL FALLS, LEHMAN TOWNSHIP. Bushkill Falls, a popular tourist attraction, opened in 1904. Bushkill is often referred to as the Niagara of Pennsylvania.

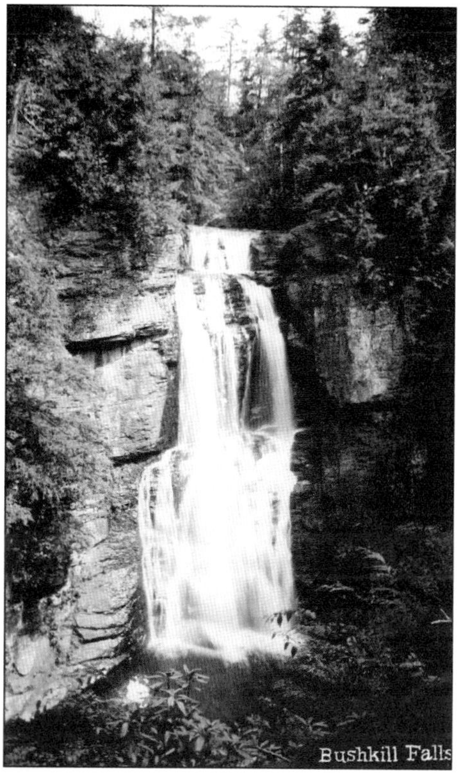

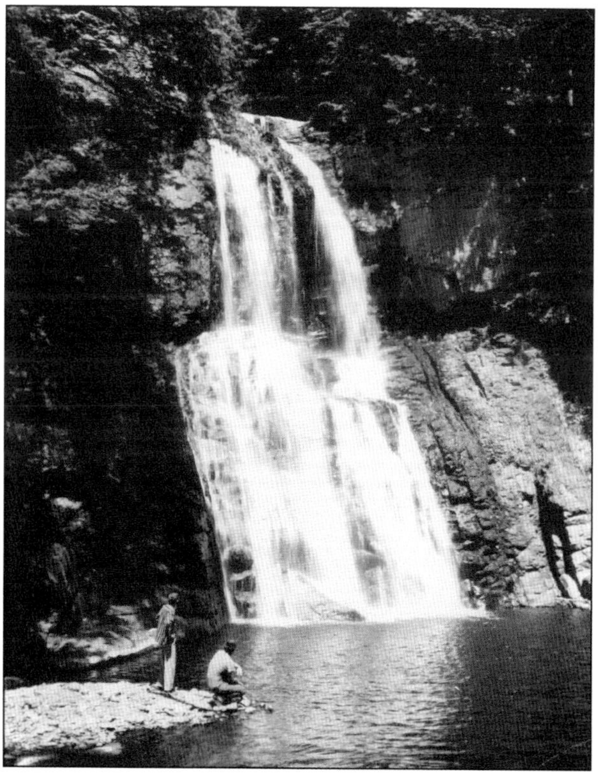

BUSHKILL FALLS. Bushkill Falls are fed by the Big Bushkill Creek and cascade over 100 feet. The sights and sound of Bushkill Falls are breathtaking.

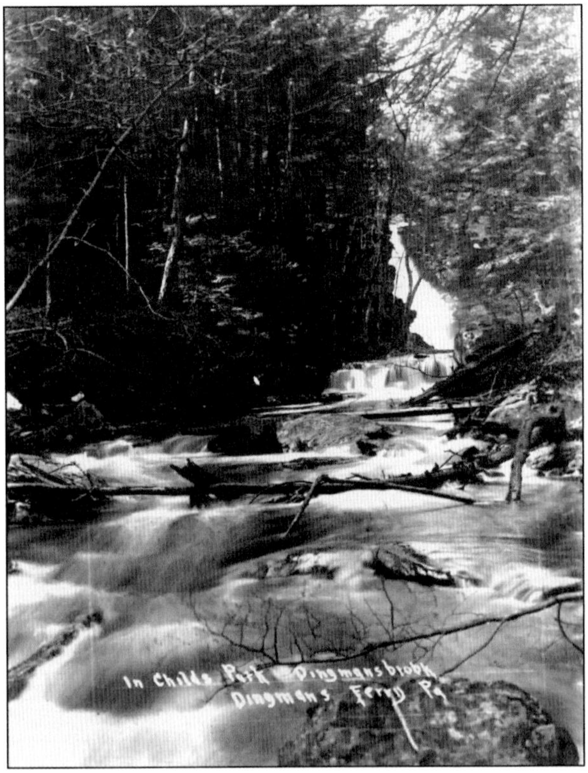

CHILDS PARK, DINGMANS FERRY. The water flowing from Dingmans Creek forms three sets of waterfalls within George W. Childs Park. Wooden-planked walkways and stairs make the falls an easy experience.

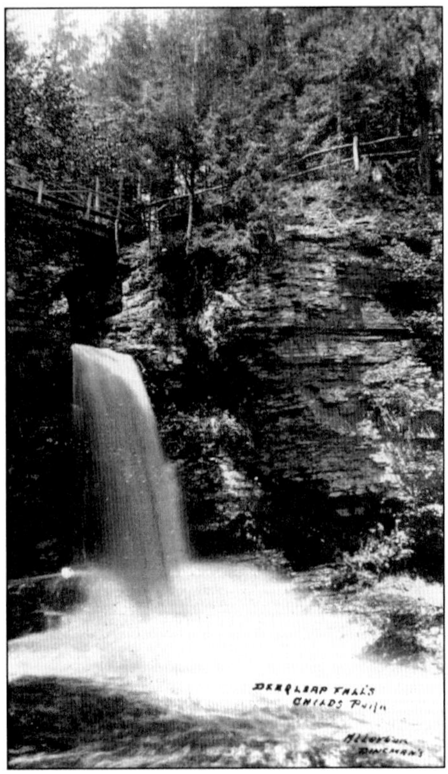

DEER LEAP FALLS, CHILDS PARK. This is a view of one of the three sets of waterfalls visible in George W. Childs Park. The park was donated by Mrs. Childs in loving memory of her husband, who was publisher of the *Philadelphia Public Ledger* and a philanthropist of note.

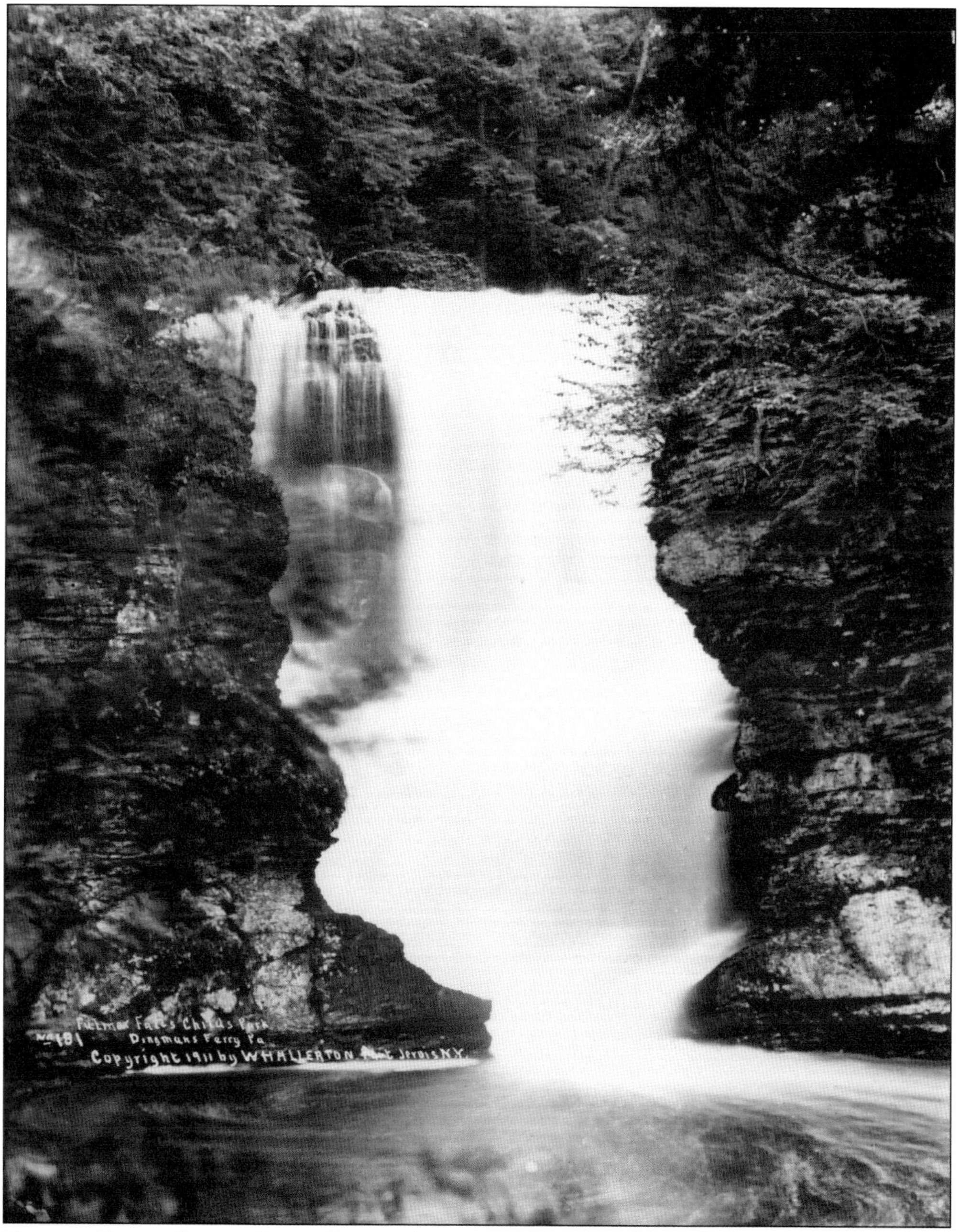

FULMER FALLS, CHILDS PARK. Yet another waterfall within the park is Fulmer Falls. Nearby Fulmerville was a town in and of itself near the falls. John Fulmer operated a tannery. A post office was established there in 1853, and a schoolhouse and store also existed. A welcome addition to the area was Phillip Fulmer, John's son. He was a practicing physician and made a great country doctor by all known accounts. By 1892, a once flourishing Fulmerville was no more.

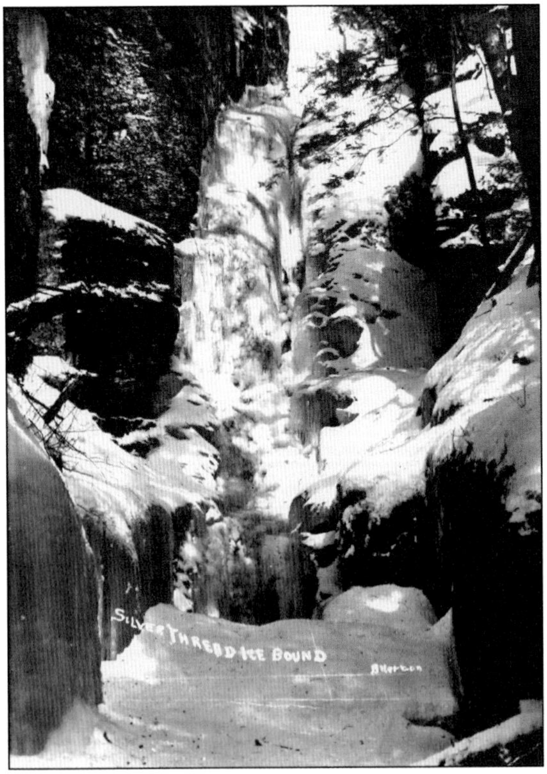

SILVER THREAD FALLS ICEBOUND. Located in Dingman Gorge, the Silver Thread Falls drop 80 feet. They are also known as the "Soap Trough."

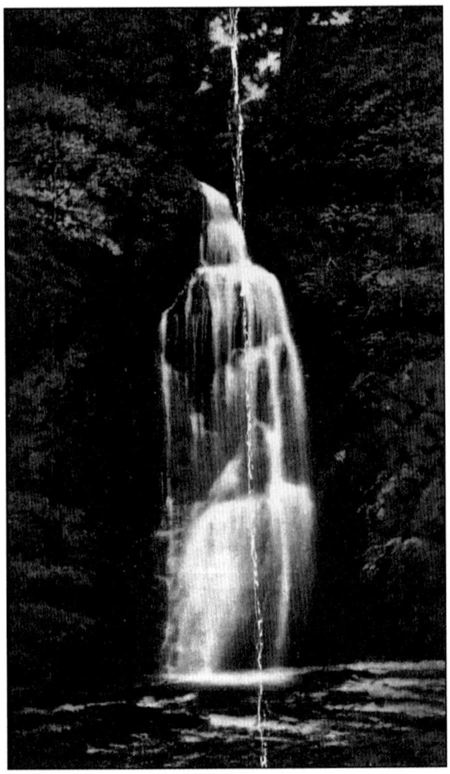

RAYMONDSKILL FALLS. These beautiful falls are found within Dingman Township and are referred to as the "Monarch of Milford Fluviarchy."

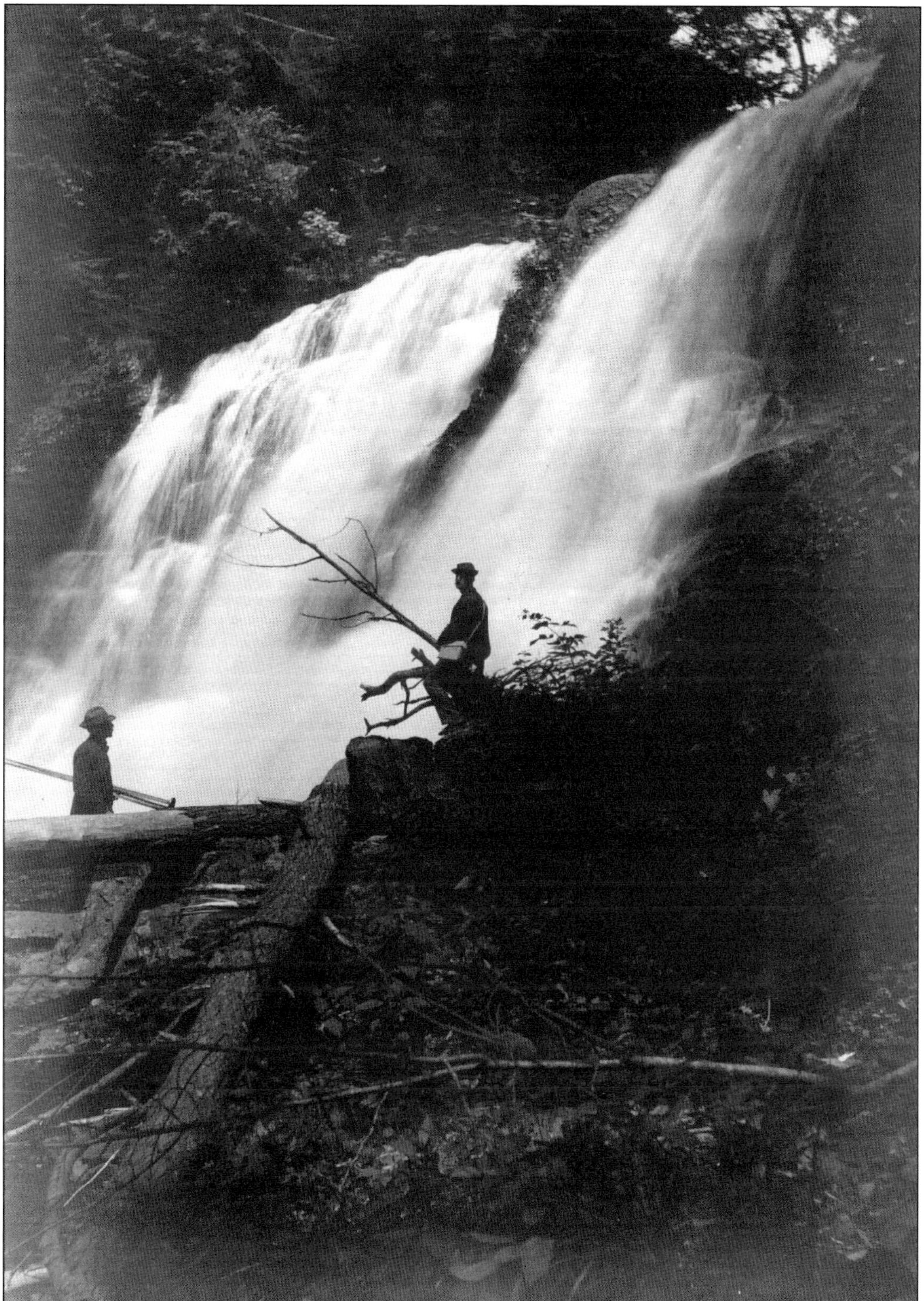

RAYMONDSKILL FALLS, 1889. Edmund C. Stedman declared that he had more pleasure in gazing at the Raymondskill Falls than at Niagara itself.

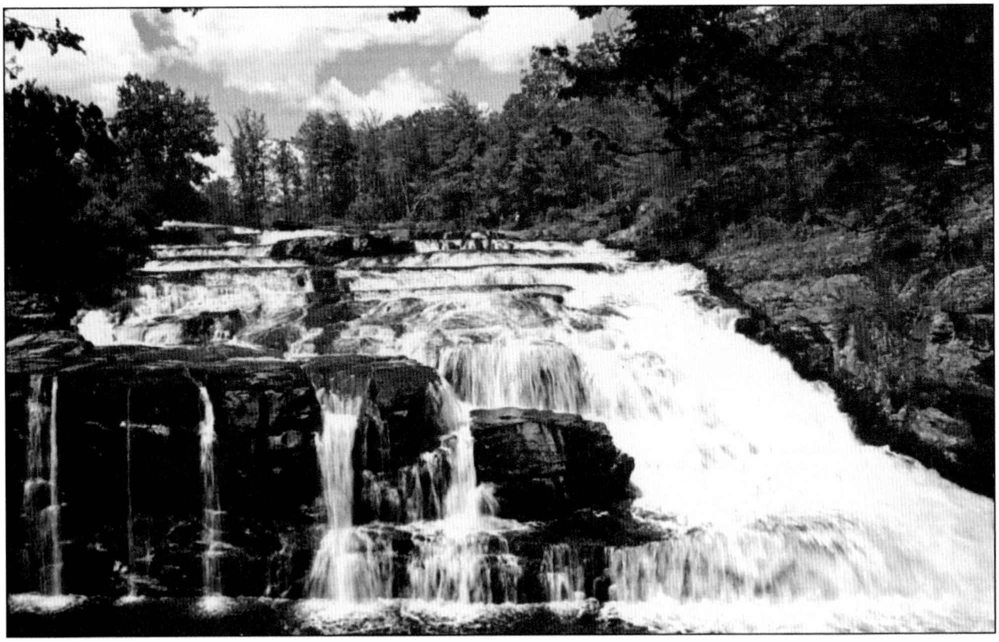

SHOHOLA FALLS. Shohola Falls differ from most Pike County falls because they drop in numerous steep ledges in succession and create a cascading effect.

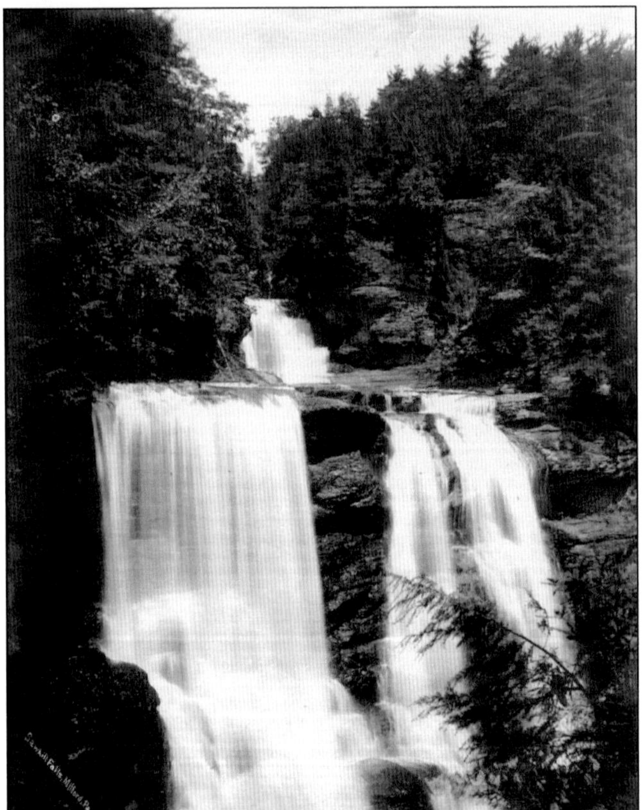

FAVORITE SPOT. Located near Grey Towers, Sawkill Falls were once a favorite spot among many residents and visitors.

SAWKILL FALLS, 1889. This 1889 scene may never be recreated, as the falls are not accessible to the public anymore, keeping one of Pike County's natural wonders at arms length.

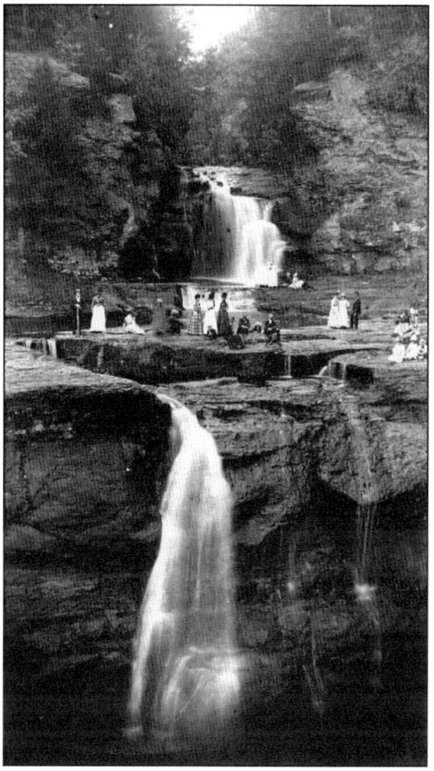

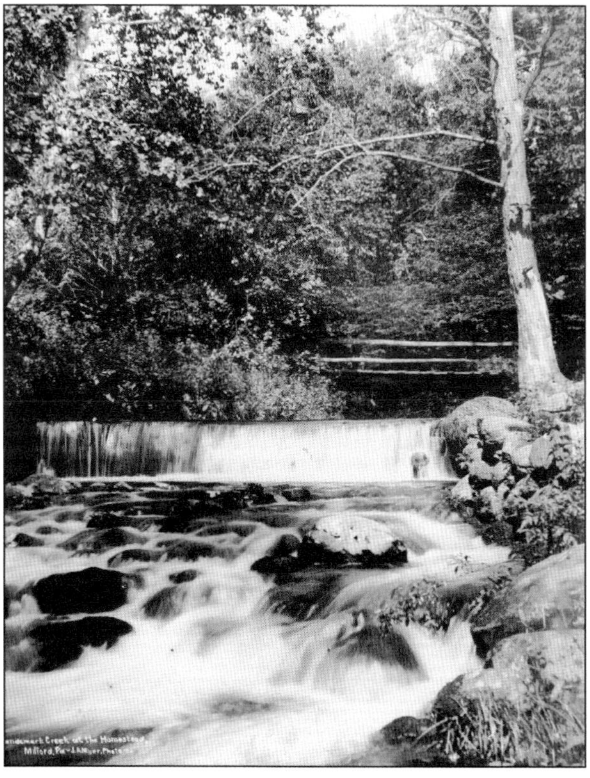

VANDERMARK CREEK. The Vandermark Creek is one of many creeks in Pike County that makes its way to the Delaware River.

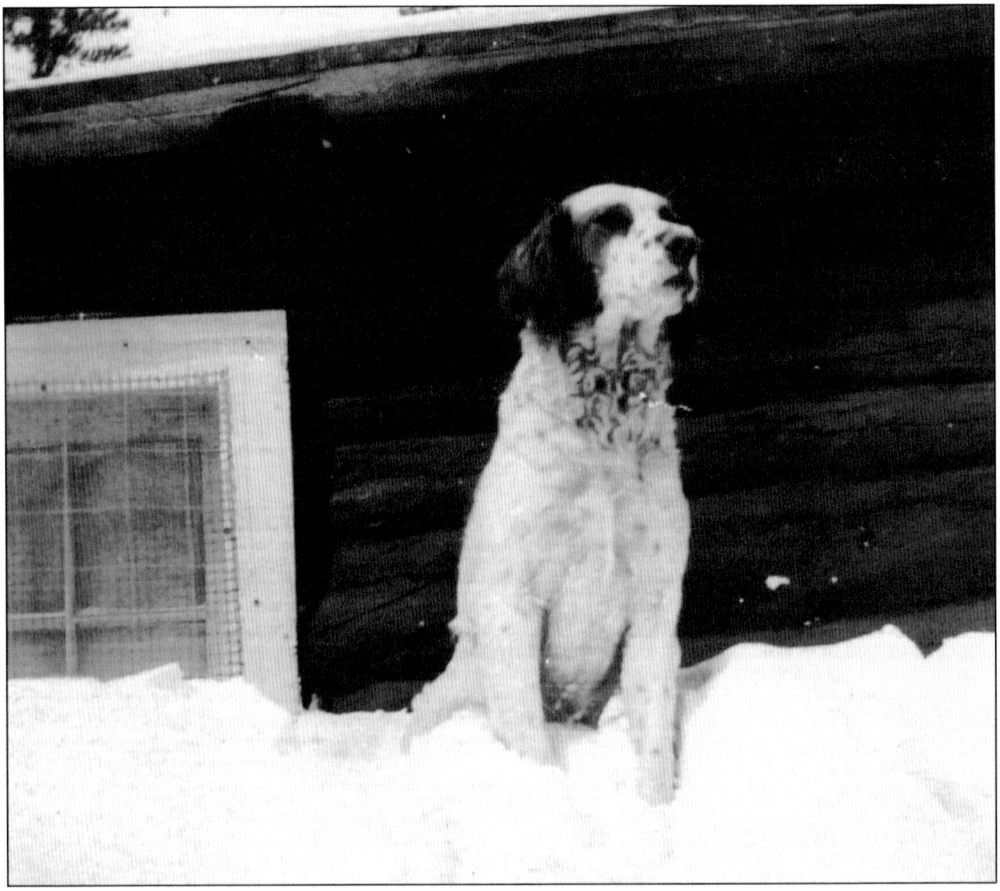

DOG. The treacherous winter conditions in Pike County are sometimes not fit for man or beast.

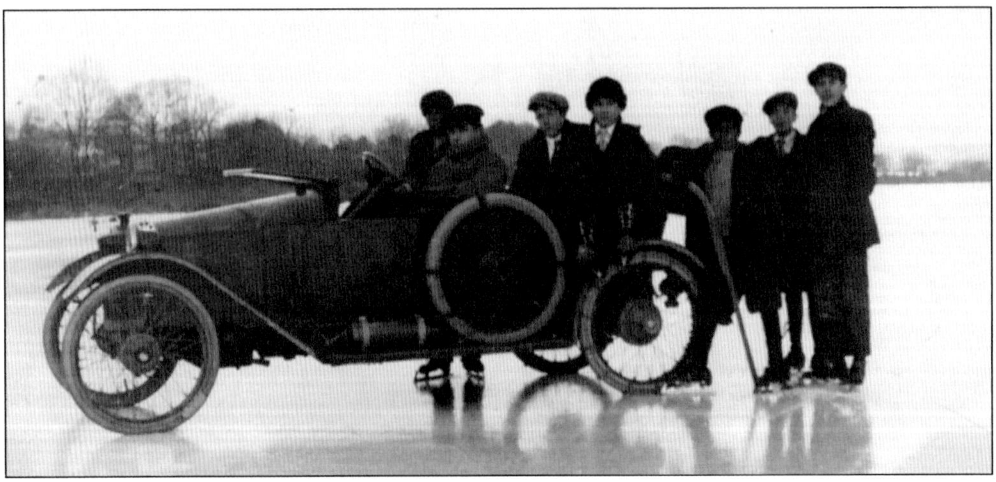

CAR ICE. Scenes such as this are an unlikely site today.

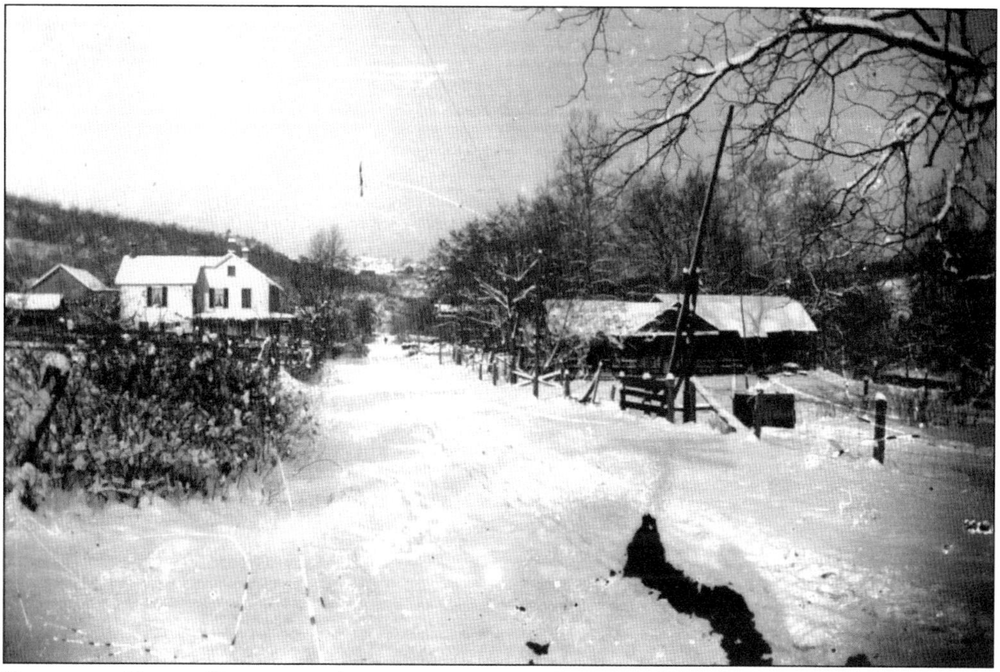

DINGMANS FERRY. Picturesque for certain, snow in winter is a Pike County staple.

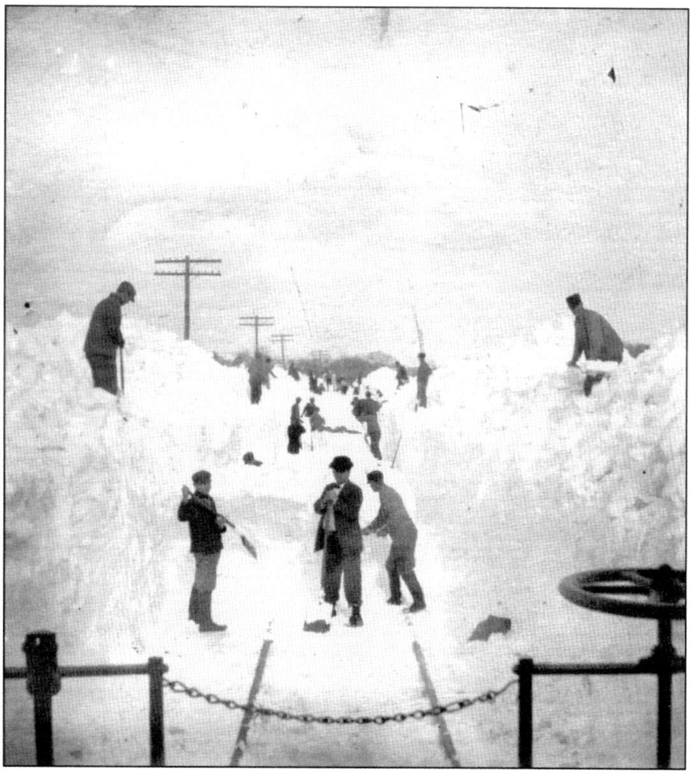

BLIZZARD OF 1914. In 1914, record snowfall brought the county to its knees.

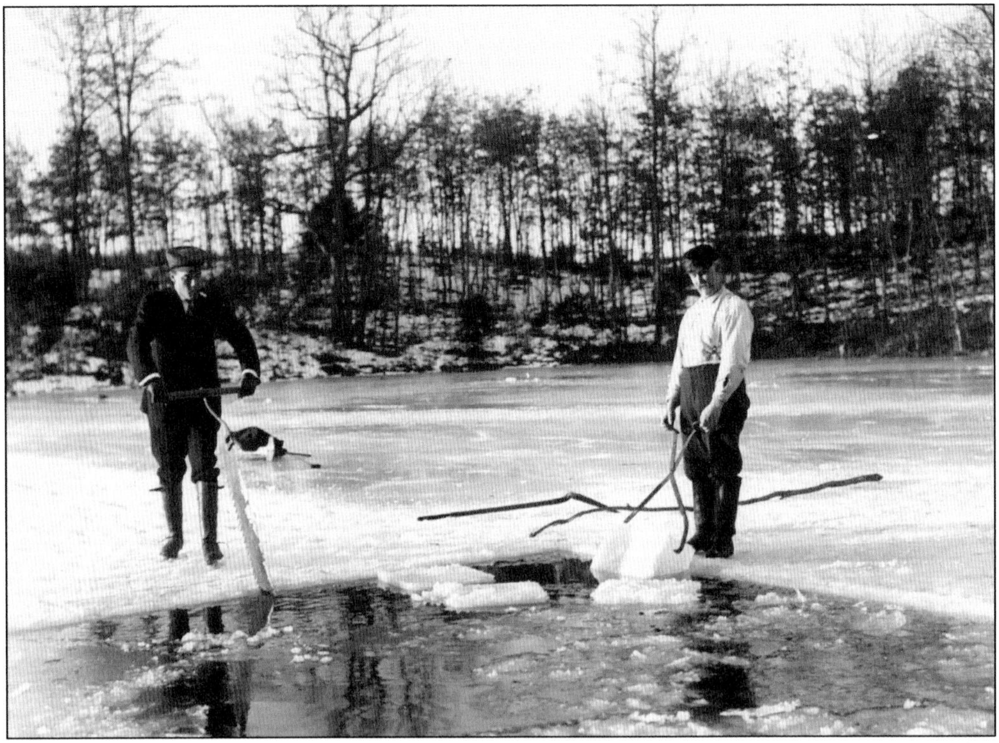

CUTTING ICE IN MILFORD. The ice industry was once a necessity in rural Pike County. This picture was taken on Christmas Day, 1910.

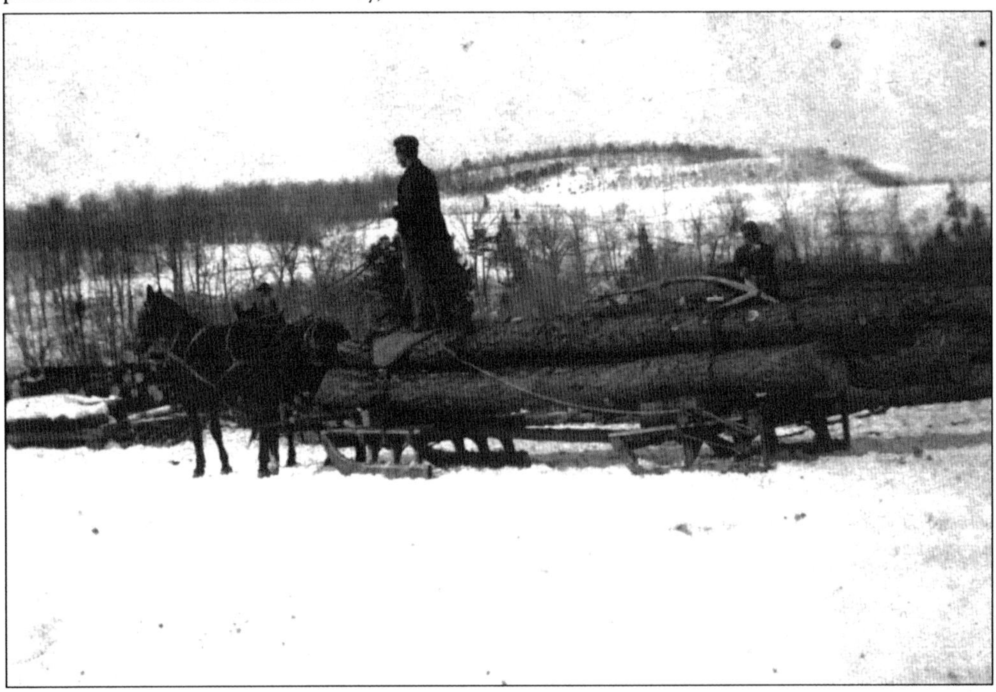

TRANSPORTING LOGS. Rain, sleet, or snow could not stop lumber from transport during the winter months, as evidenced here.

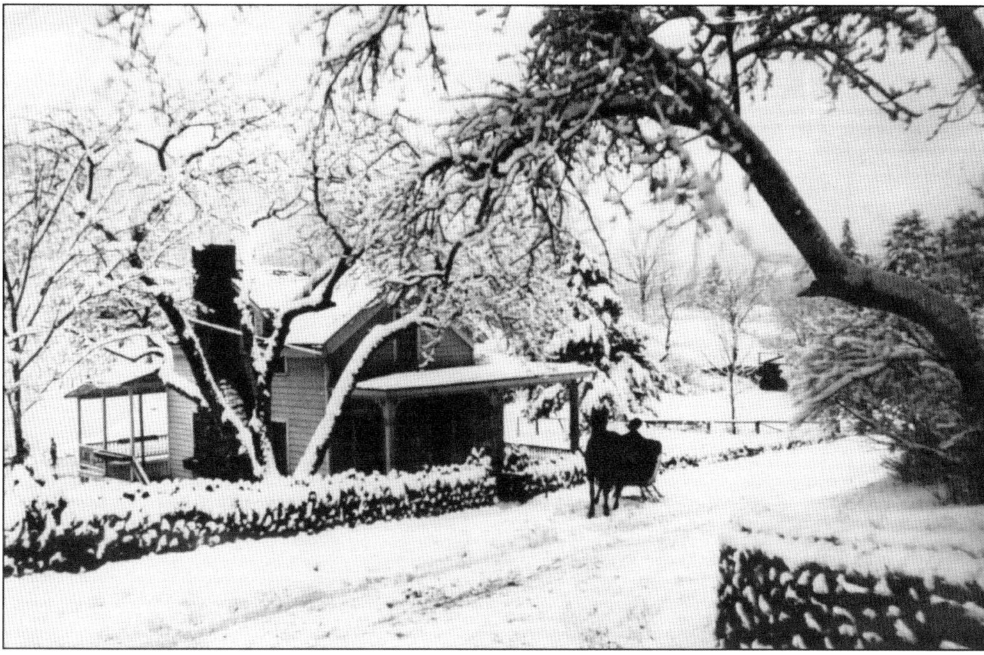

Snow Scene. Snowmelt also adds to water levels, and the annual spring thaw can prove an added complication to flood concerns.

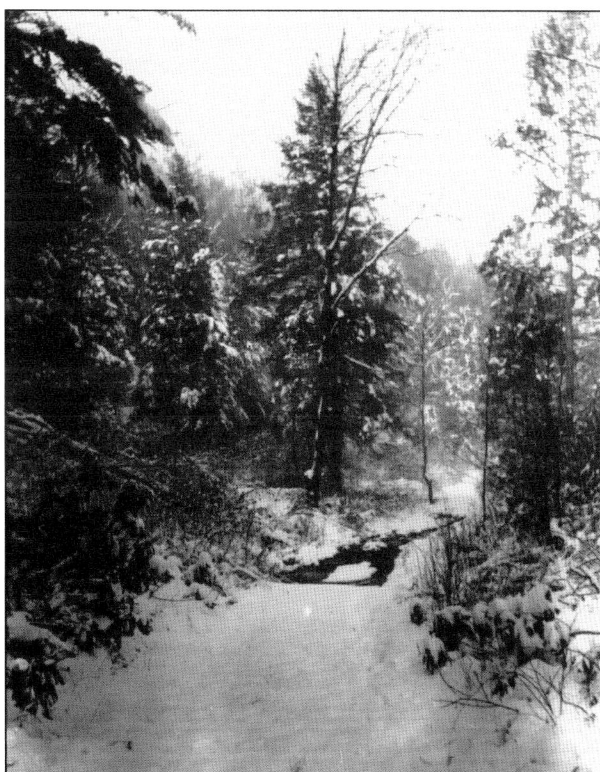

Silver Thread Pond. The environs encompassed by Silver Lake Pond and Falls were once described as enchanting.

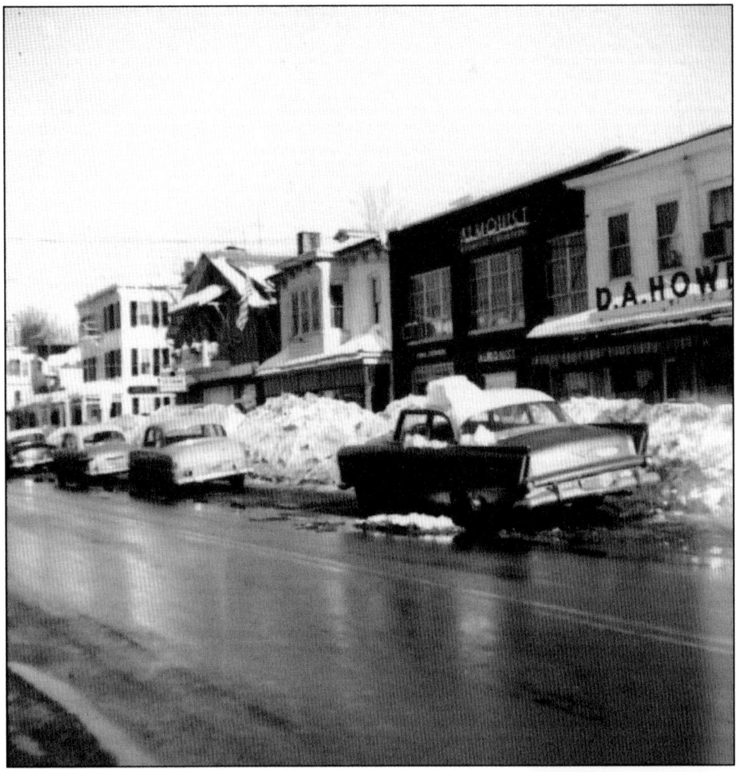

MILFORD, 1950. Seen here is the aftermath of snowfall.

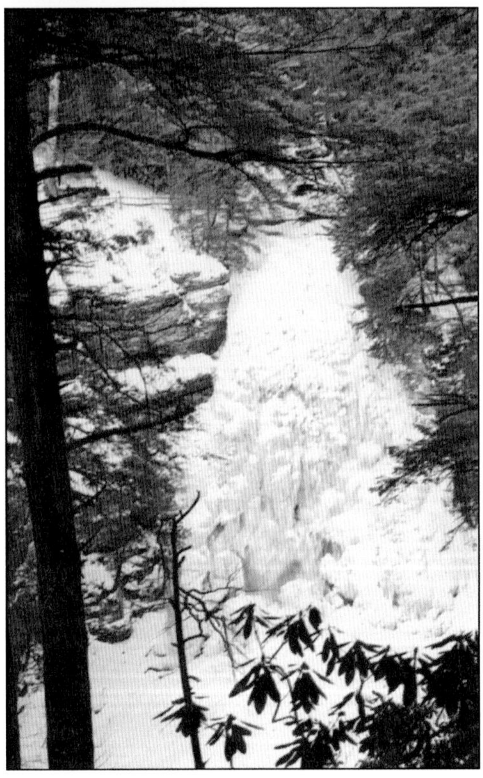

BUSHKILL FROZEN. The weather has to be rather cold for such fast-moving water to freeze.

Five

Talk about Tocks

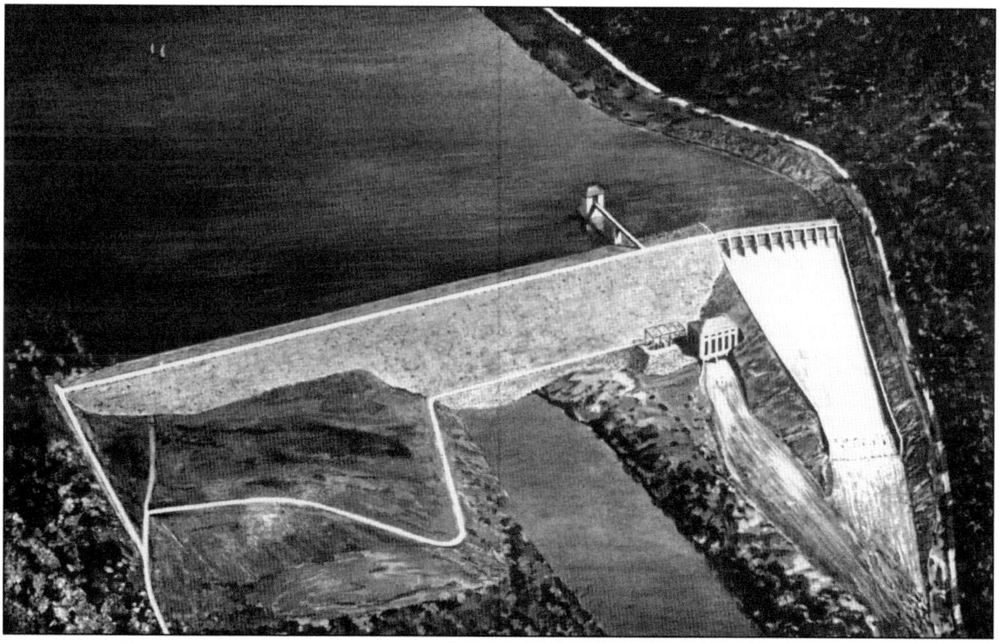

Artist's Rendering of the Tocks Island Dam. In 1962, Congress authorized the construction of a 160-foot-high dam across the Delaware River near Stroudsburg. The goal of the Tocks Island Dam was to create a 35-mile, 12,000-acre reservoir.

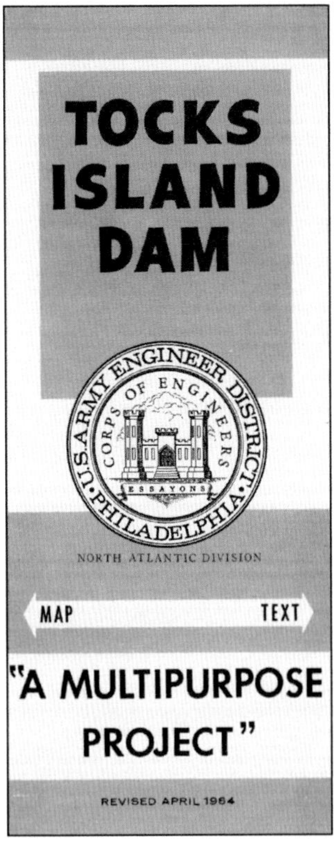

TOCKS ISLAND PAMPHLET, APRIL 1965. The Tocks Island Dam Project caused quite a stir. An ambitions project authorized by Congress, it would have created a 30-mile-long lake to the Delaware River above the Delaware Water Gap. A dam would be built on the Upper Delaware River. The previous floods were cause for the initiation of the project, as were water supplies, recreation, and power.

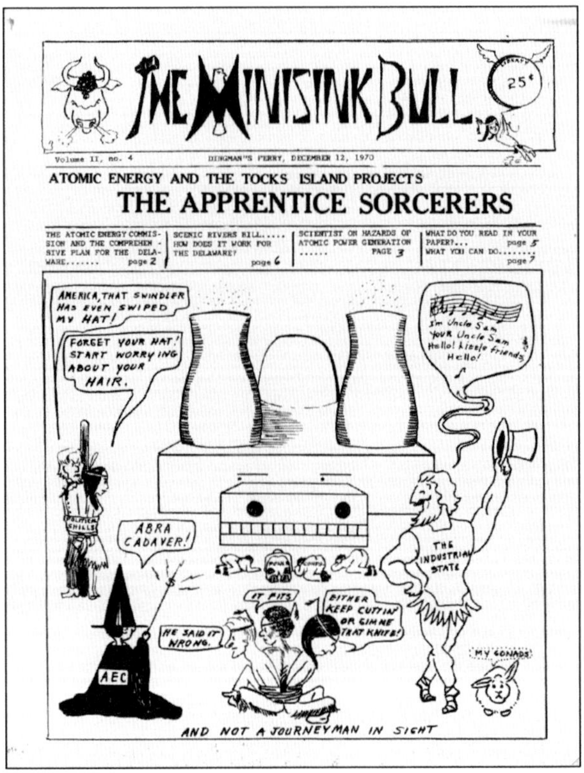

MINISINK BULL, ATOMIC ENERGY ISSUE. The potential environmental impact the reservoir would cause brought to light many unanswered questions, such as regulating pollution, transportation, development, and the economy of the impacted area.

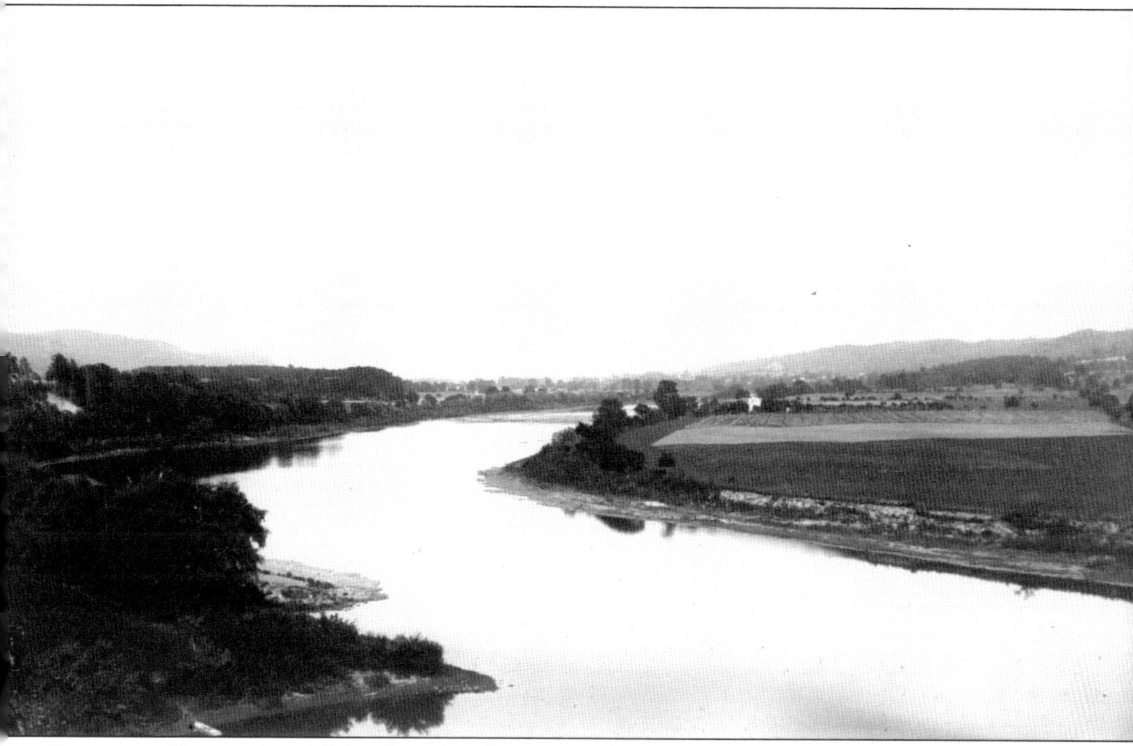

Delaware River, 1884. The thought of turning a beautiful, free-flowing river segment with white water stretches into a stagnant lake garnered much opposition from area residents.

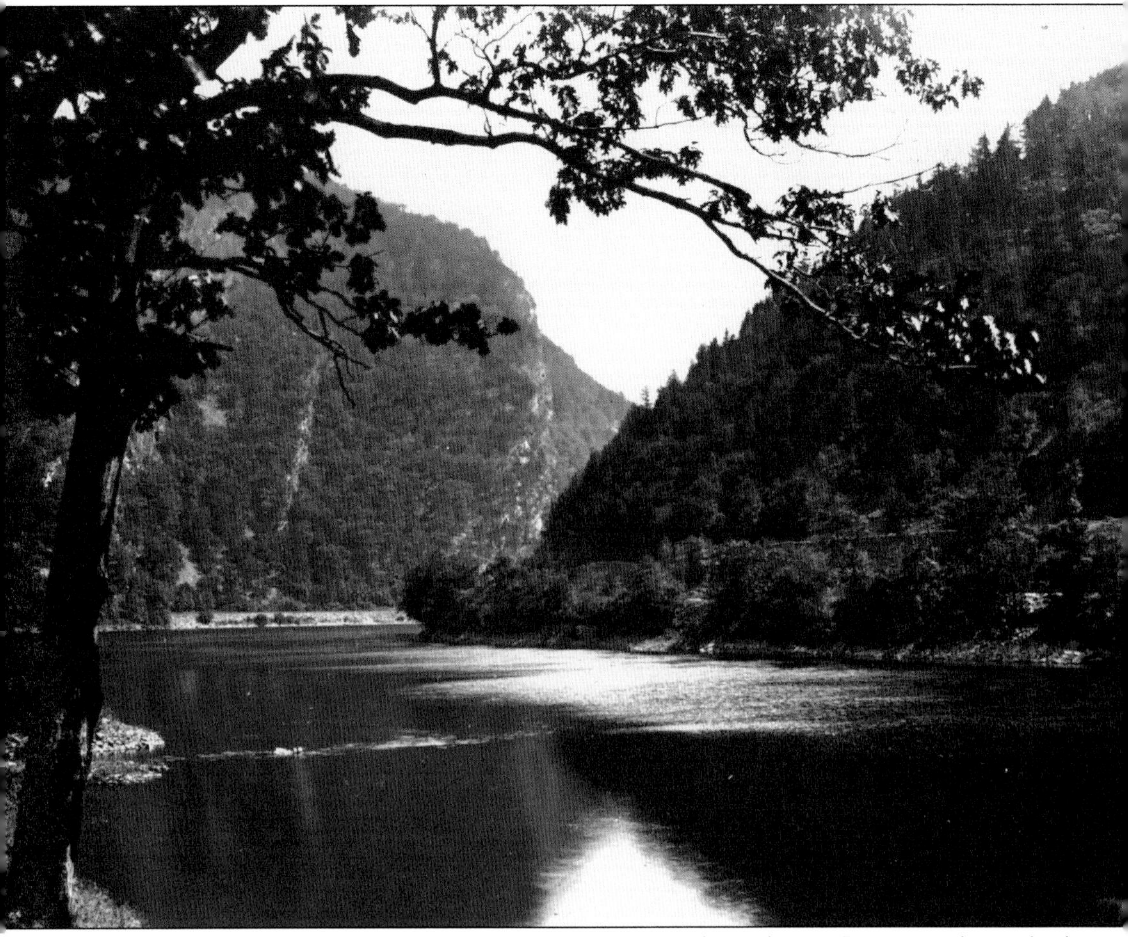

DELAWARE RIVER AT DELAWARE WATER GAP, 1898. The Delaware River travels nearly the same course today as it did over 200 million years ago when it made its way across the Schooley Penaplain and eventually reached the ocean.

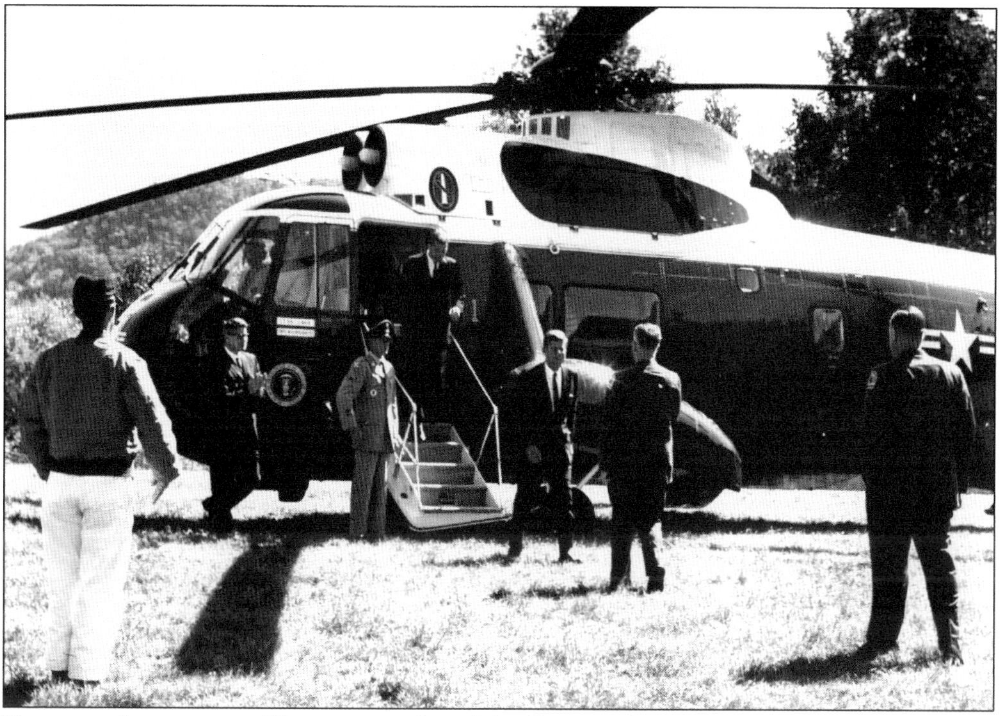

KENNEDY ARRIVAL VIA HELICOPTER. Pres. John F. Kennedy supported the Tocks Island Dam Project in 1963 at his visit to Grey Towers.

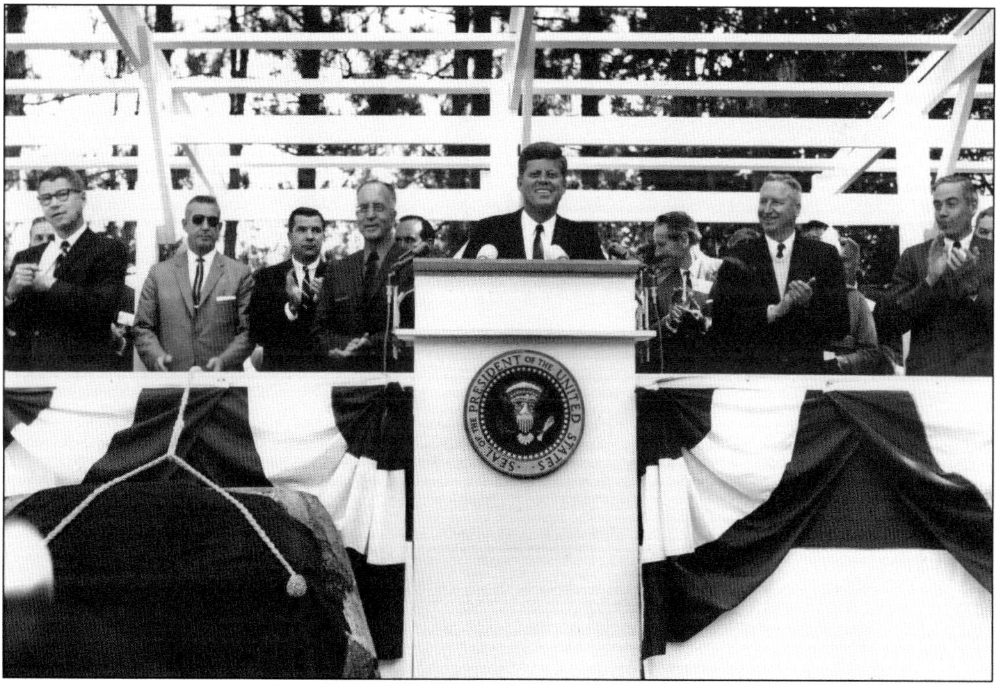

KENNEDY AT PODIUM. On September 24, 1963, President Kennedy visited Pike County to dedicate Grey Towers as the Pinchot Institute for conservation studies. He spoke of many conservation projects and touted the Tocks Island Dam Project as one he endorsed.

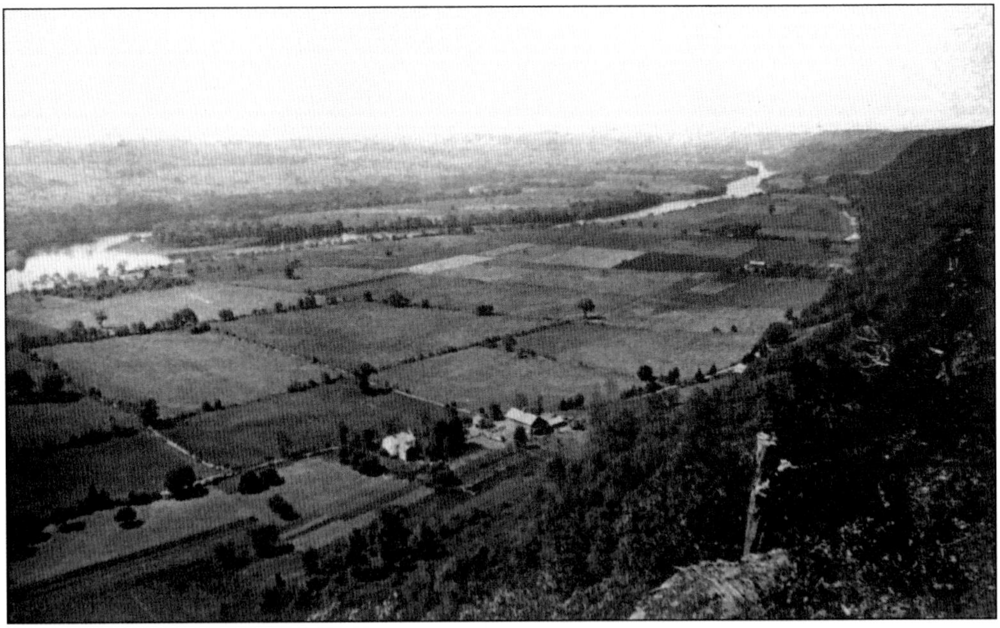

AERIAL VIEW OF MODEL FARM. Farming the highly fertile soils along the Delaware River lowland would no longer be an option if the Tocks Island Dam Project became a reality.

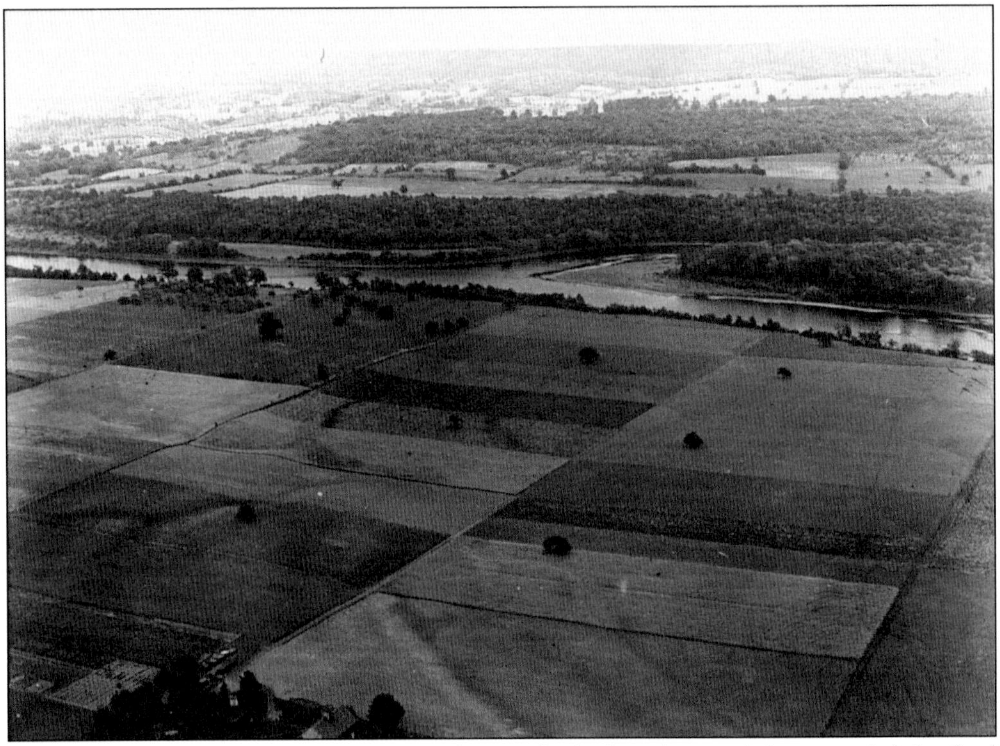

AERIAL VIEW OF DIETRICH FARM. Dietrich Farm had a burial ground that provided the final resting place for many early Pike County settlers whose names would be carried on by descendants through many years to follow. The farm also had one of the finest shad fisheries on the Delaware River. Shad were sold for 15¢–60¢, depending on size.

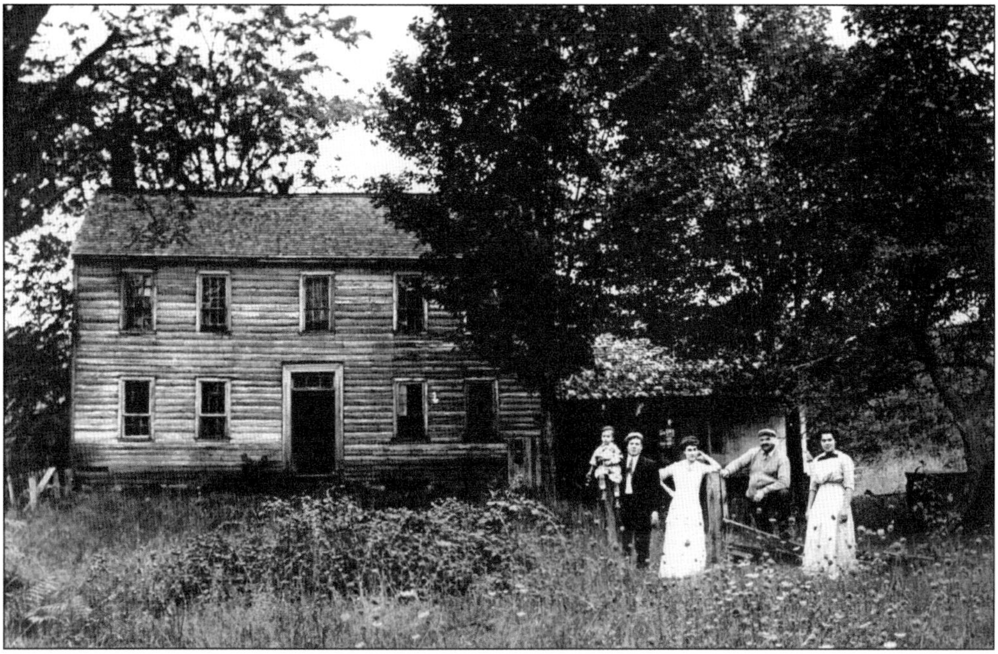

THE DIETRICH HOME. Within the boundaries of the Tocks Island proposal was the Dietrich house. This two-story frame house had a fireplace in every room.

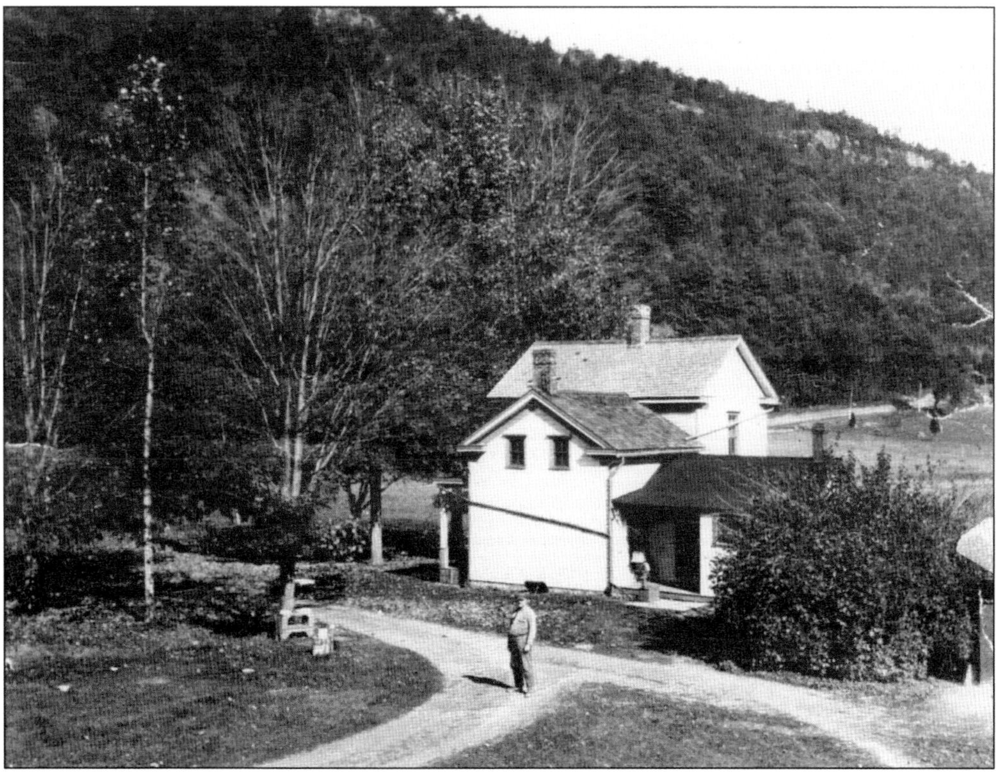

TENANTS' HOUSE. The Dietrichs bought their property in 1860, and it was farmed by John and Moses Dietrich.

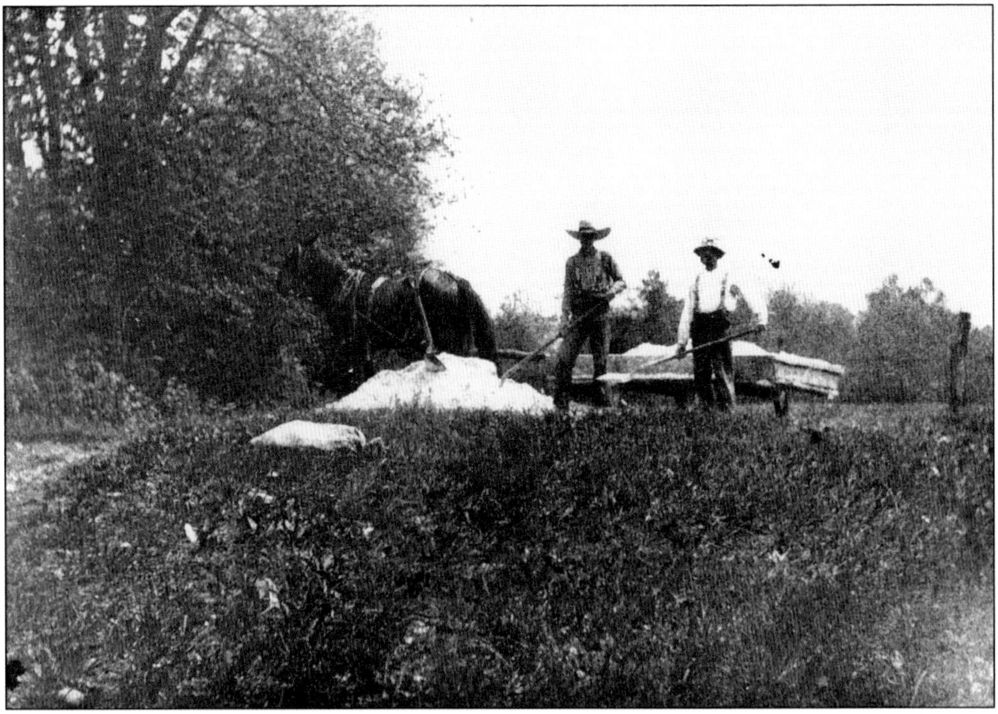

SPREADING LIME IN BUSHKILL. So much farm land would be lost to the Tocks proposal. Once occupied by the Native Americans, the Dutch named Bushkill, which was an outpost of the Pennsylvania frontier, during the French and Indian War.

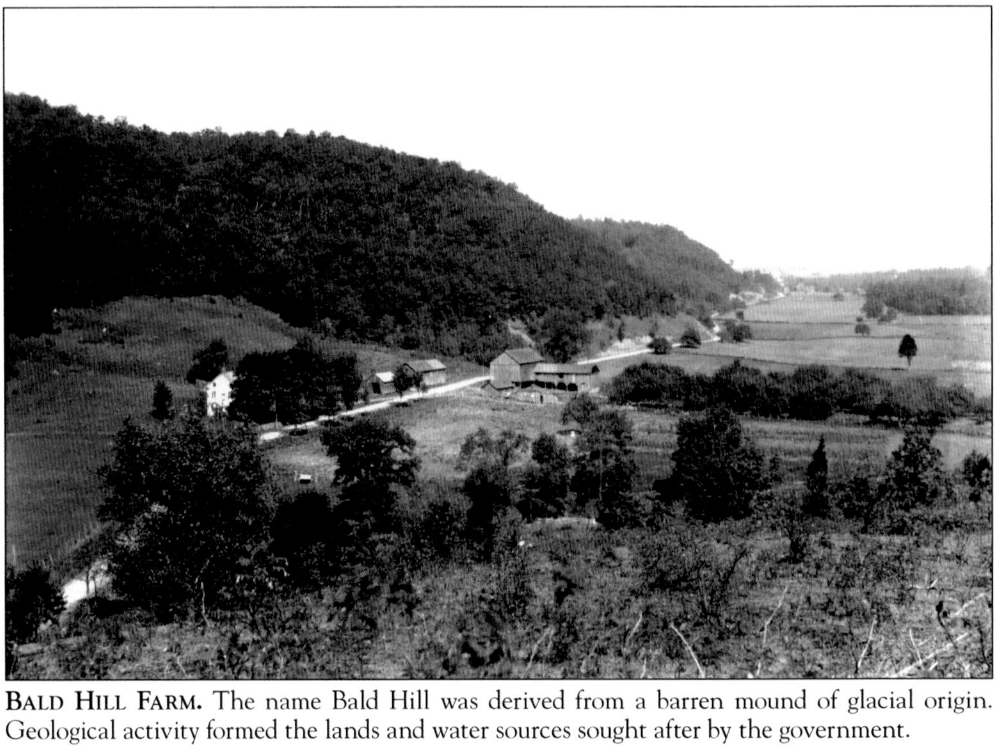

BALD HILL FARM. The name Bald Hill was derived from a barren mound of glacial origin. Geological activity formed the lands and water sources sought after by the government.

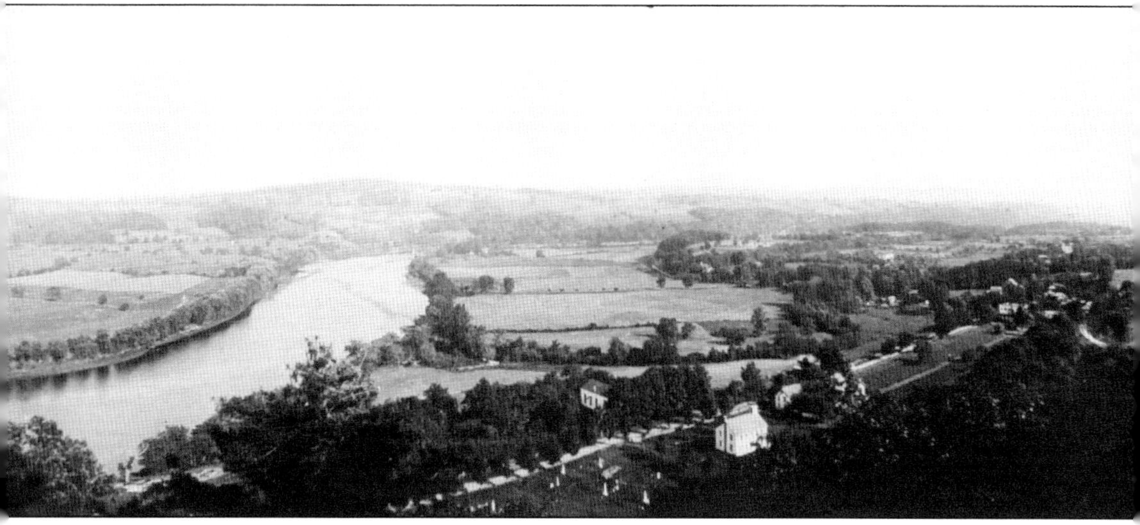

DINGMANS FERRY WITH RIVER CEMETERIES. If the proposed Tocks Island Dam Project was completed, the land now contained within the boundaries of the Delaware Water Gap National Recreation Area would be submersed in a lake created by the dam.

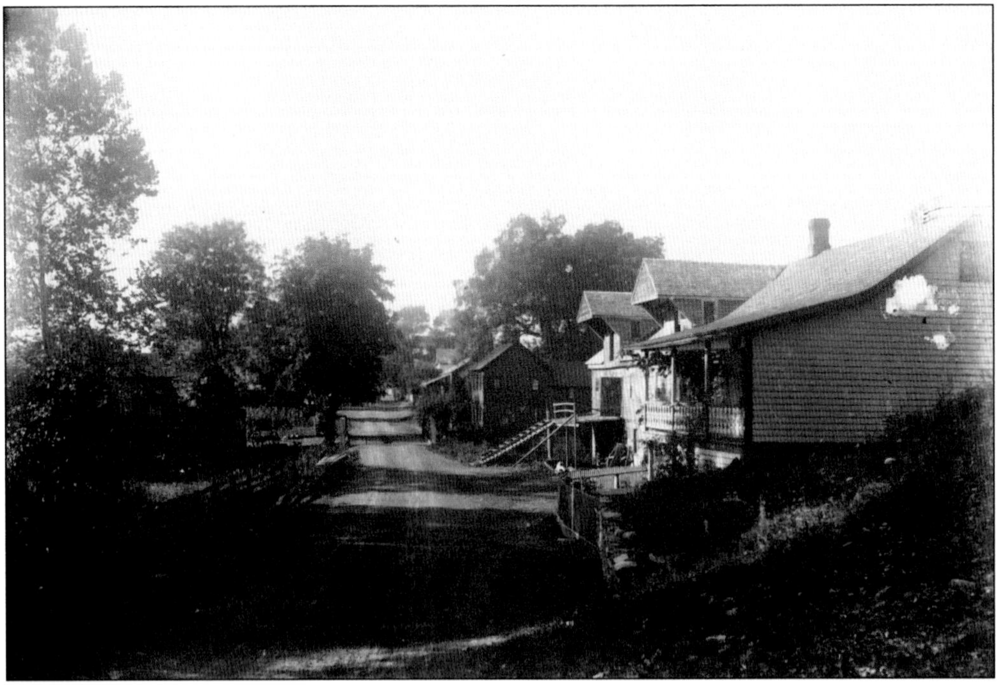

MAIN STREET, DINGMANS FERRY. The project was de-authorized by Congress in 1992, but not before many people were displaced after their homes were destroyed in preparation for the project.

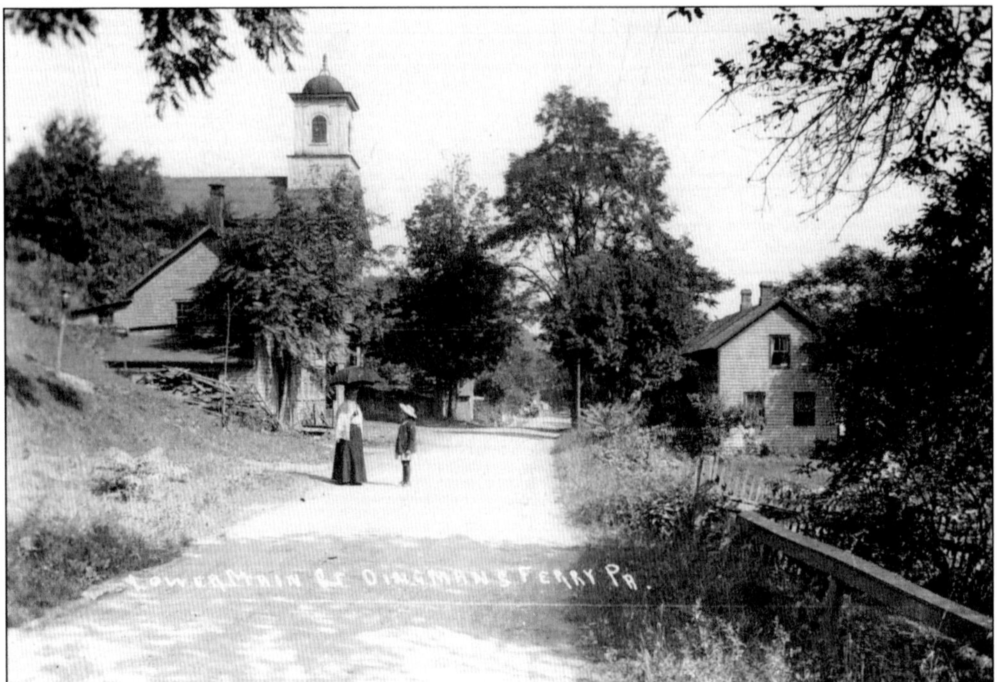

LOWER MAIN STREET DINGMANS FERRY. Main Street in Dingmans Ferry featured inns, shops, and residences, all of which were destroyed in the wake of the Tocks Island Dam Project.

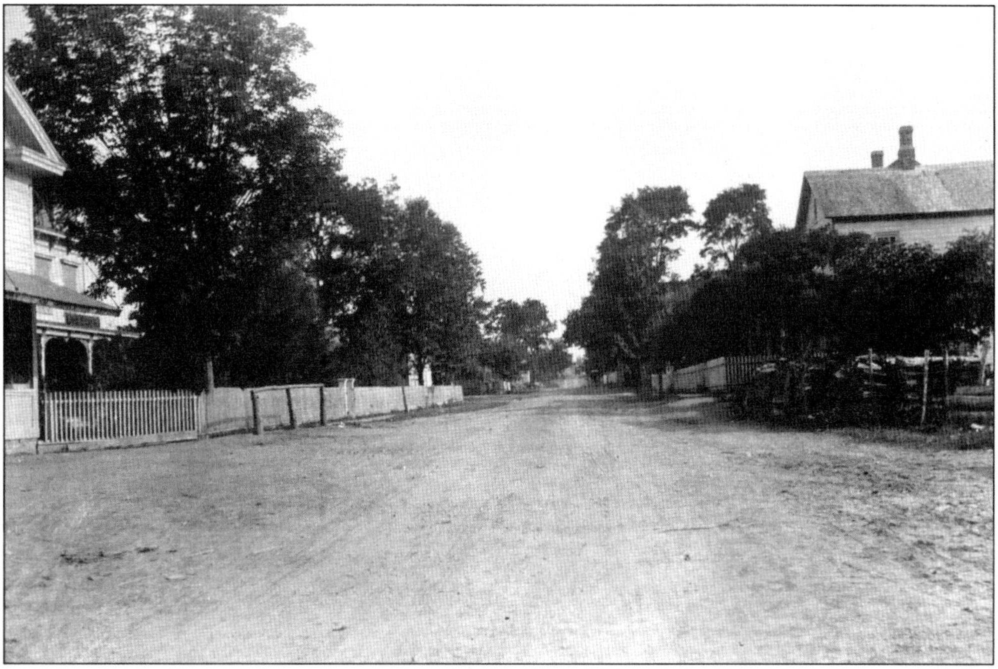

MAIN ROAD, DINGMANS FERRY, 1889. The task of removing residents from their Dingmans Ferry homes was left up to the U.S. Army Corps of Engineers. The wrecking ball moved swiftly though the area.

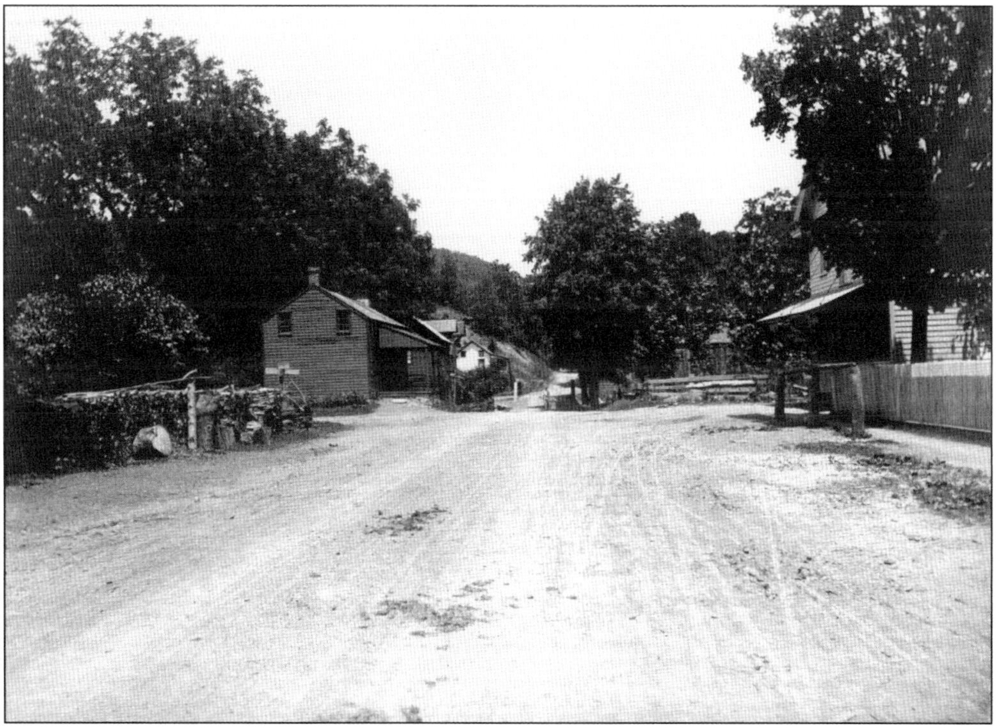

DINGMANS FERRY, 1889. The lands contained within the Delaware Water Gap National Recreation Area may have been developed if not for the scrubbed project.

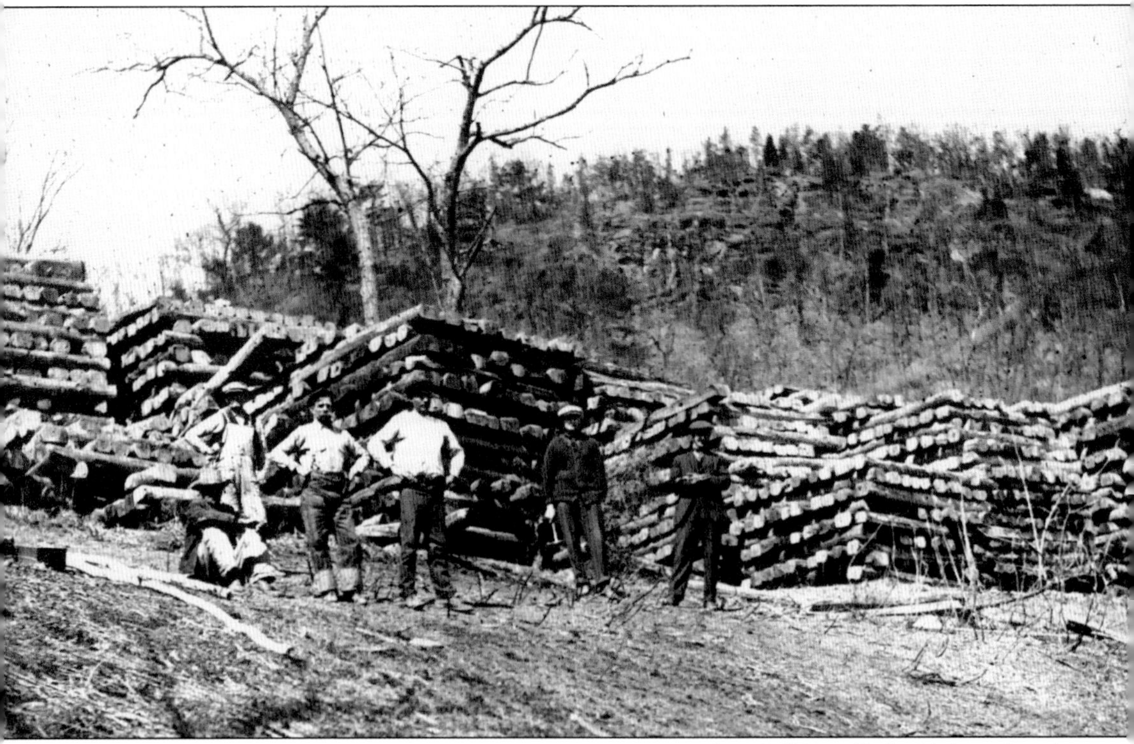

THE YARD AT THE EDDY, DINGMANS FERRY, 1910. Pictured are Bill Retallick, Alpheus Bensley, Andrew Dingman, Fred Middaugh, and Carl Edsel. An inspector and Wesley Angle are seated. These family names are deeply rooted in Dingmans Ferry history; their homesteads would be taken away from them by 1970.

Six

In the Movies

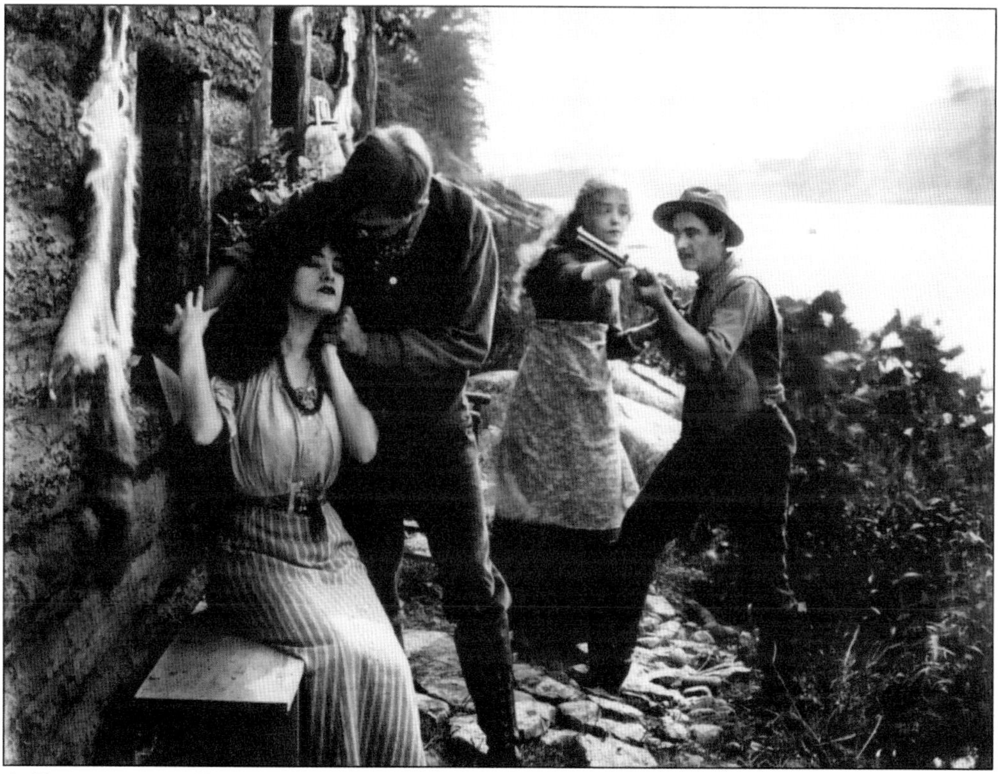

A Feud in the Kentucky Hills. In 1912, filmmaker David Wark Griffith came to Pike County with his troupe of some 40 actors known as the Biograph Players to make two movies. The players, including Mary Pickford, Lillian and Dorothy Gish, Francis X. Bushman, and Harry Carey, stayed at the Sawkill House in Milford and filmed many scenes around town, as well as on the Knob overlooking the Delaware River. Many locals were used as extras in the film, including Ernest Wood. During 1916–1917, two silent films were made, *A Feud in the Kentucky Hills* and *The Informer.*

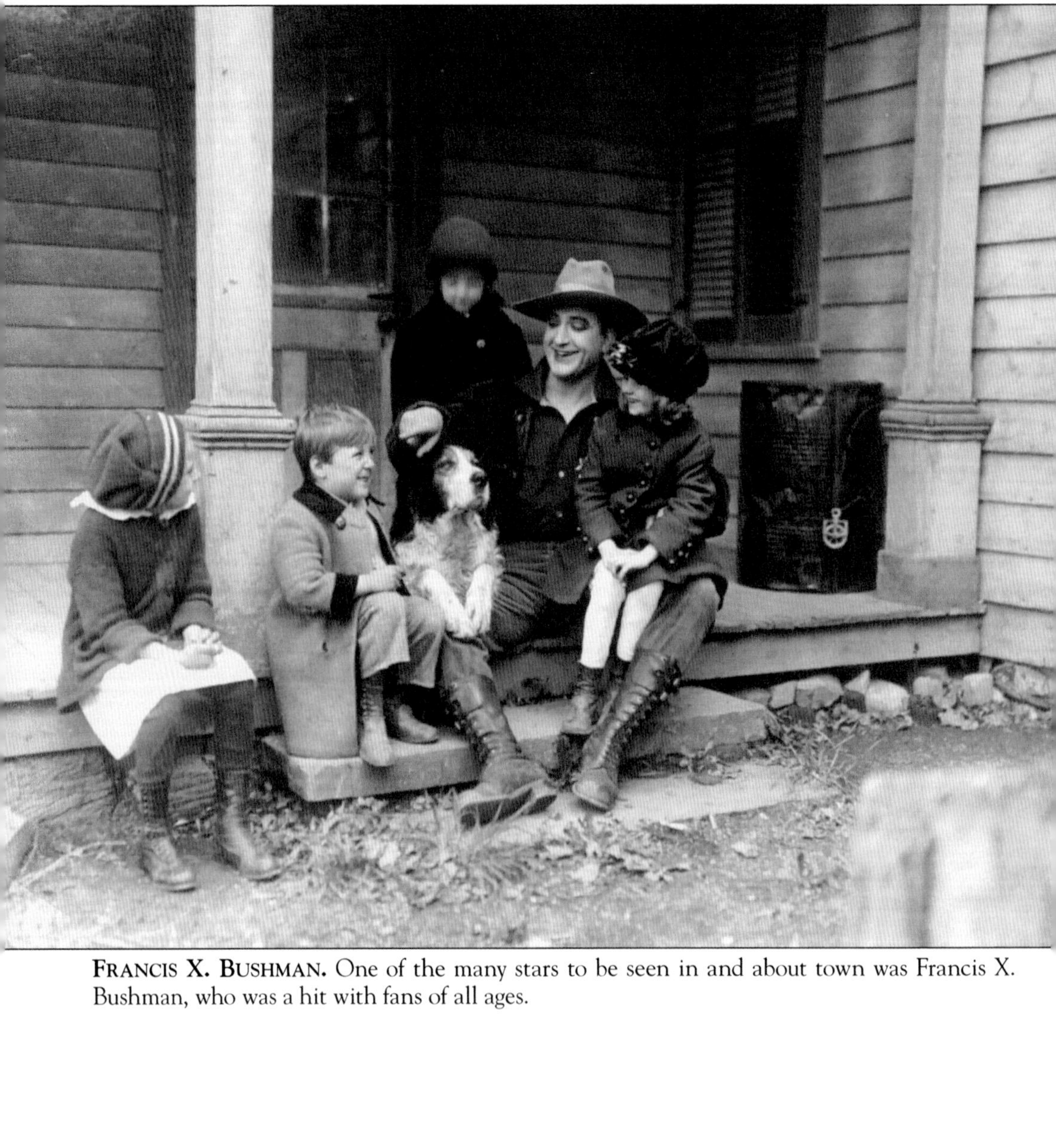

FRANCIS X. BUSHMAN. One of the many stars to be seen in and about town was Francis X. Bushman, who was a hit with fans of all ages.

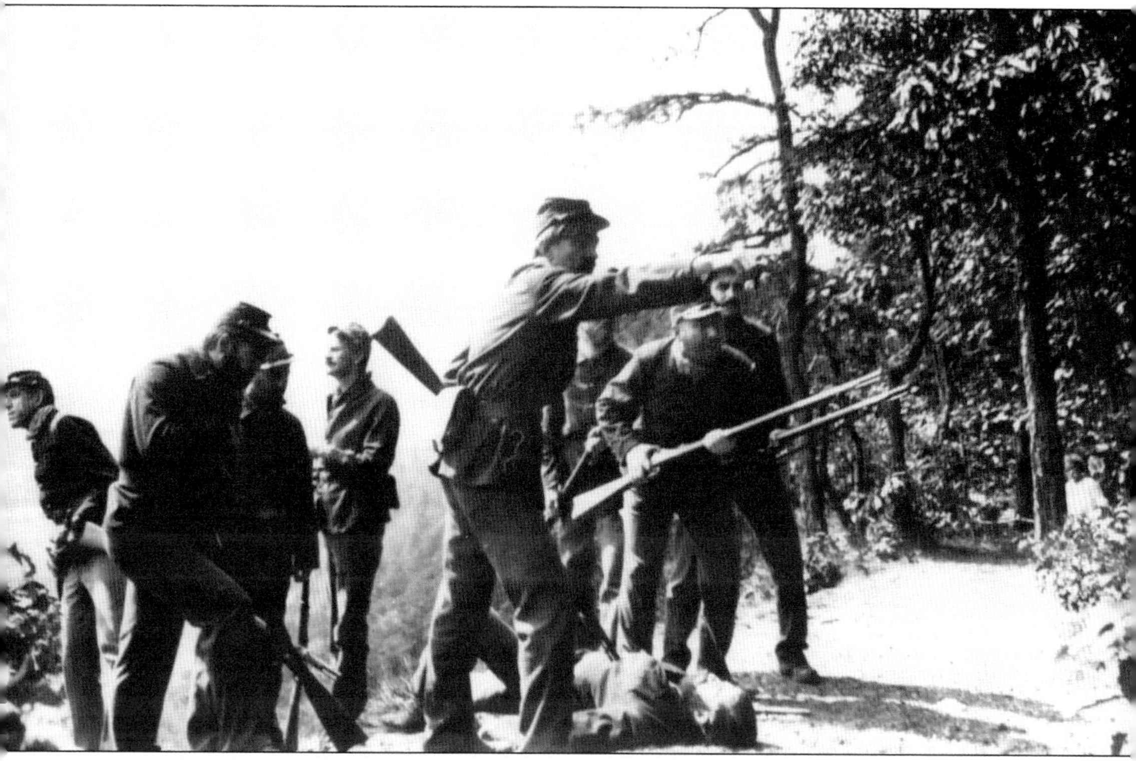

THE INFORMER. One of two movies filmed during their visit, *The Informer* was a Civil War tale. In this image, depicting the climactic and action-packed battle scene filmed on and around the cliffs overlooking the river, it seems as though D. W. Griffith has a bit of "Hitchcock" in him. Could that be Griffith pictured on the left in this still?

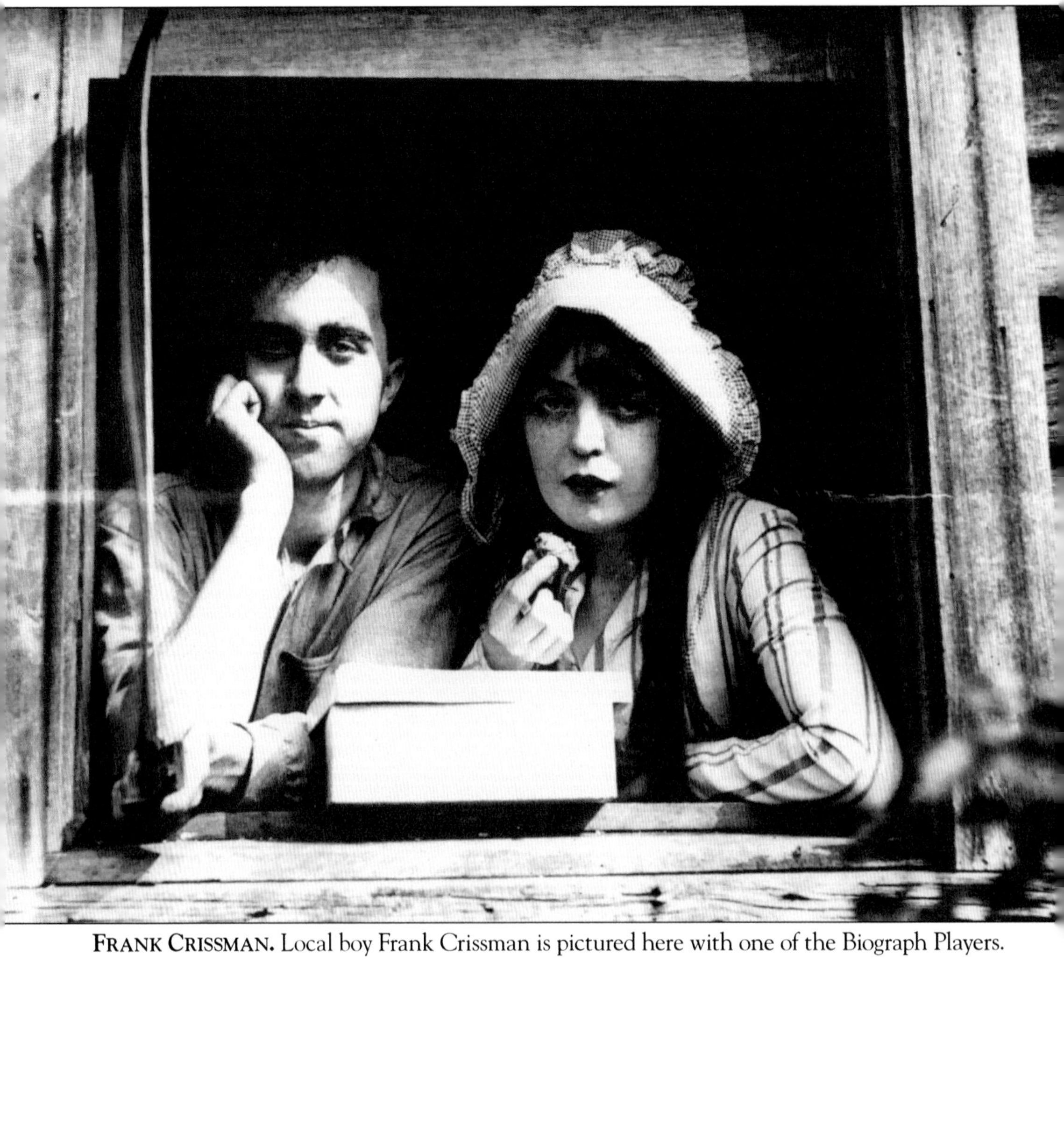

FRANK CRISSMAN. Local boy Frank Crissman is pictured here with one of the Biograph Players.

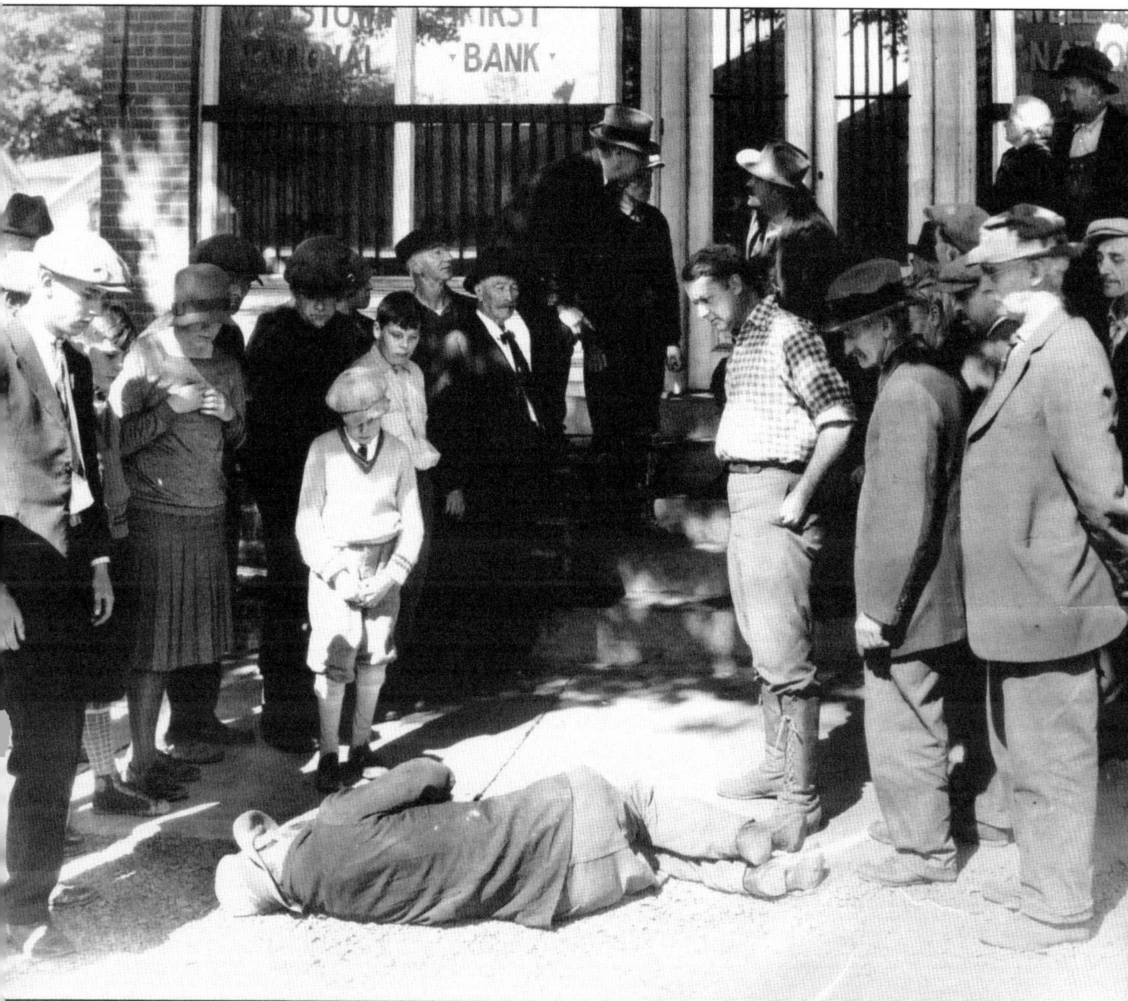

THE STRENGTH OF THE WEAK, 1927. The film was rolling once again in 1927 in Pike County when the movie *The Strength of the Weak* was filmed. Many locals were once again used in the film.

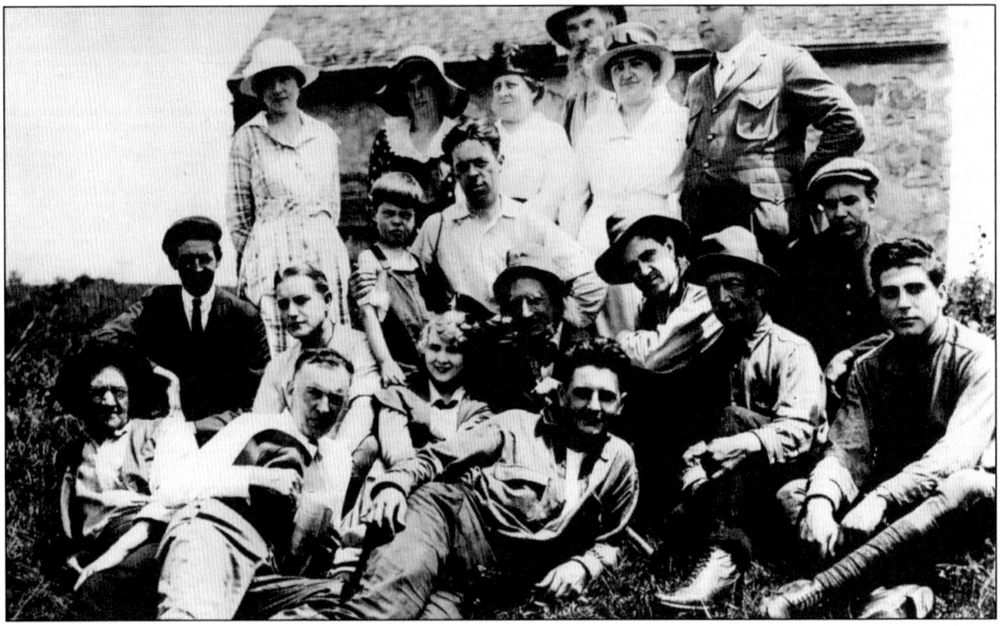

Gladys Leslie, You are Lovely. Pictured here is the cast of a movie on break. Included are Gladys Leslie and Ernest Wood, of course. The film title was *Nymph of the Foothills.*

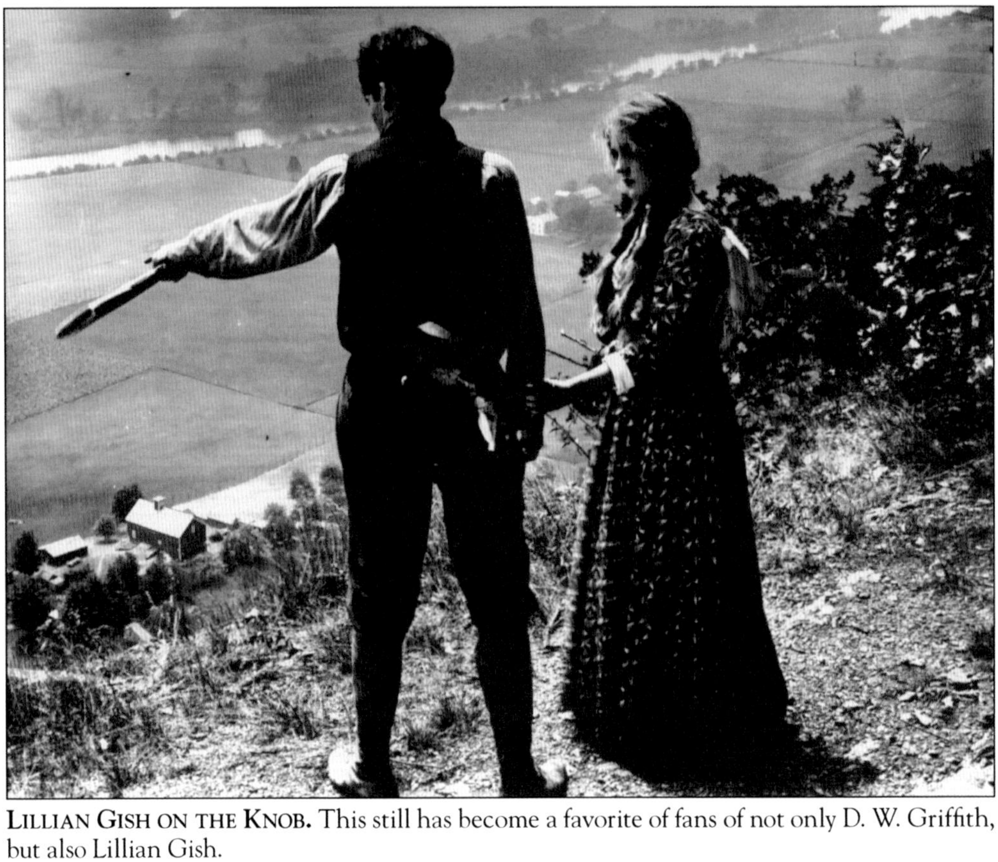

Lillian Gish on the Knob. This still has become a favorite of fans of not only D. W. Griffith, but also Lillian Gish.

ALLYN JOSLYN. Born in Milford, Allyn Joslyn (1901–1979) fared well as an actor in many genres. He first performed at the age of 17 and went on to be quite successful in both stage and screen. His list of credits is seemingly endless.

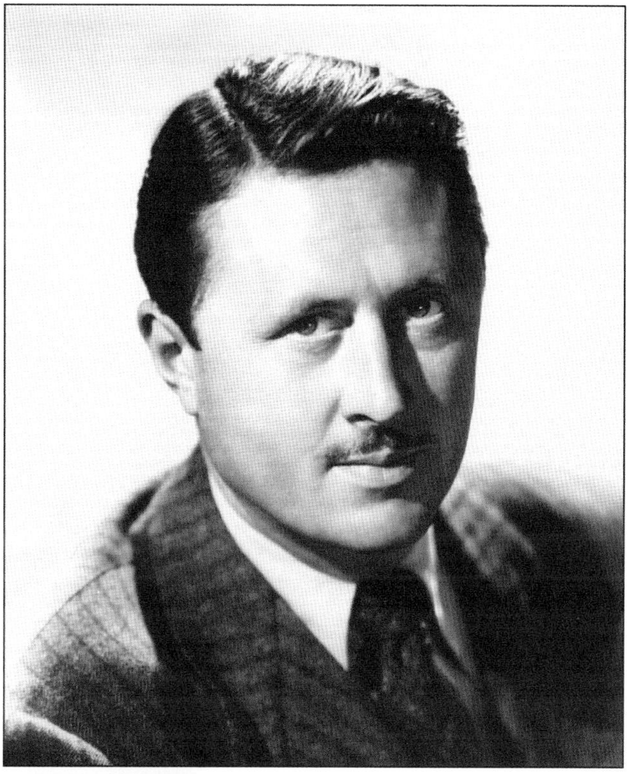

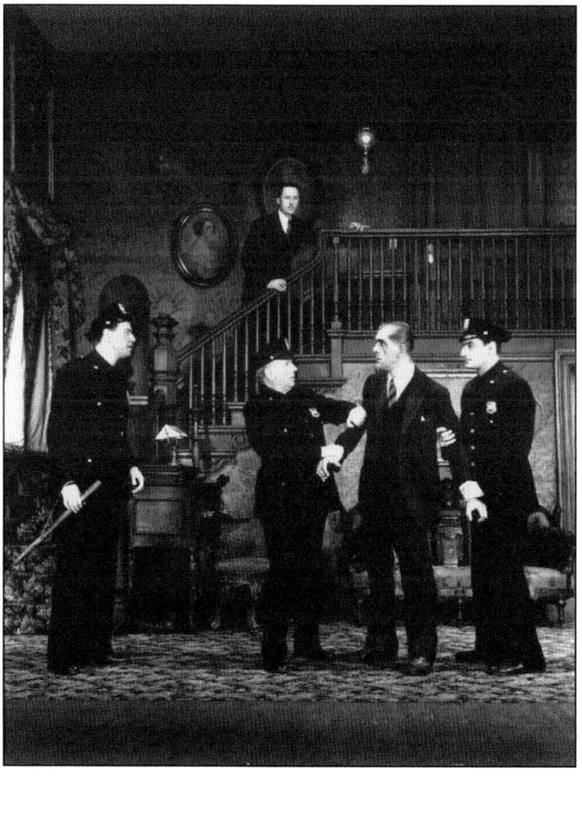

ADDAMS FAMILY. Although he has many screen credits, Joslyn is also remembered for a reoccurring role in the *Addams Family* sitcom. Pictured here with Boris Karloff, his list of costars is quite impressive.

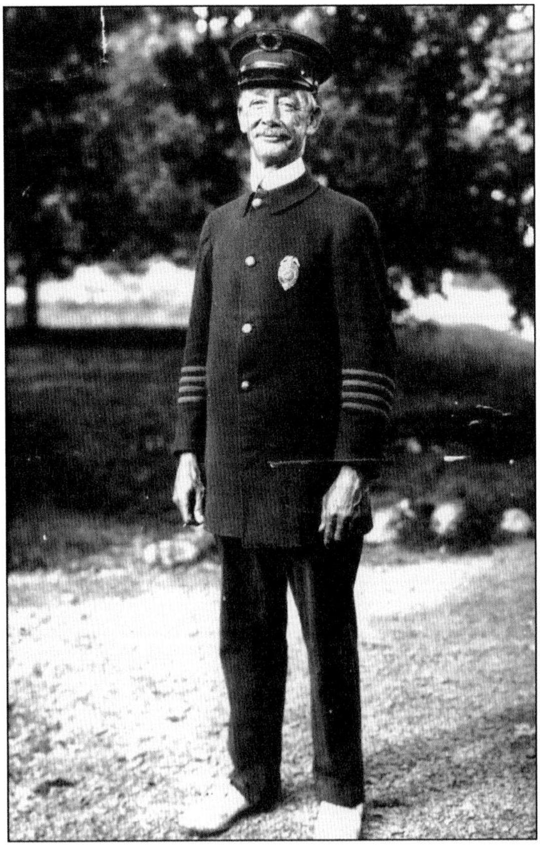

ERNEST WOOD. Ernest Wood was not a movie star; he was a police officer and high constable. However, he is quite photogenic and appears in several photographs used in this book.

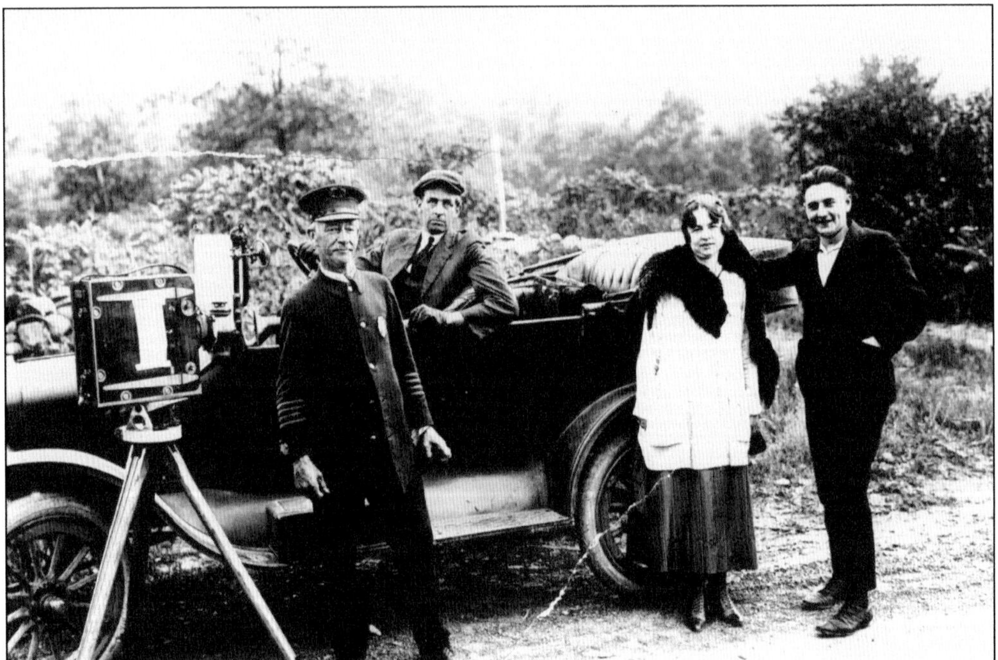

Seven

PIKE PEOPLE

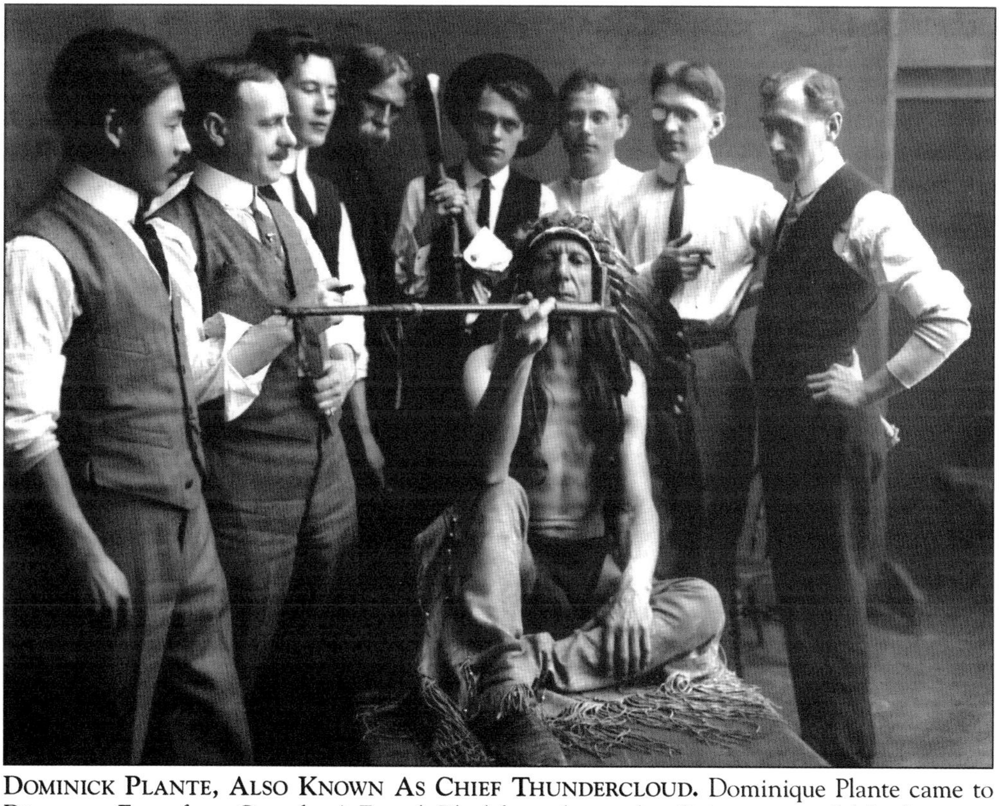

DOMINICK PLANTE, ALSO KNOWN AS CHIEF THUNDERCLOUD. Dominique Plante came to Dingmans Ferry from Canada. A French-Blackfoot who made a living as a model, he later was part of Buffalo Bill's Wild West Show. Through modeling, he was the subject of artists of the day, such as Frederic Remington. He was also the model for the last $5 gold piece made. Between 1872 and 1876, he enlisted in the U.S. Army to be a scout. He met and married artist Henrietta Heshigan while serving as her model. (Courtesy of Dingmans Ferry Delaware Township Historical Society.)

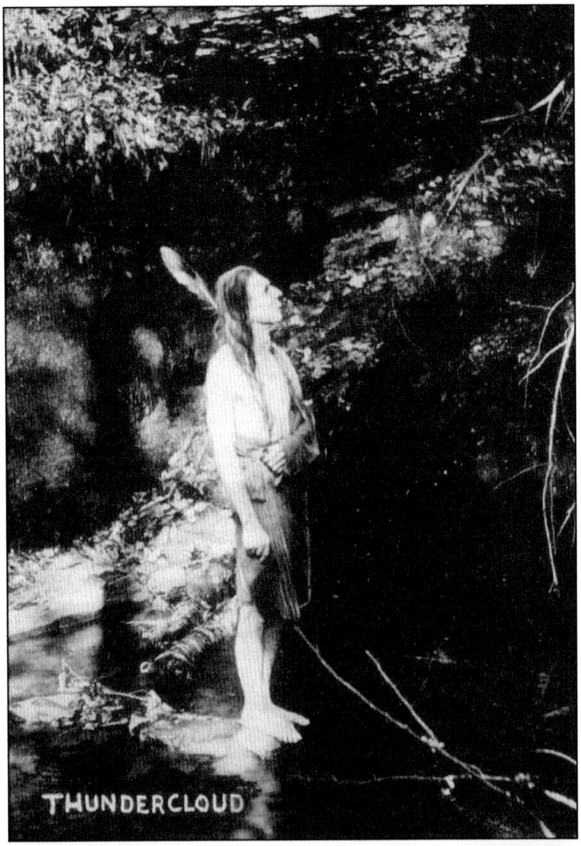

THUNDERCLOUD ON THE CLIFFS. This was a popular Pike County postcard in the early 1900s.

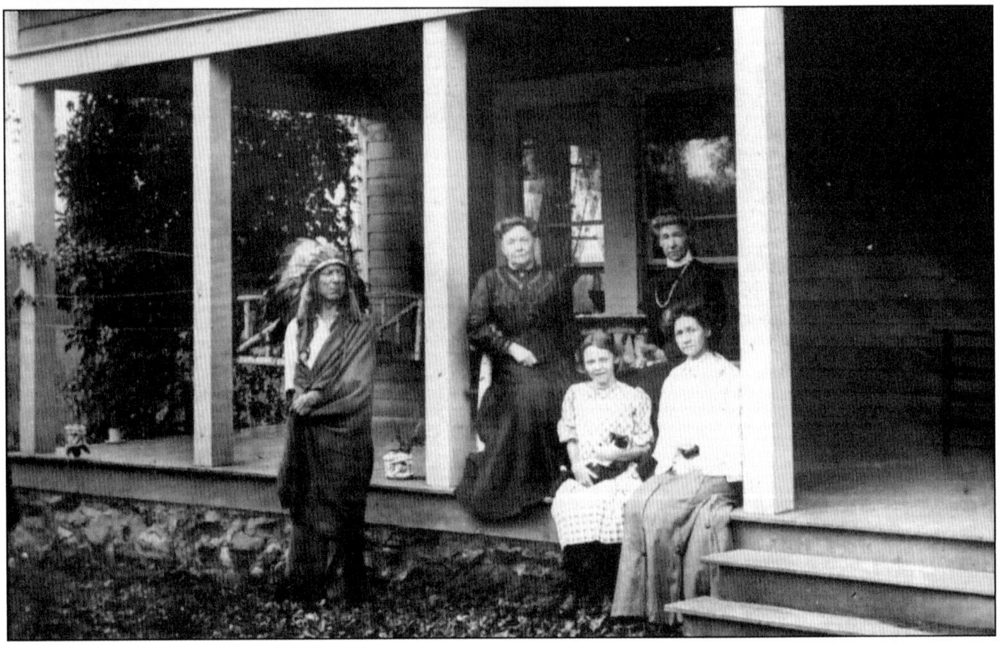

THE FAMILY. After Dominique Plante's marriage to Henrietta, the couple moved into her mom's family home in Delaware Township.

WANITA PLANTE. Pictured in traditional papoose is Chief Thundercloud's pride and joy, Wanita Plante. She was born in 1899 and was the apple of her daddy's eye.

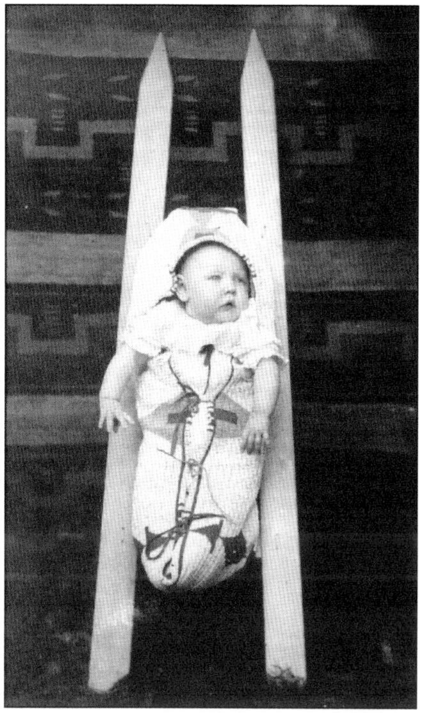

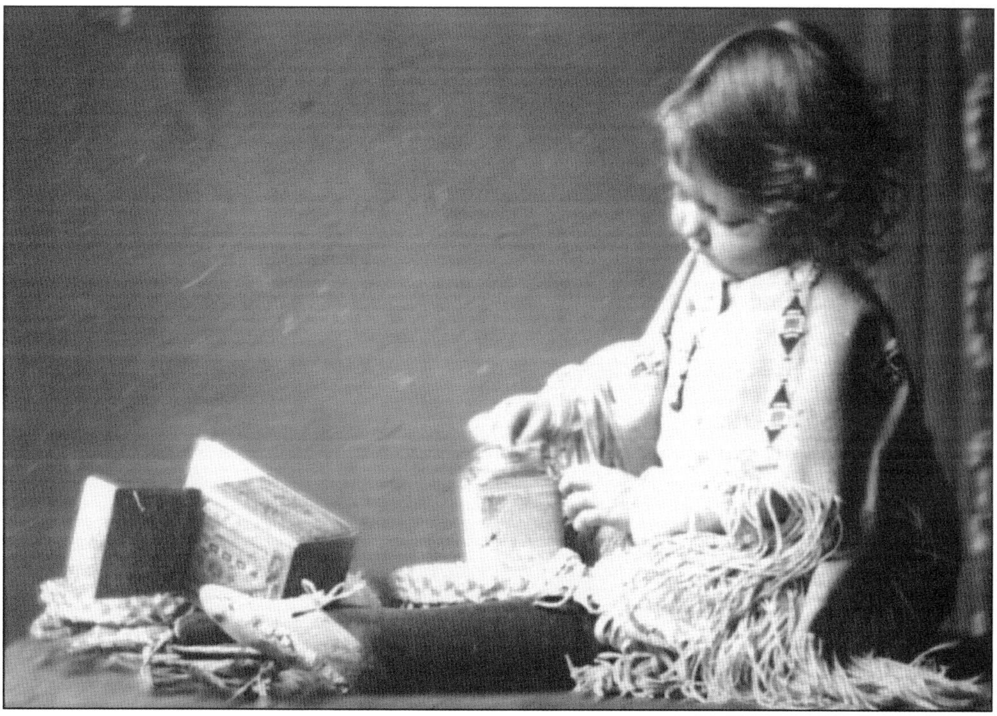

TAKING AFTER DAD. Wanita makes a lovely model, just like her dad. Thundercloud died in 1916 on the road while traveling with Buffalo Bill's Wild West Show. He is buried in Dingman Cemetery where his grave is often found to have gifts placed upon it from admirers and fellow Native Americans. (Courtesy of Mim Carpenter.)

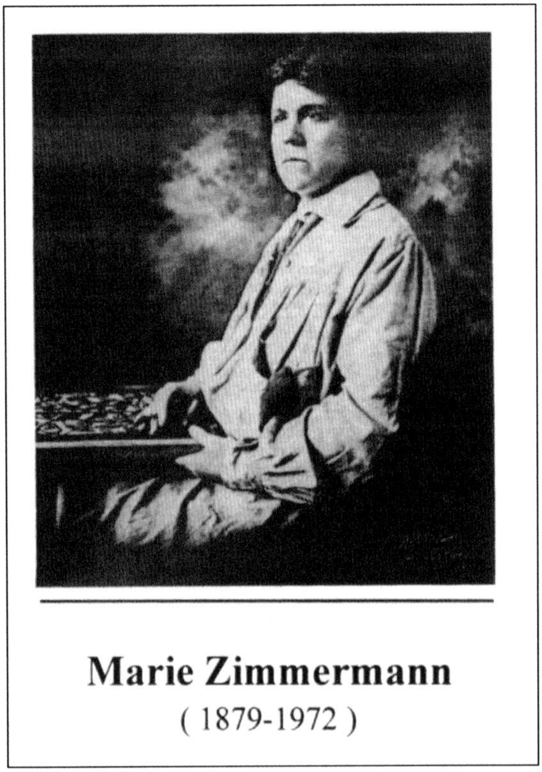

MARIE ZIMMERMANN. One of the most introspective artists of her time, Marie Zimmermann (1879–1972) lived on a farm in Delaware Township. She was one of the first women to be a master metal and iron worker, creating ornamental fences and gates, candlesticks, vases, and jewelry.

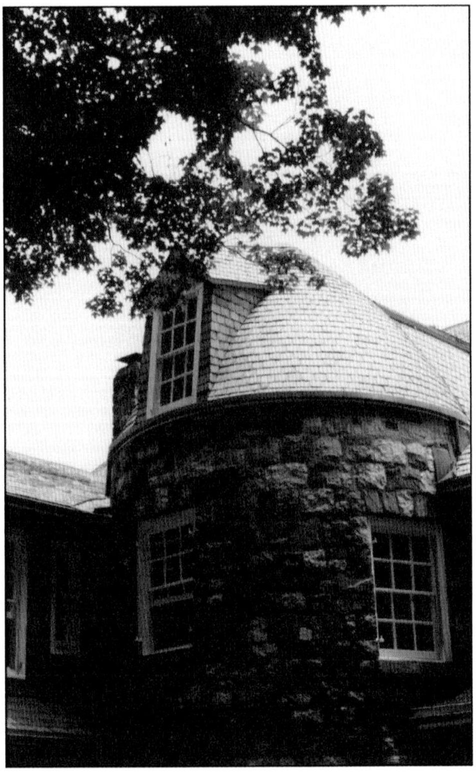

ZIMMERMANN BARN. Zimmermann's father, a wealthy New York businessman, proposed she either go to law school or art school, and thankfully she became an artist and craftswoman. Her jewelry has been offered at Sotheby's for quite a hefty price.

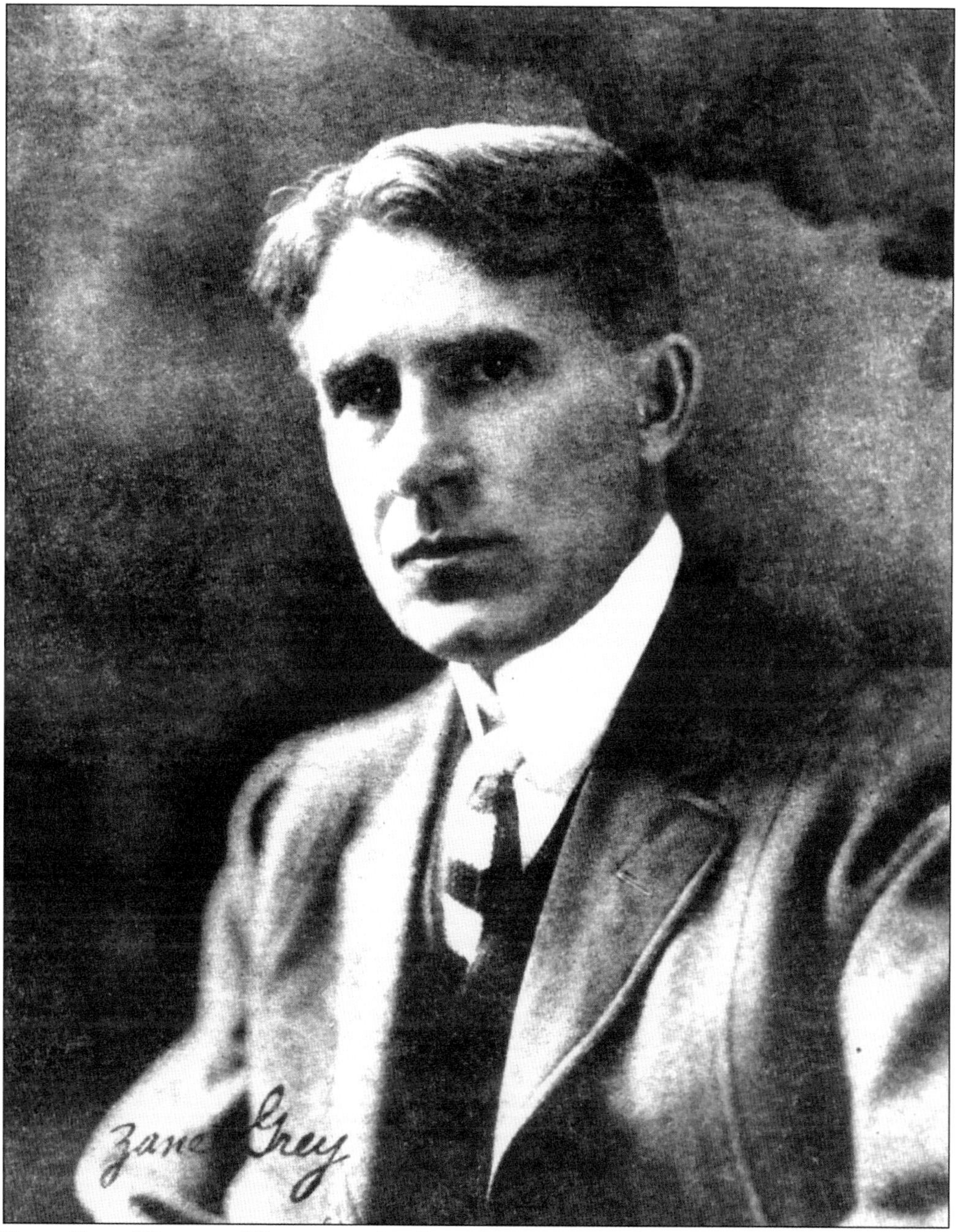

ZANE GREY. The great Western novelist Zane Grey spent much time in Lackawaxen as a boy. He had a great love of fishing, and in addition to his many books, he wrote several essays on fishing. His real first name was Pearl.

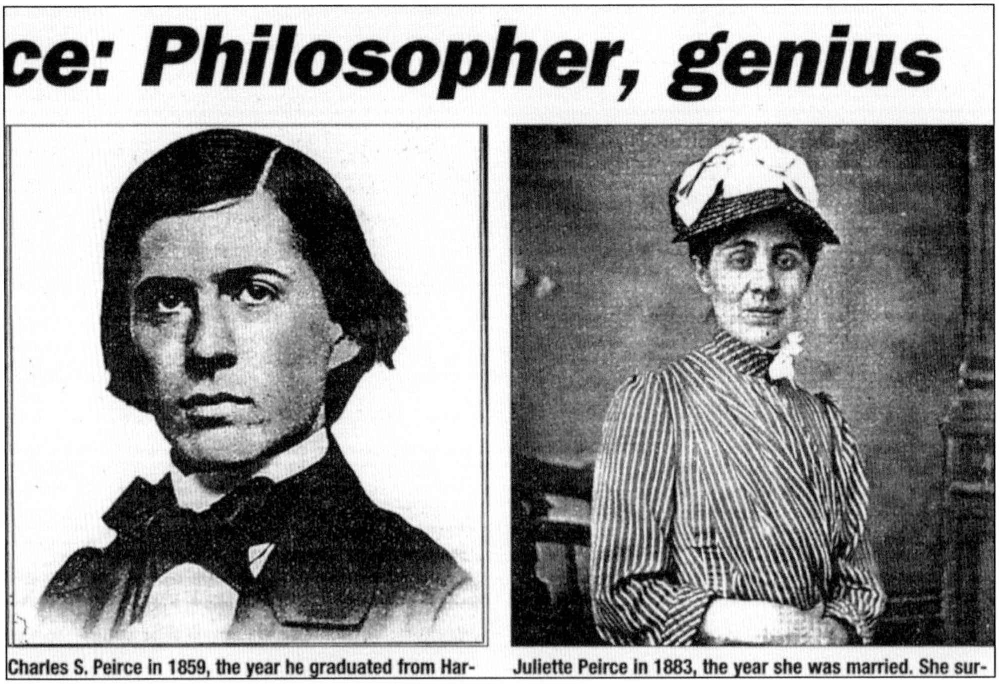

ce: Philosopher, genius

Charles S. Peirce in 1859, the year he graduated from Har-

Juliette Peirce in 1883, the year she was married. She sur-

CHARLES SAUNDERS AND JULIETTE PEIRCE. Charles Saunders is responsible for initiating the theory of pragmatism. A brilliant man, he was a philosopher and mathematician. His wife, Juliette, has become famous in her own right. A woman shrouded in mystery and known to dabble in the tarot, she was said to possess the deck of tarot cards that foretold the downfall of Napoleon.

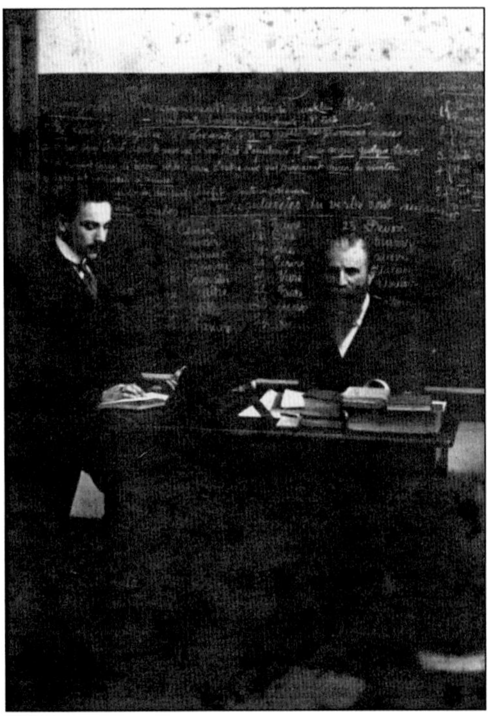

CHARLES PEIRCE WITH STUDENT. This photograph was taken in 1902. Charles and Juliette Peirce purchased a home in Westfall Township which they referred to as Arisbe, paying tribute to Homer. After Charles's death, Juliette lived out her last days at Arisbe in squalor. The remains of their possessions are housed at the Pike County Historical Society where it is said that Juliette can be found, in spirit, roaming the second floor hallway.

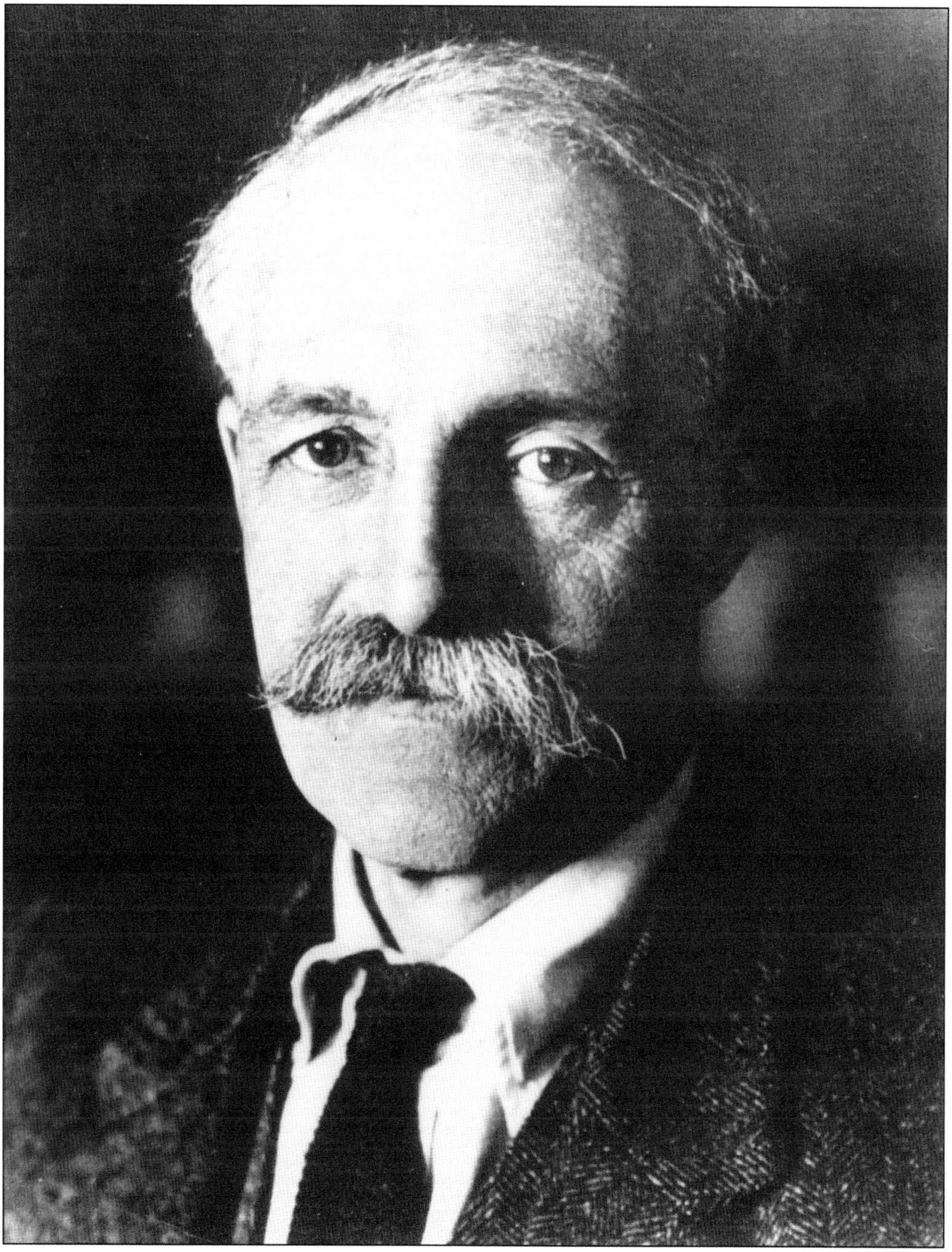

GIFFORD PINCHOT. The Pinchot family came to Pike County from France as early as 1817. Gifford Pinchot was encouraged by his parents, James and Mary, to pursue his love of forestry and later became governor of Pennsylvania, twice. Gifford's slogan in one of his campaigns was "everybody knows Gifford Pinchot." He had a great interest in forestry and after attending Yale went abroad to study further, as there was no forestry school in the states.

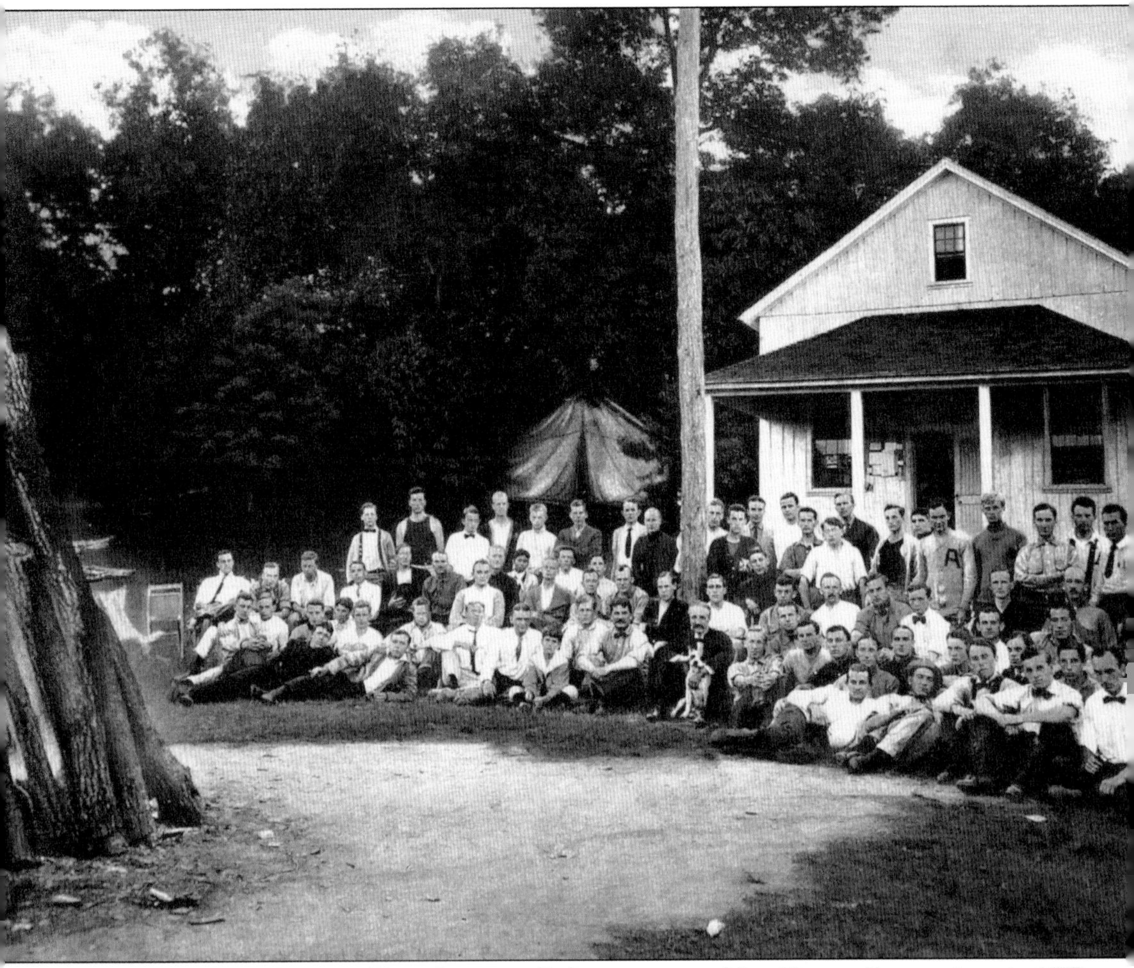

YALE FORESTRY SCHOOL, PIKE COUNTY. Before moving to New Haven, Connecticut, in 1927, the Yale Forestry School offered courses in the introduction to forestry on the Pinchot family estate grounds.

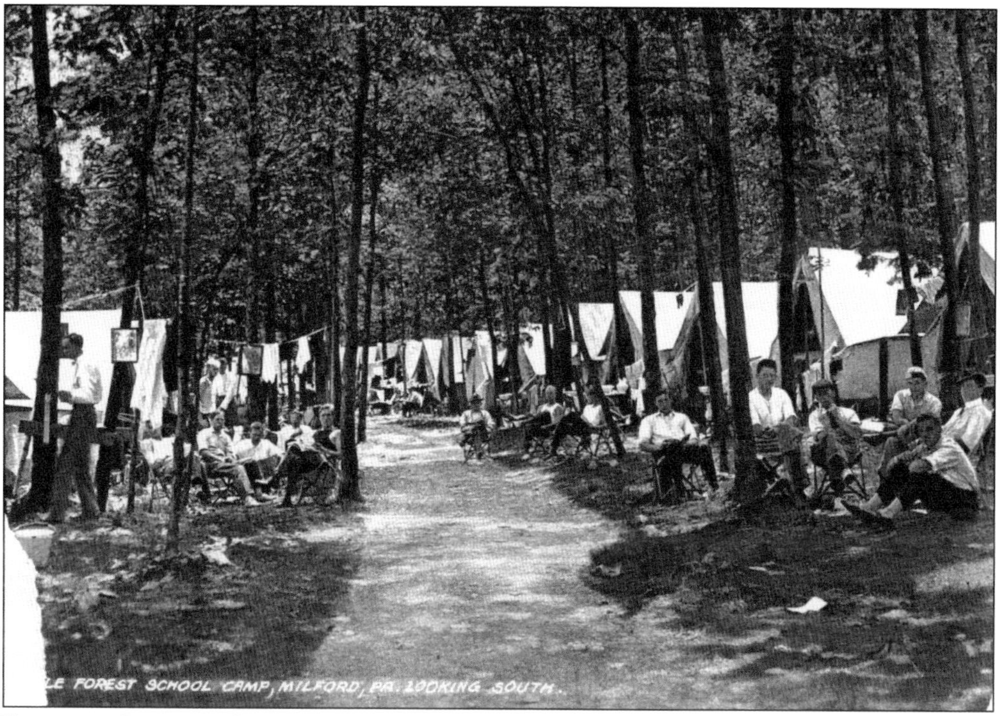

FORESTRY SCHOOL. This "tent city" served as housing for students.

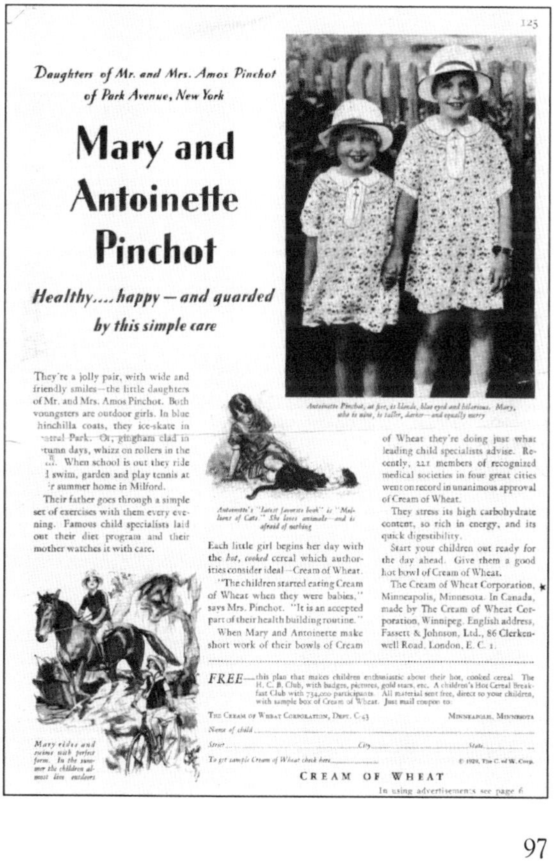

MARY AND ANTOINETTE PINCHOT. In 1929, Mary and Antoinette Pinchot were advocates for Cream of Wheat. In adulthood, Mary was linked romantically with Pres. John F. Kennedy. It may be just that connection that caused her death. She was murdered walking along the Chesapeake and Ohio Towpath in the Georgetown neighborhood of Washington, D.C., in 1964.

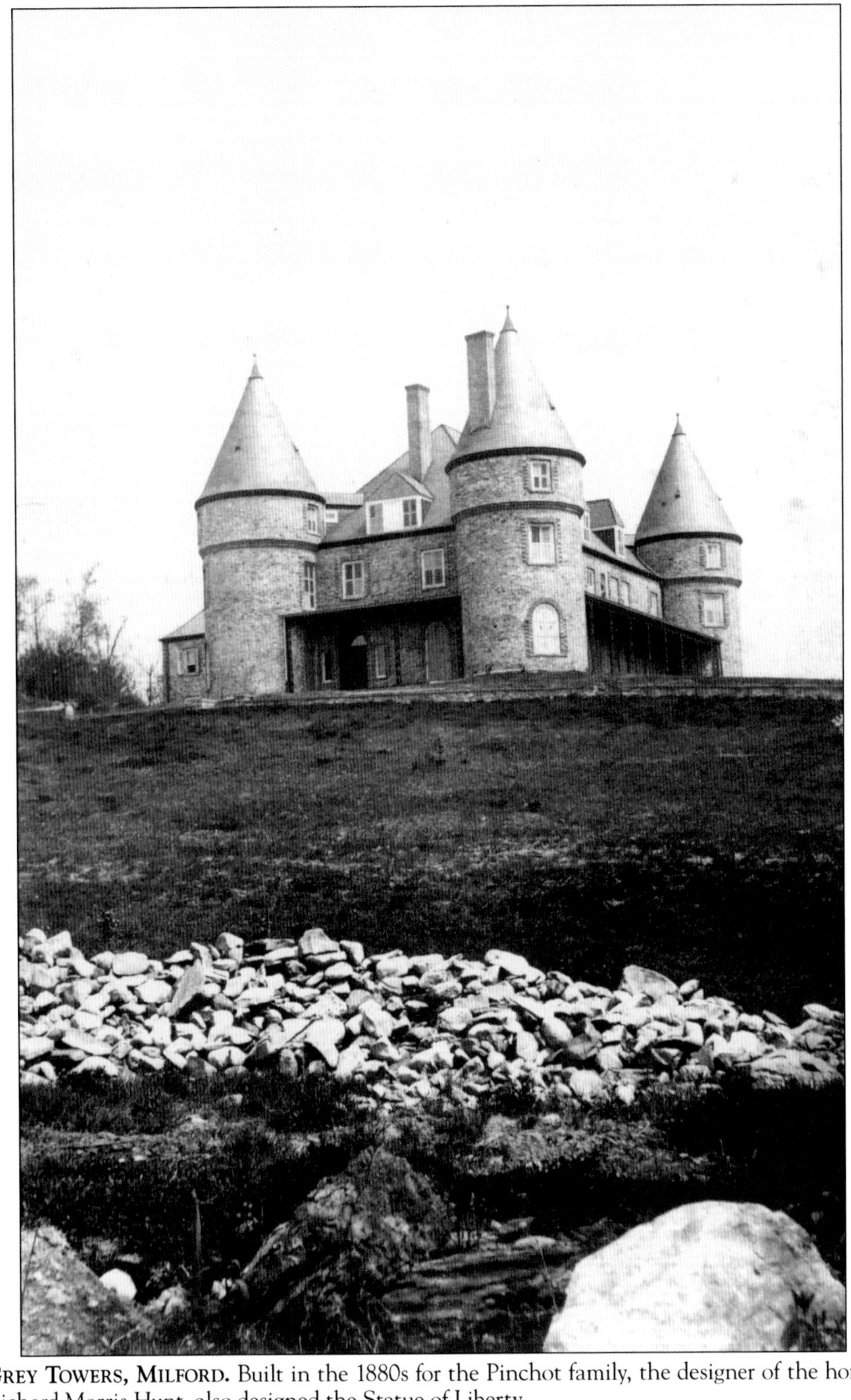

GREY TOWERS, MILFORD. Built in the 1880s for the Pinchot family, the designer of the home, Richard Morris Hunt, also designed the Statue of Liberty.

DAVID IRWIN. In 1935, David Irwin was considered "the year's most thrilling true story." He and three sled dogs made a trek across the top of the world to the magnetic North Pole, encompassing 3,600 miles.

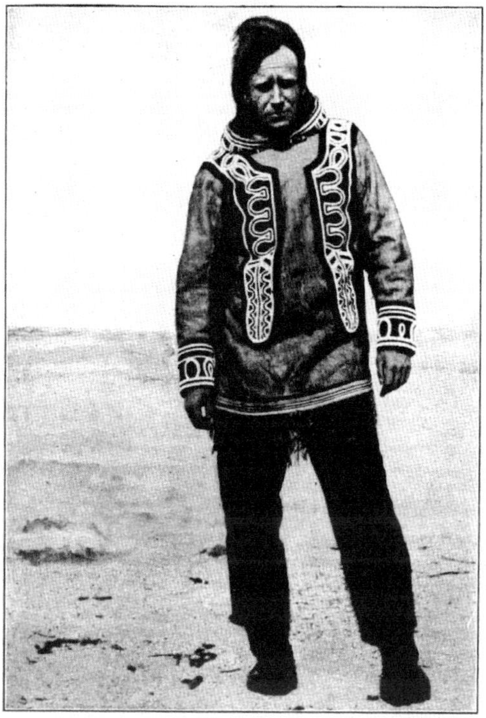

"It was a lonely feeling, watching the *Trader* disappear in the fog."

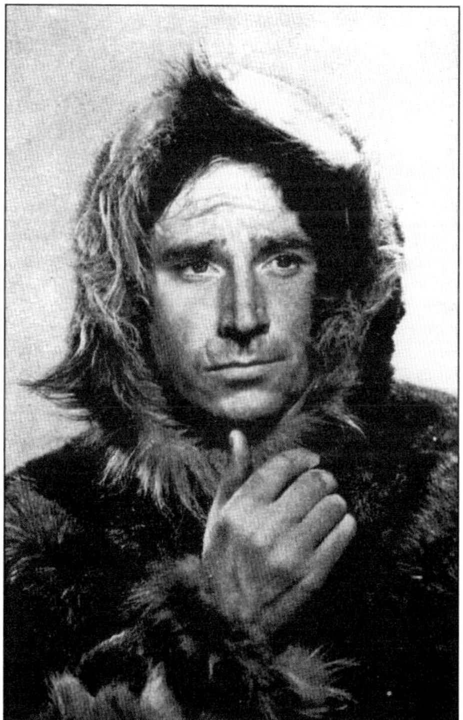

David Irwin

SETTLING DOWN. The three-year trek saw Irwin faced with death upon many occasions. After his journey, he settled in Pike County and opened the North Pole Animal Farm just outside of Stroudsburg.

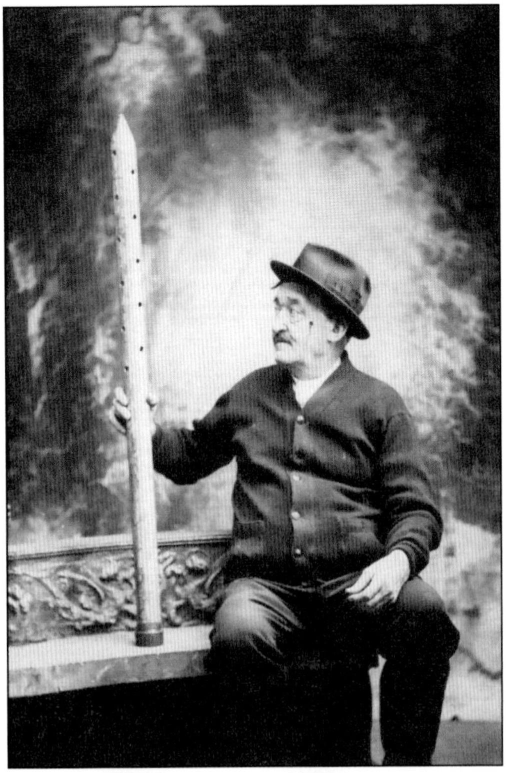

Eugene Octave Boillotat. Pictured here in 1925, Eugene Octave Boillotat invented a tool used in watering and feeding trees. Trees have always been revered along the shaded streets of Milford Borough. Tree Bees were held in the early days, and there is even a Shade Tree Commission still in existence today. New plantings in Milford are encased in a zippered bag in their early growth, which allows for water to be stored. This may be a modern day take on Boillotat's idea.

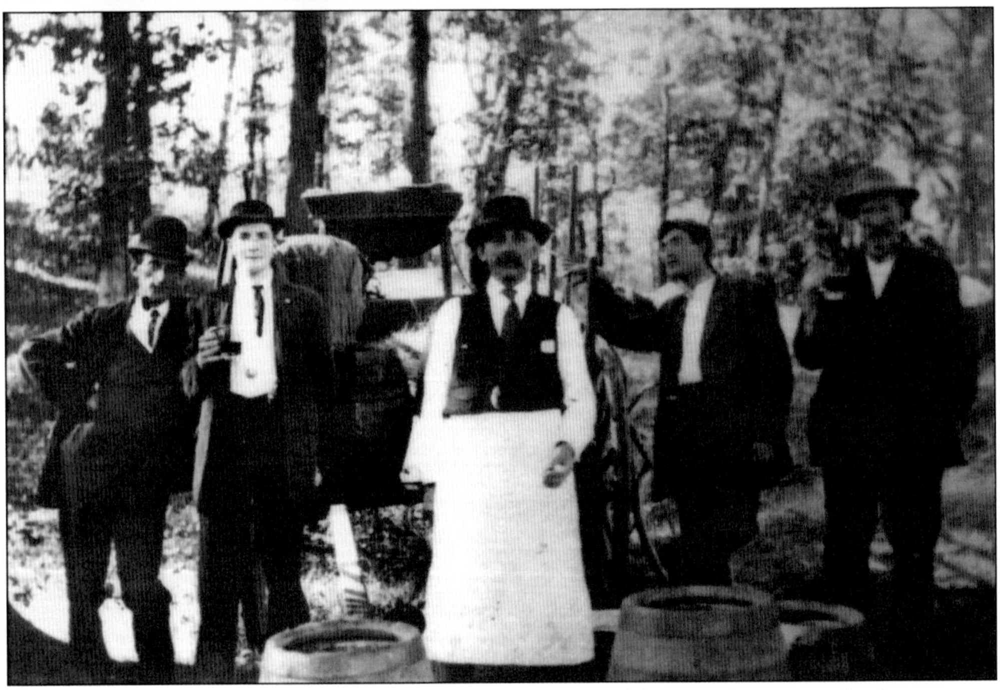

Herman Paul Schultz. In 1897, Herman Schultz (center) became known as the first man to be hanged in the county seat of Milford. After a lengthy trial, he was found guilty of murdering and shooting to death his wife, Lizzie, at Wohlforth's Country Inn in Shohola.

LETTER TO THE SHERIFF. Many people wrote letters asking to witness Schultz's hanging. It was described as "a carnival like atmosphere in Milford" at the hanging. Over 100 people attended, and the town was buzzing with excitement.

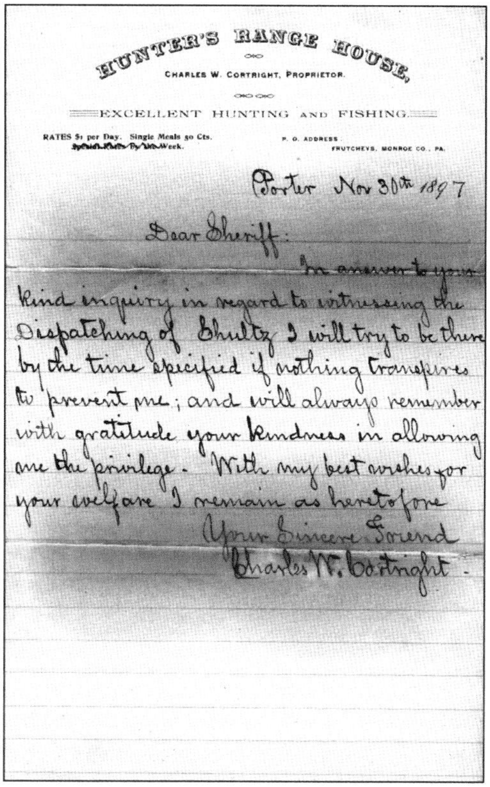

HUNTER'S RANGE HOUSE,

CHARLES W. CORTRIGHT, PROPRIETOR.

EXCELLENT HUNTING AND FISHING.

RATES $1 per Day. Single Meals 50 Cts. [illegible] Week.

P. O. ADDRESS FRUTCHEYS, MONROE CO., PA.

Porter Nov 30th 1897

Dear Sheriff:

In answer to your kind inquiry in regard to witnessing the Dispatching of Shultz I will try to be there by the time specified if nothing transpires to prevent me; and will always remember with gratitude your kindness in allowing me the privilege. With my best wishes for your welfare I remain as heretofore

Your Sincere Friend

Charles W. Cortright.

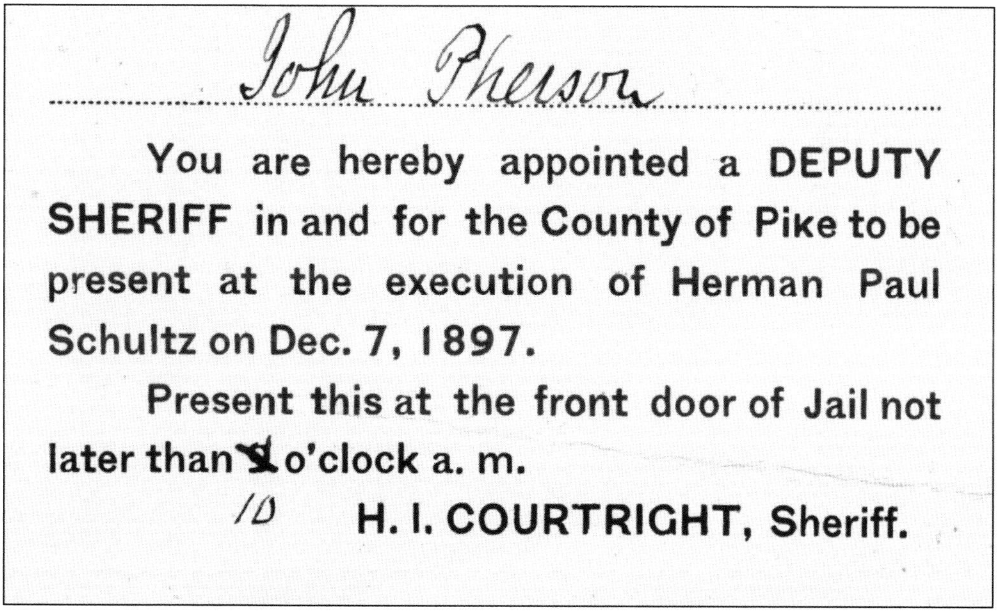

John Pherson

You are hereby appointed a DEPUTY SHERIFF in and for the County of Pike to be present at the execution of Herman Paul Schultz on Dec. 7, 1897.

Present this at the front door of Jail not later than 10 o'clock a. m.

H. I. COURTRIGHT, Sheriff.

DEPUTY FOR A DAY. Attendees received passes to the hanging. In a strange turn of events during the gathering of evidence, Lizzie's head was lopped off for the purpose of performing an investigation as to the entry of her head wound. Herman's last request was to have his wife's head buried with him. That request was denied. It is not clear what became of Herman's body after the hanging. Recent evidence has surfaced that his bones are in the courthouse safe.

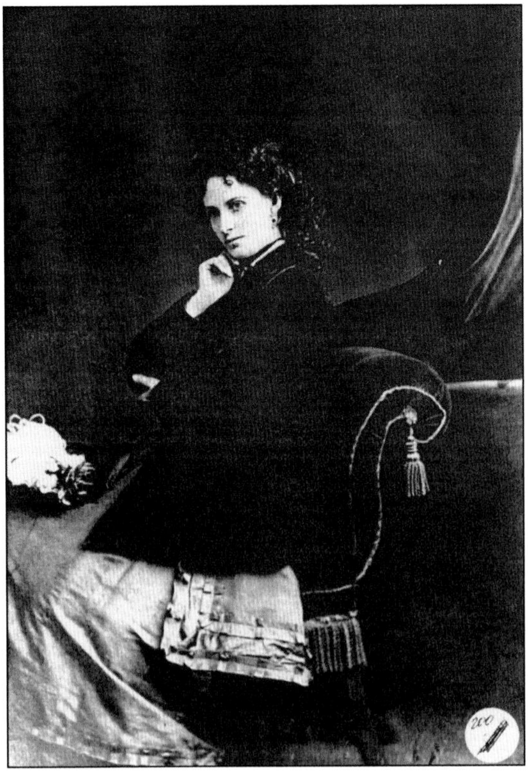

Jeannie Gourlay Struthers. Jeannie Gourlay Struthers was a young actress waiting in the wings to come on stage at Ford's Theatre the night of Pres. Abraham Lincoln's assassination.

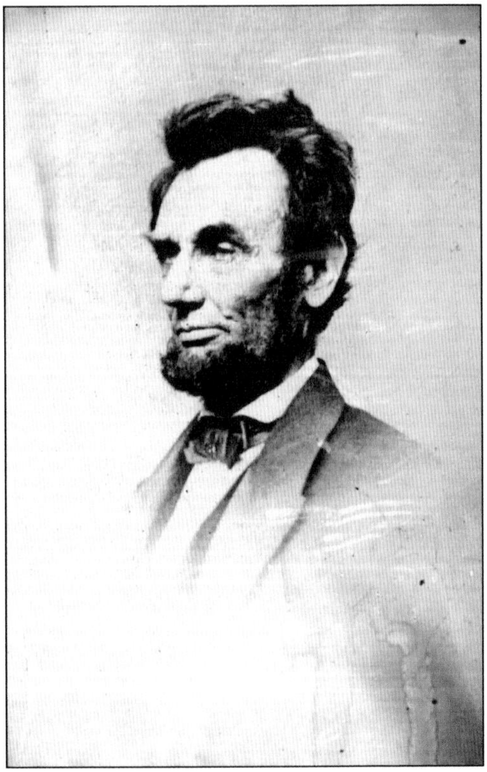

Abraham Lincoln. After President Lincoln was shot, an American flag that was used as bunting around the presidential box was placed under Lincoln's head to cushion it. There were actually five flags in the theater that evening. All five disappeared.

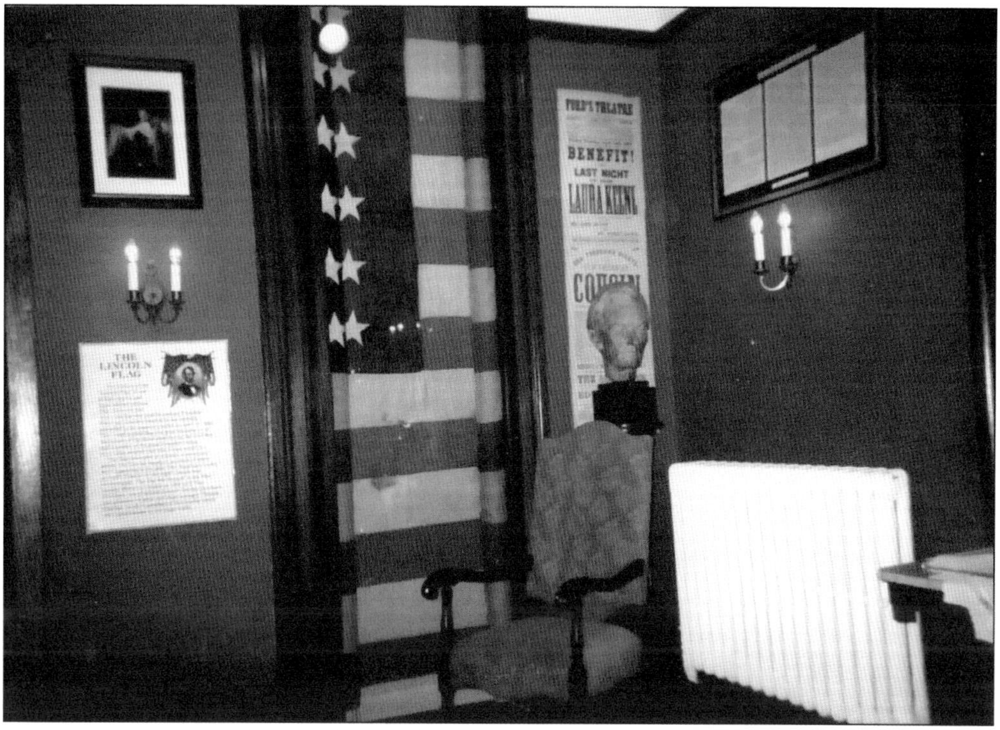

THE LINCOLN FLAG. Thomas Gourlay, Jeannie's father and theater manager at Ford's, took the flag that was placed under Lincoln's head after the president was removed from the theater. He kept this bloodstained flag until his death, after which it became the property of Jeannie, who brought it with her to Milford in 1888.

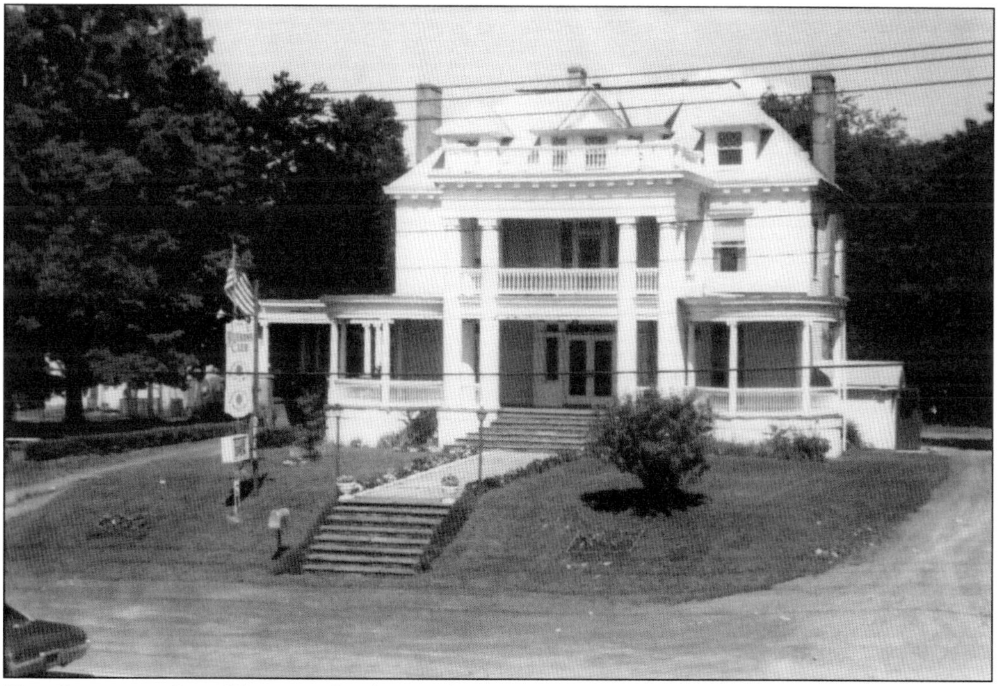

THE COLUMNS. In 1955, years after his mother's death, Vivian Paul Struthers gave the flag, along with three stage costumes belonging to his mother Jeannie to the Columns Museum in Milford. The flag remains on display there to this day.

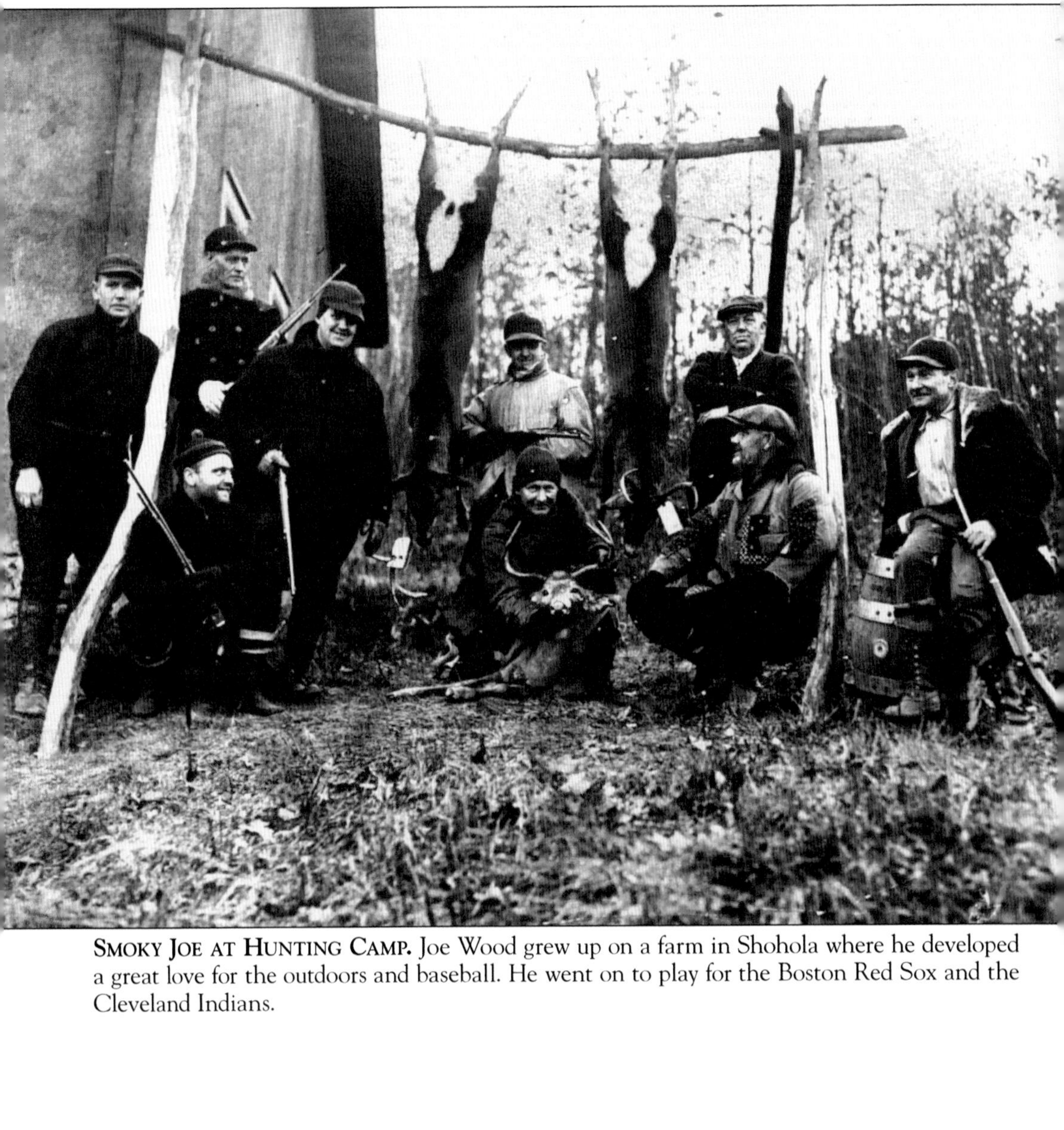

Smoky Joe at Hunting Camp. Joe Wood grew up on a farm in Shohola where he developed a great love for the outdoors and baseball. He went on to play for the Boston Red Sox and the Cleveland Indians.

CIGAR CARD. Wood's best season came in 1912, when he pitched his way to 34 wins, 16 of them coming in succession. October 25 is officially deemed "Smoky" Joe Wood Day in Pike County.

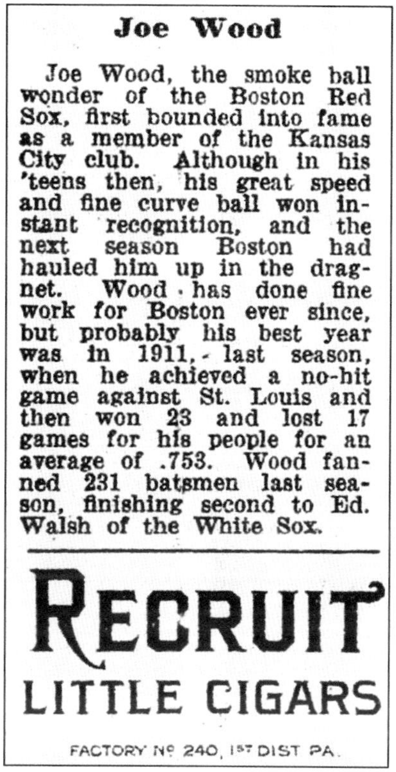
Joe Wood

Joe Wood, the smoke ball wonder of the Boston Red Sox, first bounded into fame as a member of the Kansas City club. Although in his 'teens then, his great speed and fine curve ball won instant recognition, and the next season Boston had hauled him up in the dragnet. Wood has done fine work for Boston ever since, but probably his best year was in 1911, last season, when he achieved a no-hit game against St. Louis and then won 23 and lost 17 games for his people for an average of .753. Wood fanned 231 batsmen last season, finishing second to Ed. Walsh of the White Sox.

RECRUIT
LITTLE CIGARS

FACTORY No 240, 1st DIST PA.

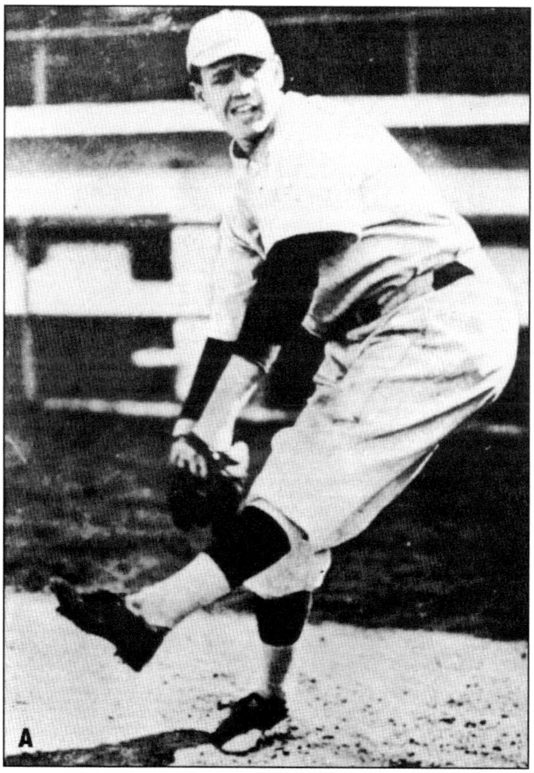

JOE WOOD. Wood earned the nickname Smoky because of the velocity of his fastball. Although he started his career as a pitcher, he finished it as an outfielder due to an arm injury. His great love of the game was evident in this transition to outfielder; he just wanted to play and did a fine job fielding and hitting in this new position.

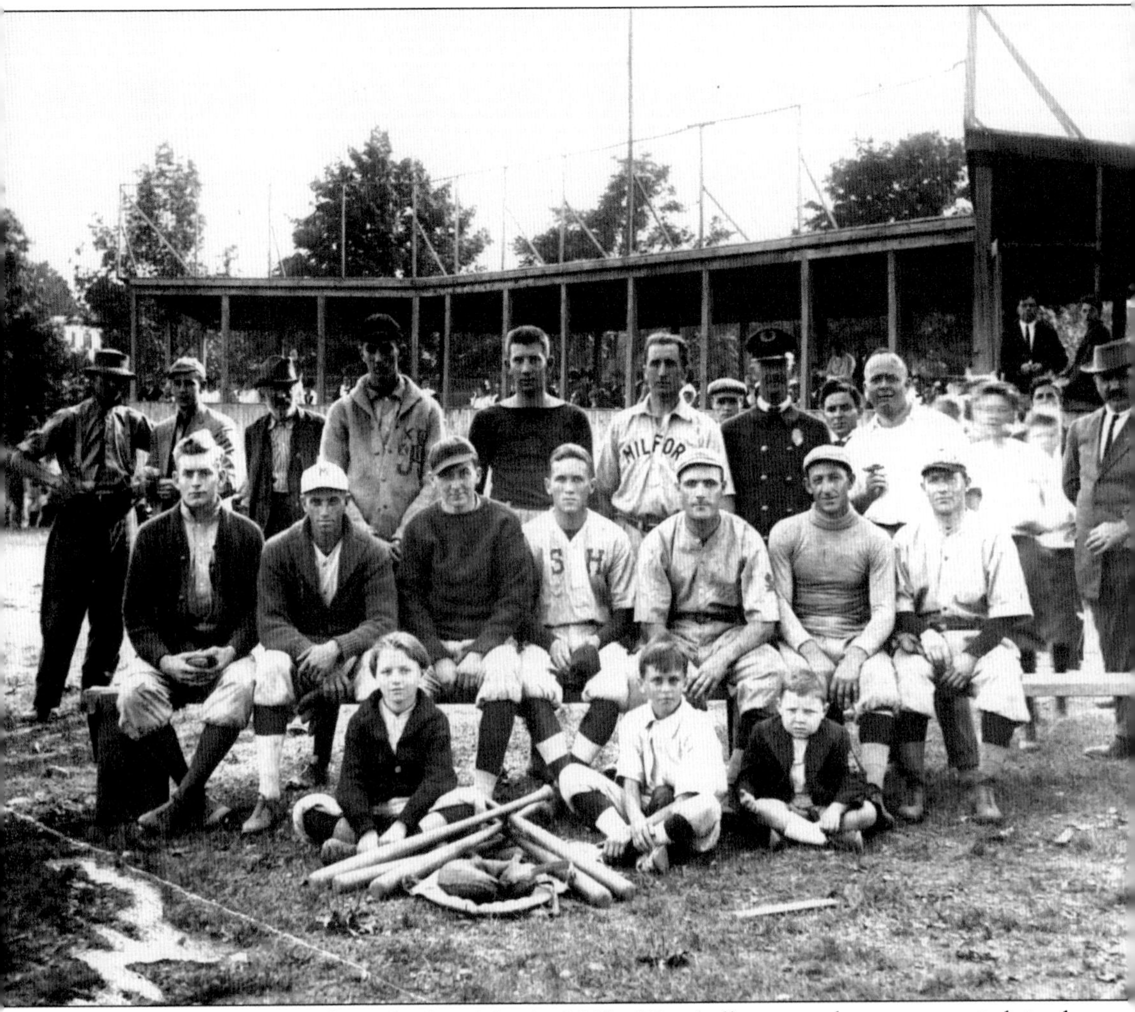

Bill Steele. "Big" Bill Steele played for the Milford Baseball team and went on to pitch in the major leagues for the St. Louis Cardinals and he Brooklyn Robins from 1910 to 1914. His life ended tragically when he was hit by a trolley car in 1949 in Overland, Missouri. Looks like Bill is standing to the right of good old Ernie Wood!.

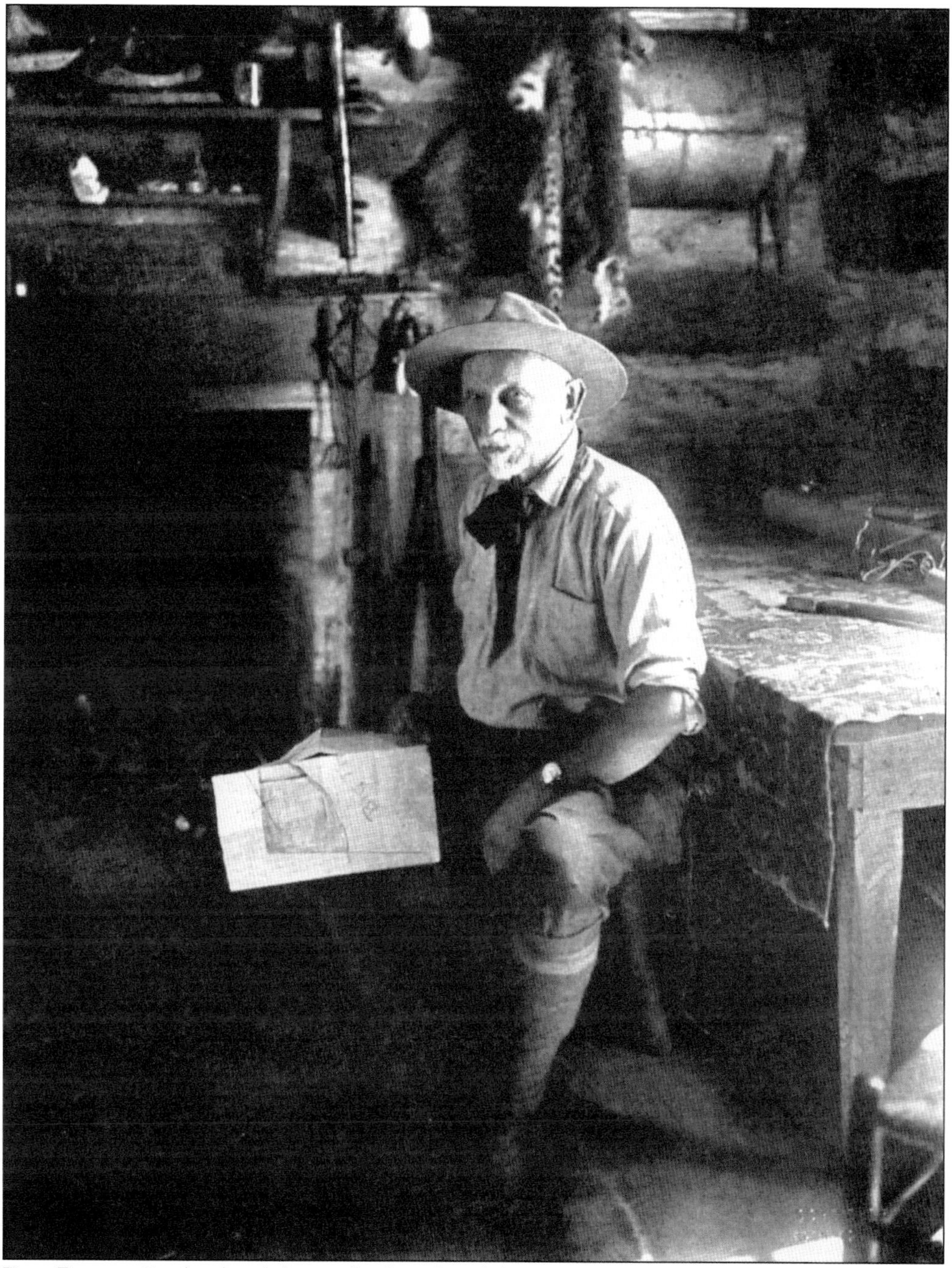

Dan Beard. Credited with being the founder of the Boy Scouts of America, Dan Beard ran an outdoor school for boys near Lackawaxen. A rugged man with a no-nonsense attitude, his goal was to turn boys into men and did not allow any "wimps or mollycoddles" into his camp.

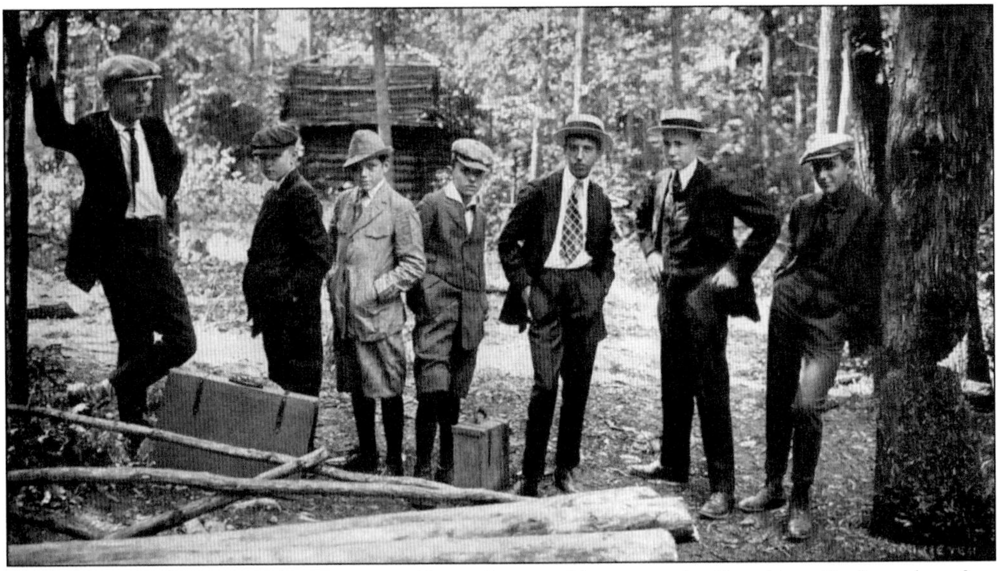

Dan Beard's Outdoor School for Boys. Pictured here are the "hooligans" when they first arrived at Dan Beard's camp.

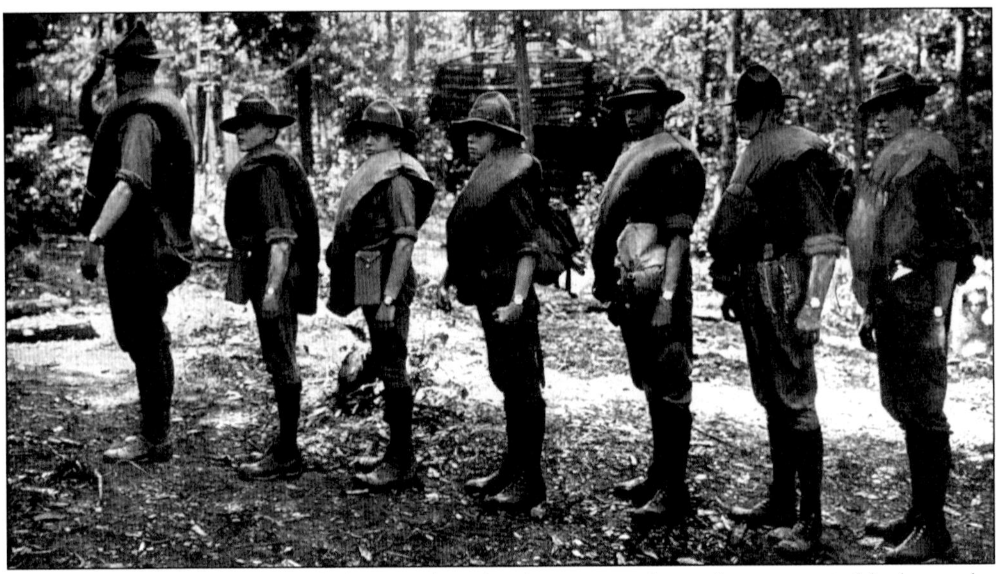

Transformation. By the end of camp, those hooligans were deemed unrecognizable due to the great transformation that occurred during their stay.

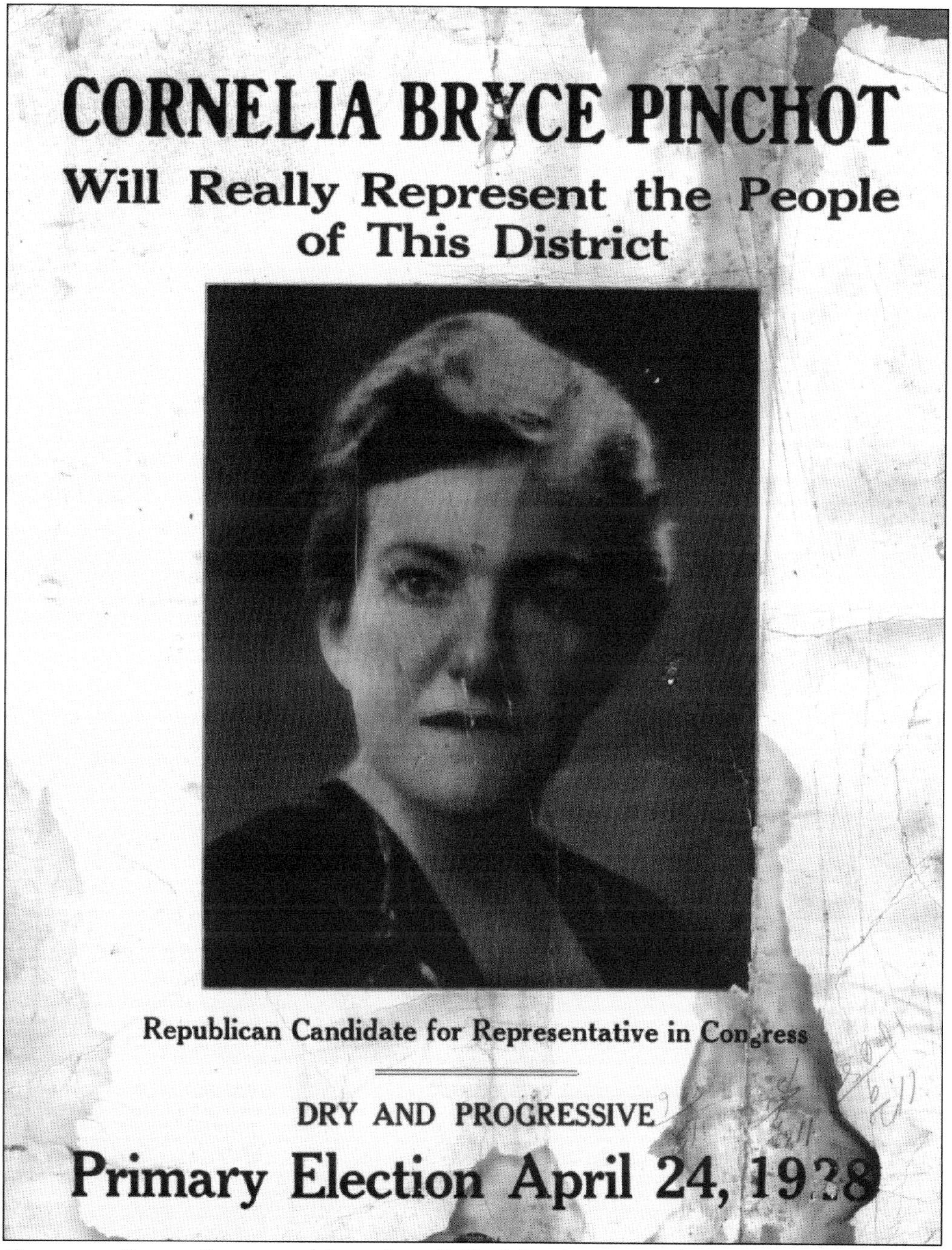

CORNELIA BRYCE PINCHOT. Married to Gifford Pinchot, Cornelia Bryce Pinchot rose to greatness in her own right. She ran for Congress and claimed to be "dry and progressive." She was very politically savvy and grew up around politics and politicians. Her bid for Congress in 1929 saw her carry Pike County but not the rest of the district. She once threw butter across the dining table at her husband while entertaining at Grey Towers. It is probably a good thing she did not drink if she exhibited this type of behavior while sober.

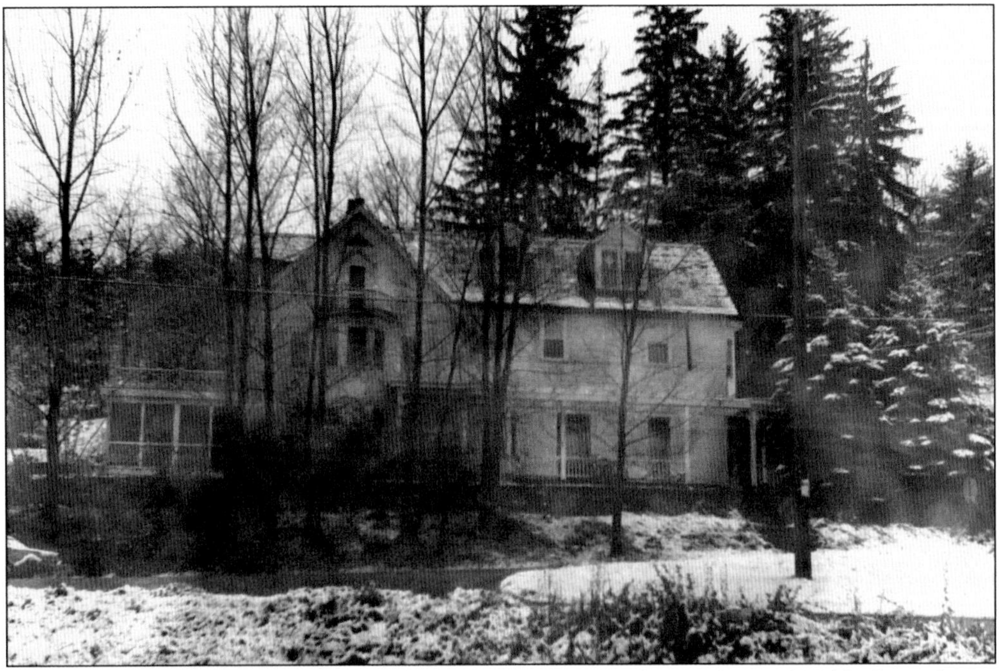

THE ANCHORAGE. Some interesting things were going on the outskirts of Milford at a house known as the anchorage when it was owned by the author Damon Knight. He, along with Milford residents Virginia Kidd and James Blish, were involved in coining a method of critiquing each others' work, known internationally to this day as "the Milford Method."

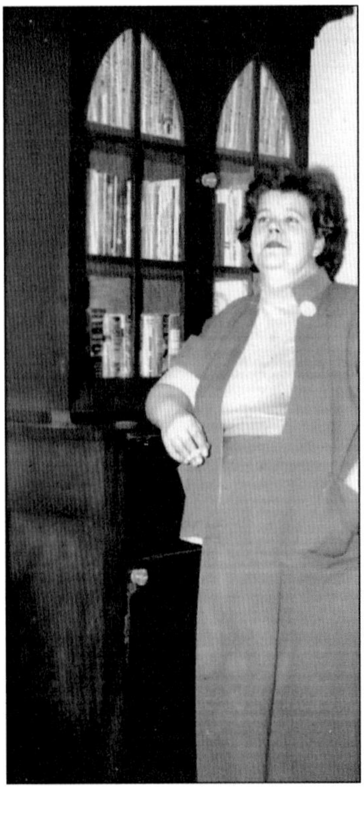

VIRGINIA KIDD. Virginia Kidd, legendary literary agent of science fiction, was an original member of the Milford science fiction community. The Virginia Kidd Agency, which she established in 1965 at Arrowhead, her home on East Harford Street in Milford, has continued to represent her clients since her death in 2004. (Courtesy of the Virginia Kidd Agency.)

FRANCIS CRAFT. Francis Craft grew up in an area of Pike County called Red Ridge. He became a medical doctor, as well as a priest. His travels took him to Sioux territory where he started an order of Native American nurses and nuns known as the Sioux Sisters.

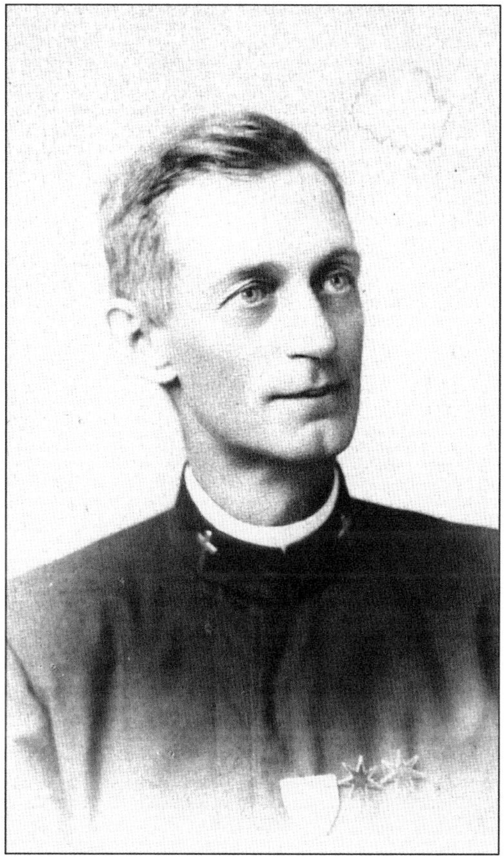

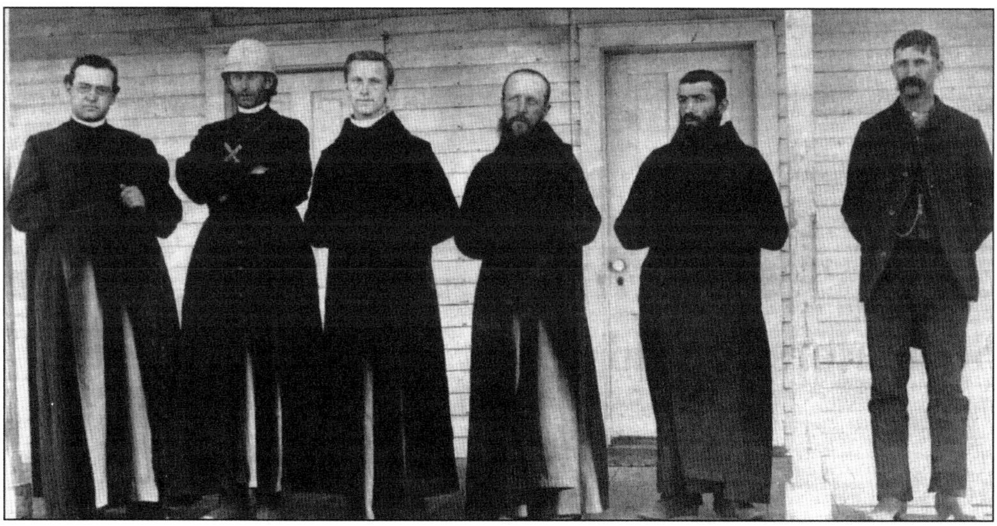

THE BENEDICTINES. Father Craft also served as liaison between the United States and the Native Americans at the Battle of Wounded Knee. He was injured in the fight and spent some of his recovery among the Sioux. He was greatly loved by the tribe and became their first white chief, Hovering Eagle.

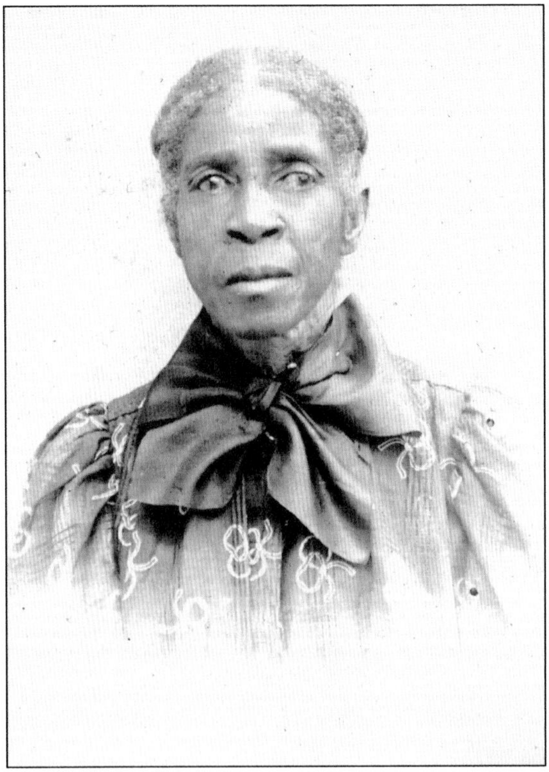

SARAH DAVIS. Sarah Davis was a woman of great fortitude and insight. She brought her family to predominantly white Milford in 1901. She had the savvy to apply for her husband, Abraham's, Civil War pension and used the money to purchase a home on High Street in Milford. She knew it would be easy for a black woman to find work in Milford at the inns and boardinghouses and also took in laundry.

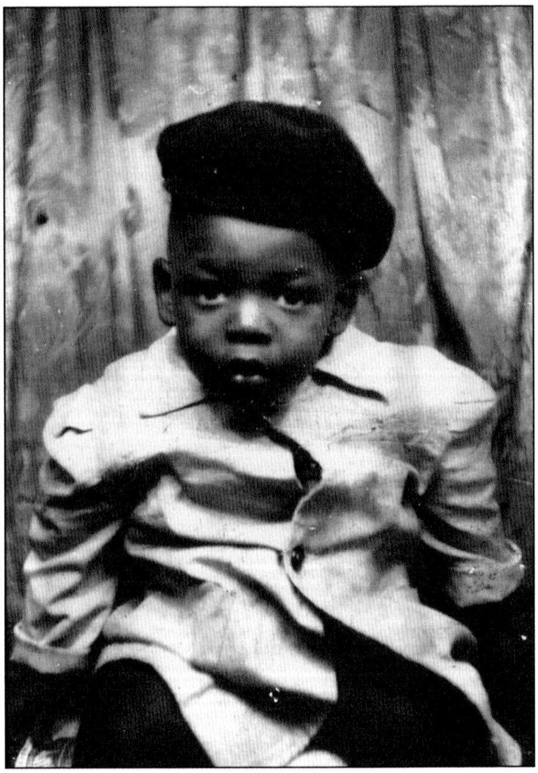

MILTON BAILEY. Sarah had four generations come to live in her house on High Street; her daughter Phoebe, granddaughter Beatrice, and great grandson Milton. All of these folks were well loved in town. Milton was a fine young man and was proud to have joined the U.S. Army and be sent off to Korea to defend his country. Milton was the only man from Milford to be killed in action. The town mourned his loss and tried to comfort his grieving mother and grandmother.

Eight

SCHOOL DAYS

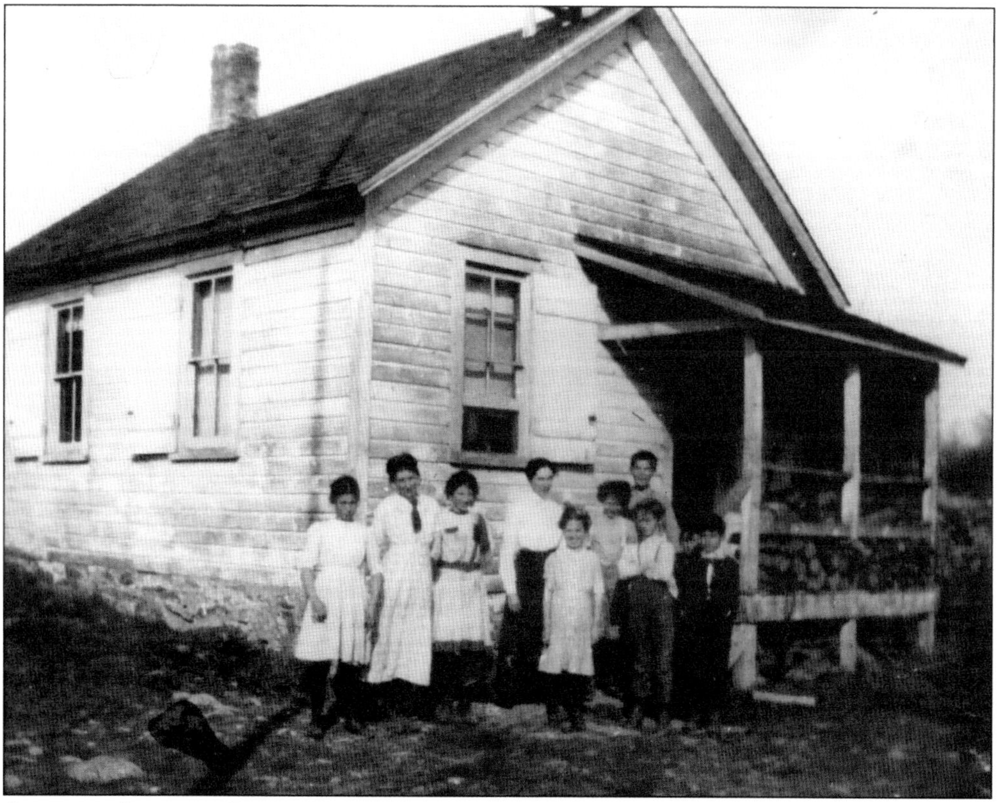

GERMAN SCHOOL, DINGMAN TOWNSHIP, 1919. This one-room schoolhouse was built before 1869. Pictured here in 1919 are Amy Auer, Arlene Simons, Jane Greening, Ross Kleinstuber, Harry Antaner, Jess Newfield, Joseph Greening, and Alber Simons. The teacher is Hazel Orben.

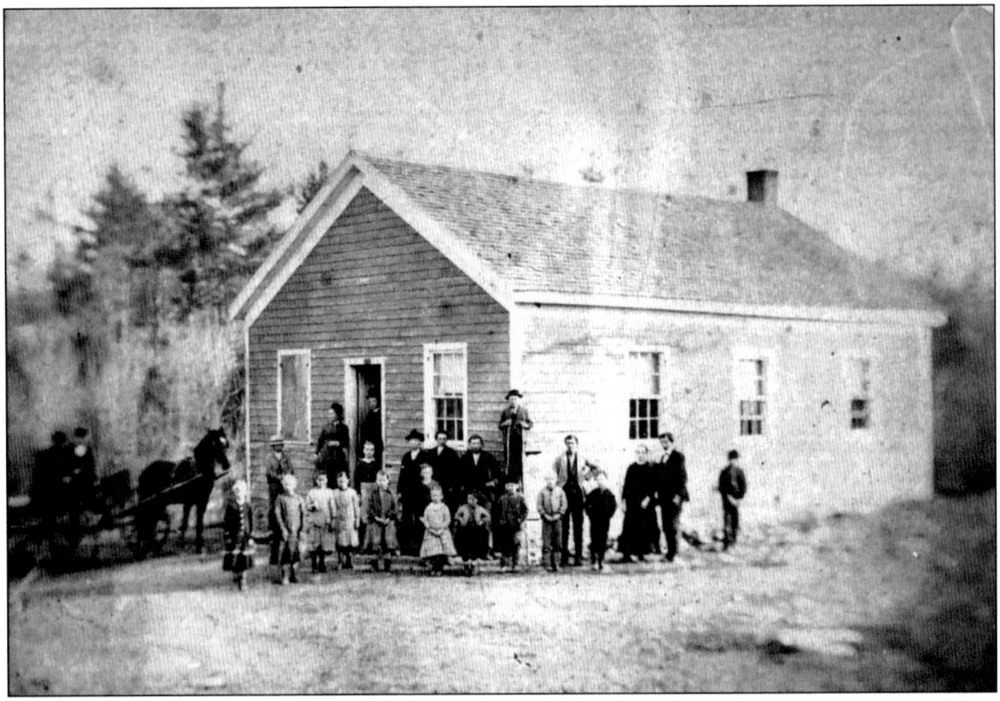

UNION SCHOOL, DINGMAN TOWNSHIP. This picture of the Union School was taken in 1905. The teacher is Louise Young.

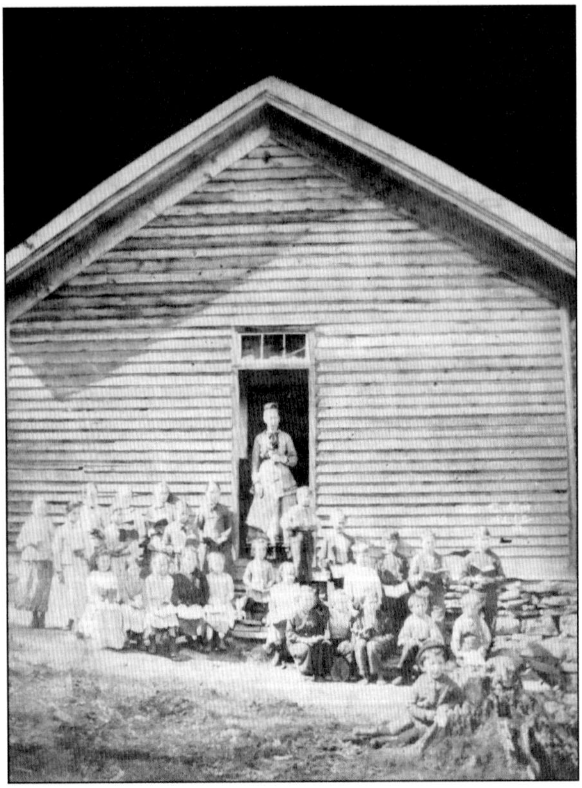

WORZEL SCHOOL. Built in 1878, the teacher of the Worzel School at the time of this picture is Rebecca Wood.

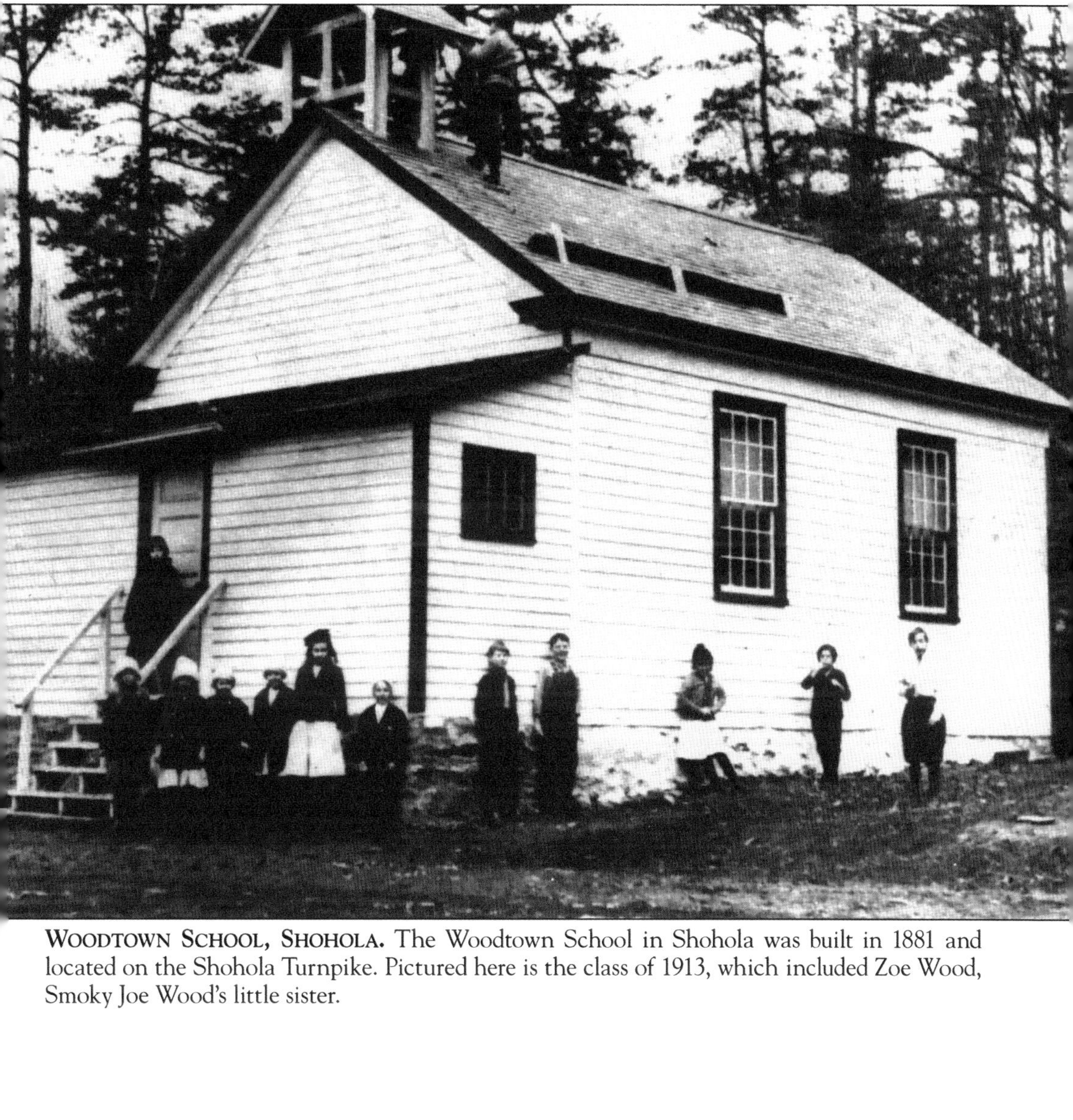

WOODTOWN SCHOOL, SHOHOLA. The Woodtown School in Shohola was built in 1881 and located on the Shohola Turnpike. Pictured here is the class of 1913, which included Zoe Wood, Smoky Joe Wood's little sister.

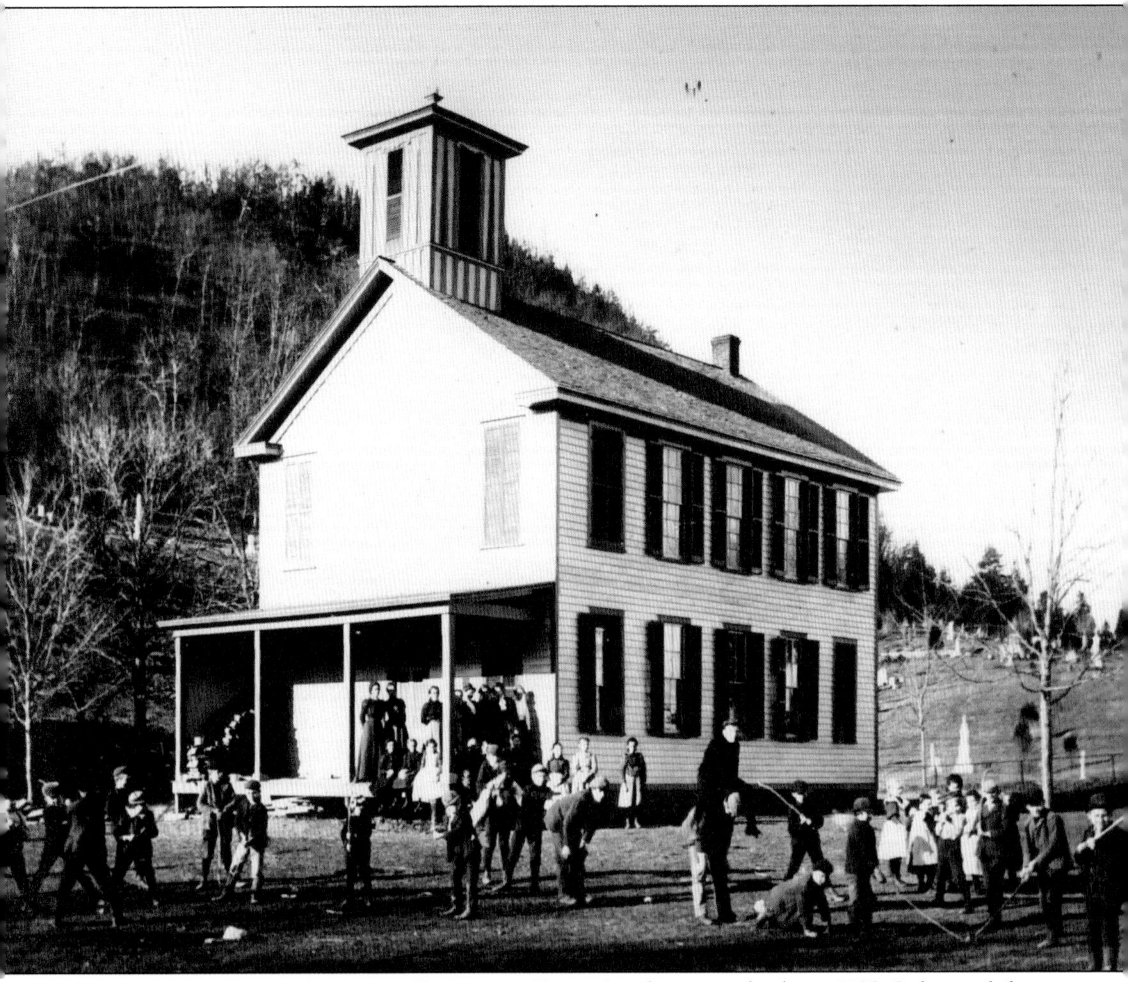

DINGMANS FERRY ACADEMY. Dingmans Ferry Academy was built in 1833. It burned down in the 1870s, was rebuilt in 1897, and then burned down once more.

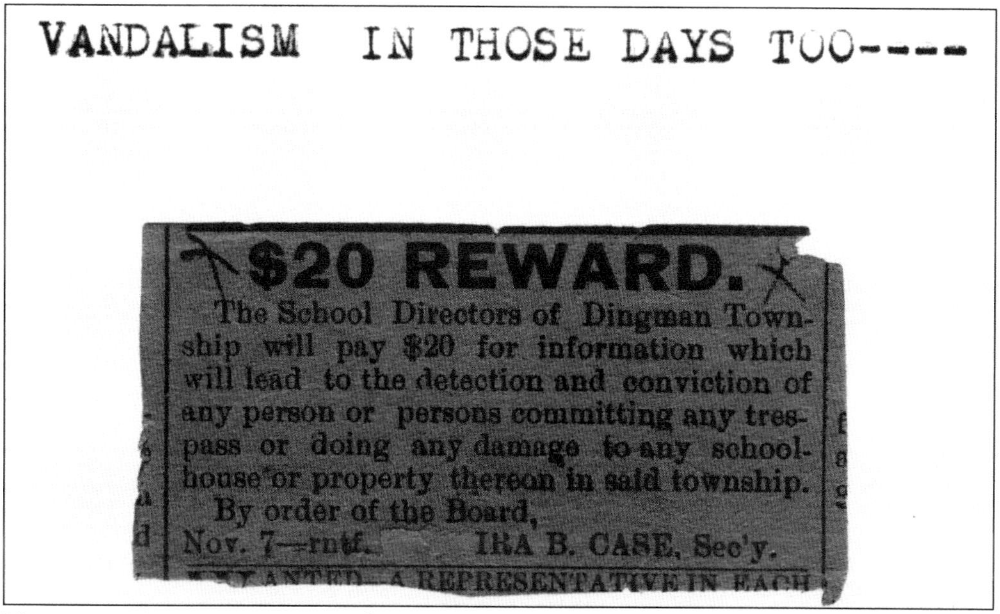

VANDALISM IN THOSE DAYS TOO----

$20 REWARD.

The School Directors of Dingman Township will pay $20 for information which will lead to the detection and conviction of any person or persons committing any trespass or doing any damage to any schoolhouse or property thereon in said township.

By order of the Board,

Nov. 7—mtf. IRA B. CASE, Sec'y.

NEWSPAPER ADVERTISEMENT. Perhaps the fate of the Dingmans Ferry Academy spurred the inclusion of this notice in the Pike County newspaper?

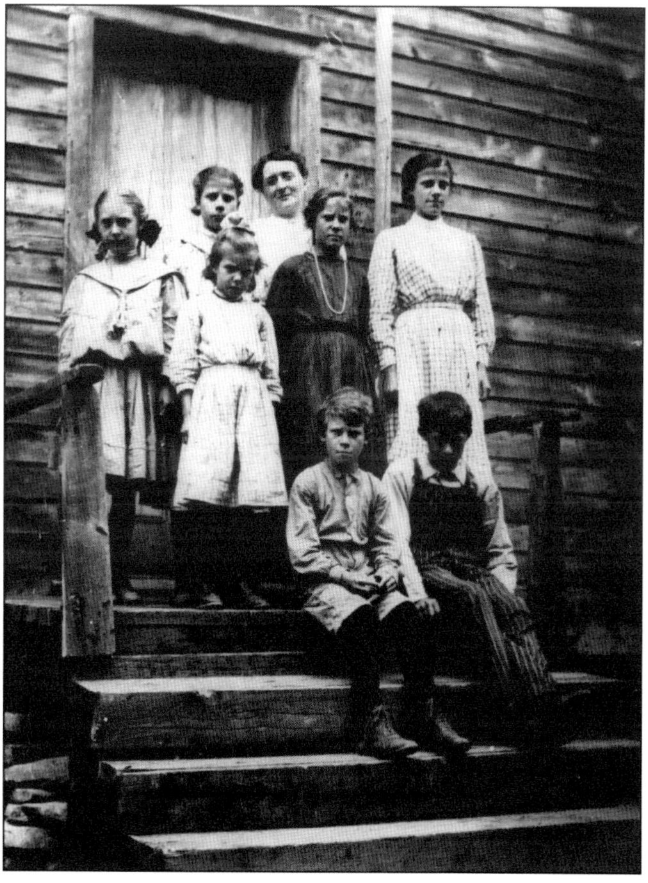

WOODTOWN SCHOOL. The class of the Woodtown School is pictured here. Shown are Willie Coursen, George Hinkel, Margaret Coursen, Alice Coursen, Harriet Coursen, Irene Haas, and their teacher Phoebe Wells.

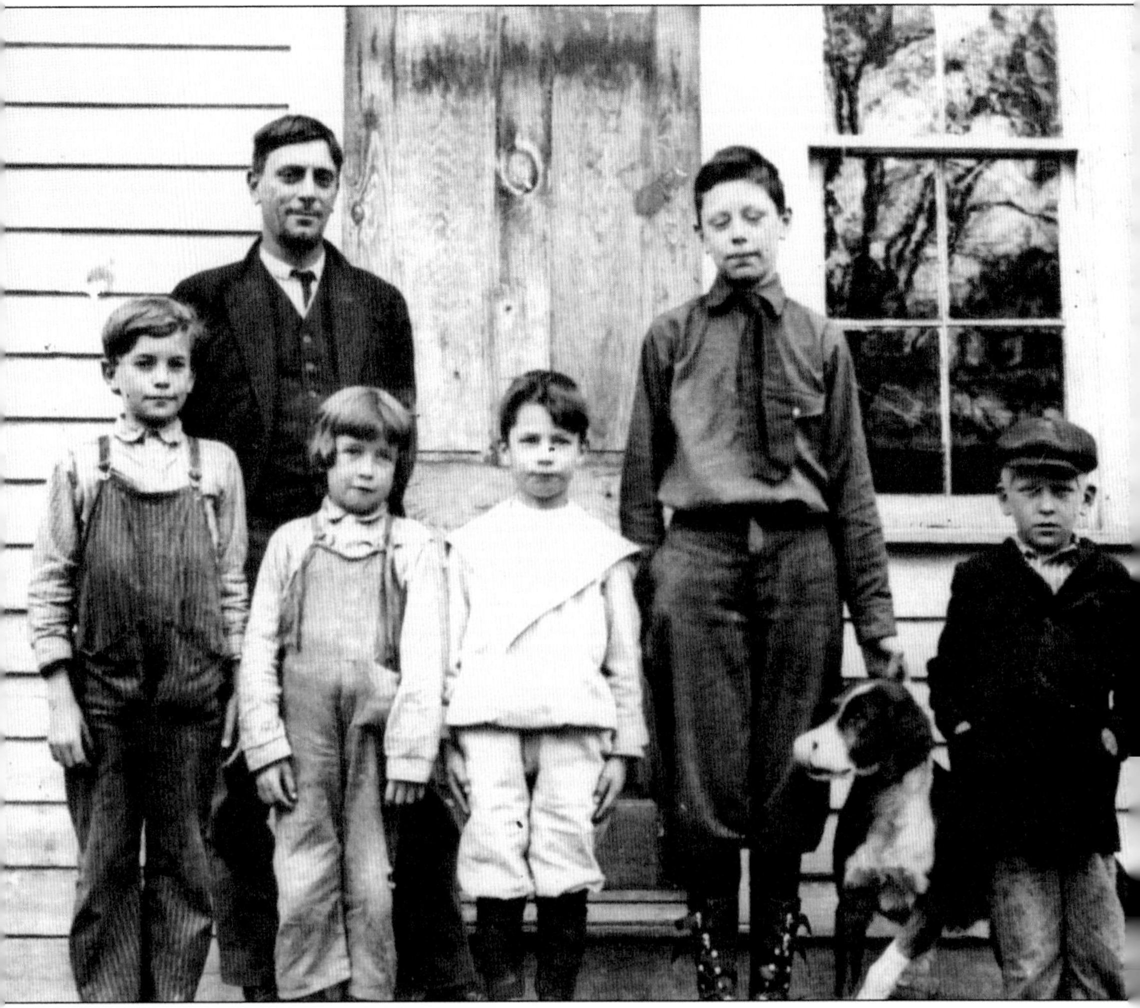

Silver Lake School. The Silver Lake School was another schoolhouse built for the children of Dingmans Ferry.

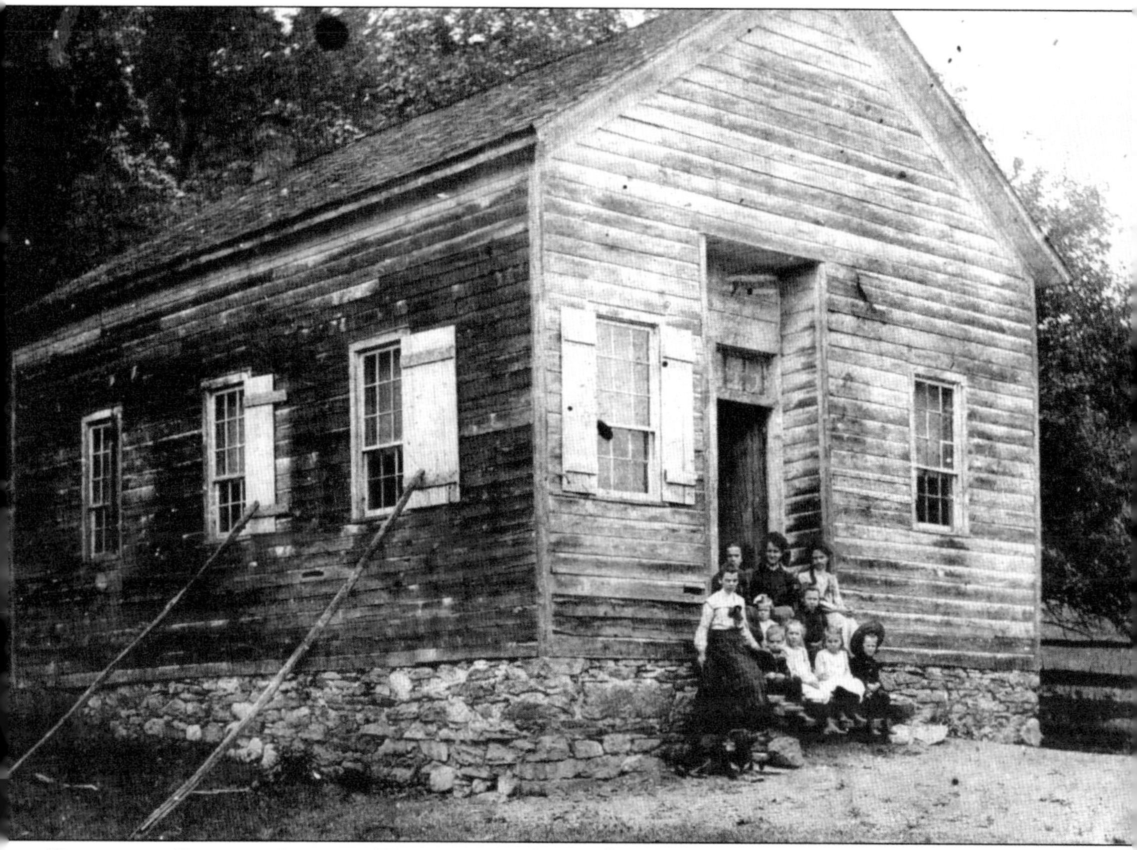

BRODHEAD SCHOOL, LEHMAN TOWNSHIP. Lulu Brodhead was the teacher at Brodhead School in 1904. Pictured here are her students Elizabeth Bensley, Mary Decker, Harry Niles, Diana Bensley, Mabel Bensley, Fannie Whitaker, Billie Briscoe, and Minnie Diermann.

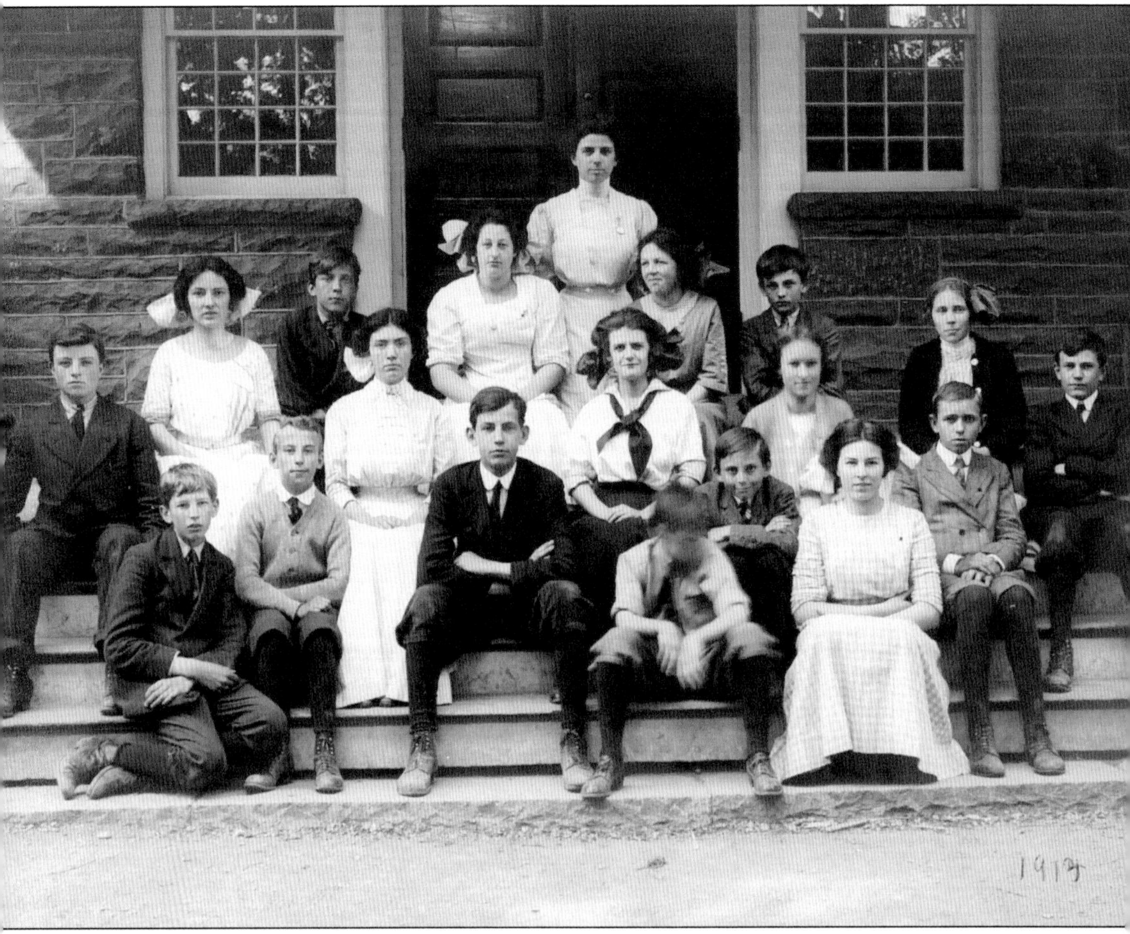

MILFORD PUBLIC SCHOOL. This photograph of the Milford Public School was taken in 1913 on the steps on the multiple-room schoolhouse built in Milford.

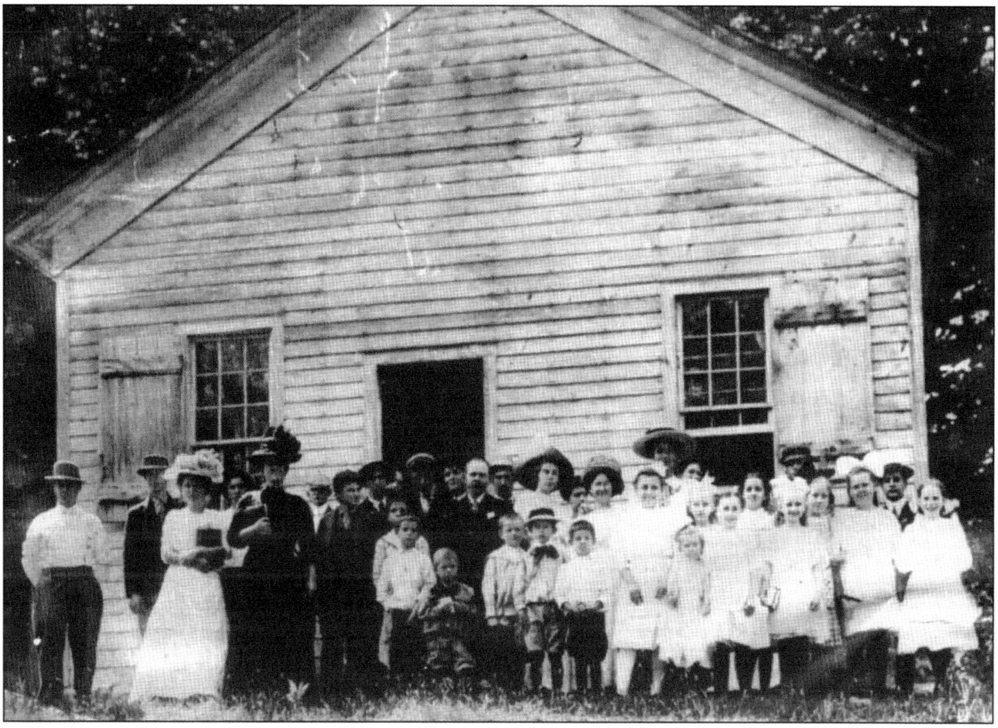

HEMLOCK GROVE SCHOOL, LEHMAN TOWNSHIP. This photograph is of the Sunday school class of 1910. Held at Egypt Mills, some of the attendees were summer boarders.

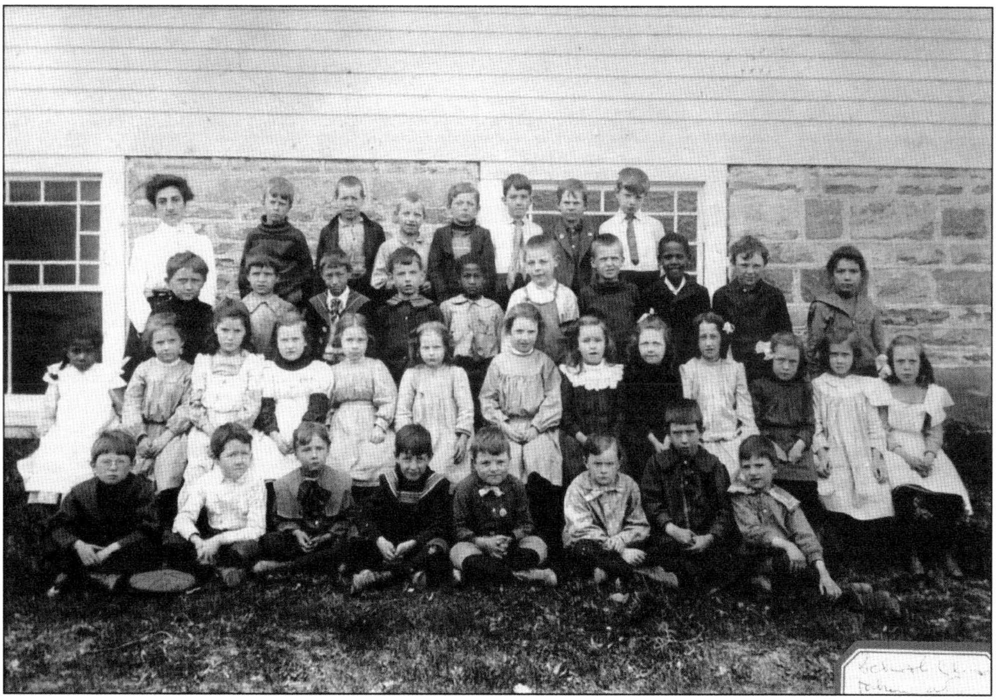

CLASS AT METHODIST CHURCH. This photograph was taken at the Methodist church in Milford.

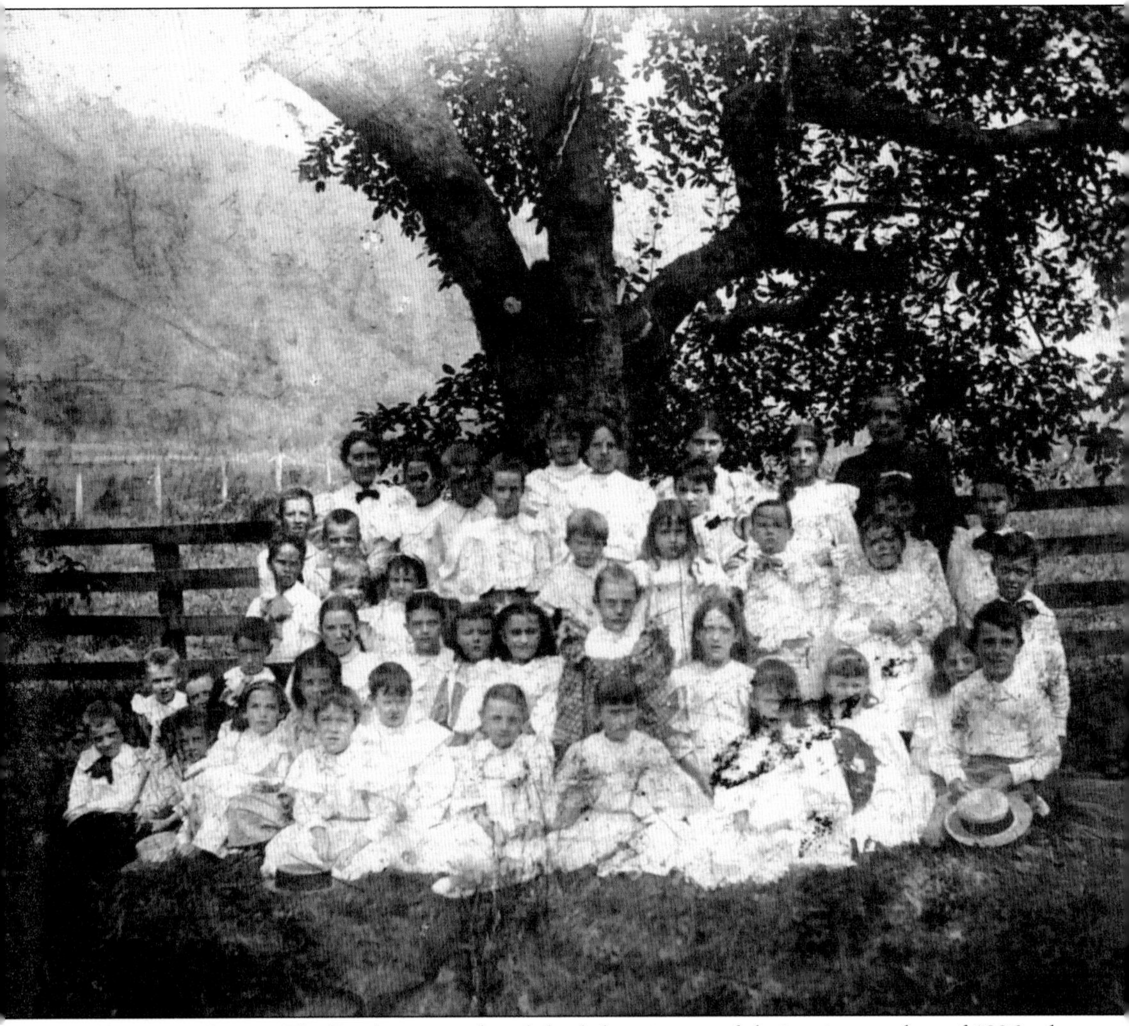

PRIMARY CLASS. The Presbyterian church had this picture of their primary class of 1896 taken at Model Farm.

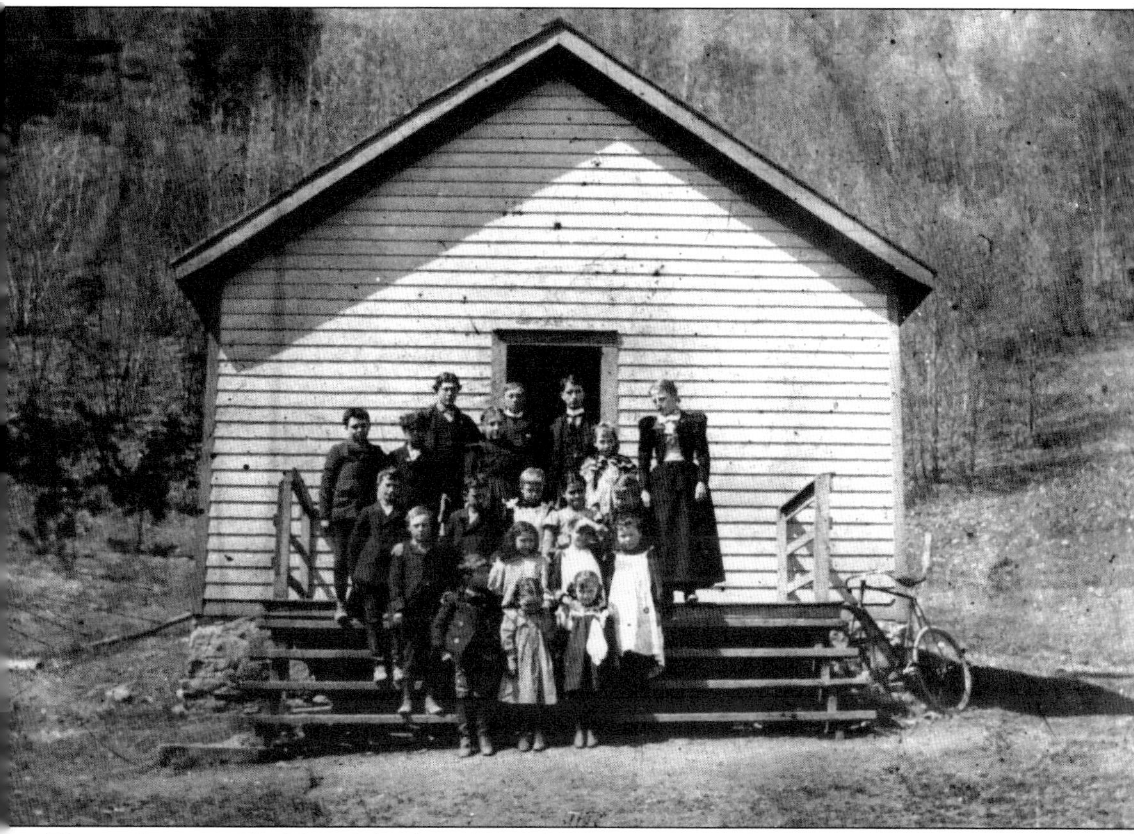

UTTER SCHOOL. The Utter School was located on Route 209 just below Milford. Pictured here is the class of 1899.

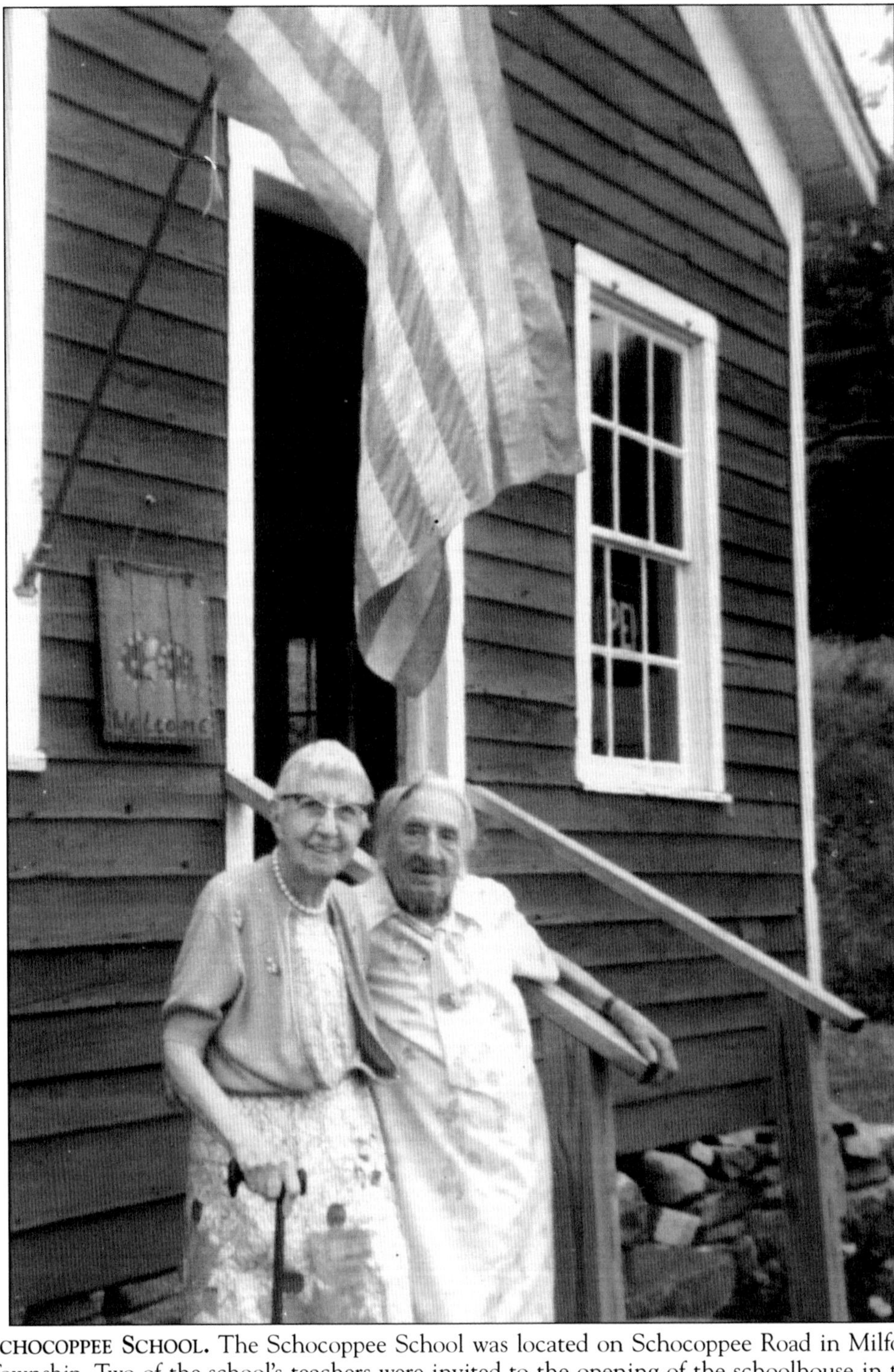

SCHOCOPPEE SCHOOL. The Schocoppee School was located on Schocoppee Road in Milford Township. Two of the school's teachers were invited to the opening of the schoolhouse in the early 1980s when it was restored and moved to a more reachable location by the Pike County Historical Society. Pictured here are Jean Struthers Newel (left), daughter of Jeannie Gourlay, and Florence Rochette Smith, who were both teachers near the dawn of the 20th century.

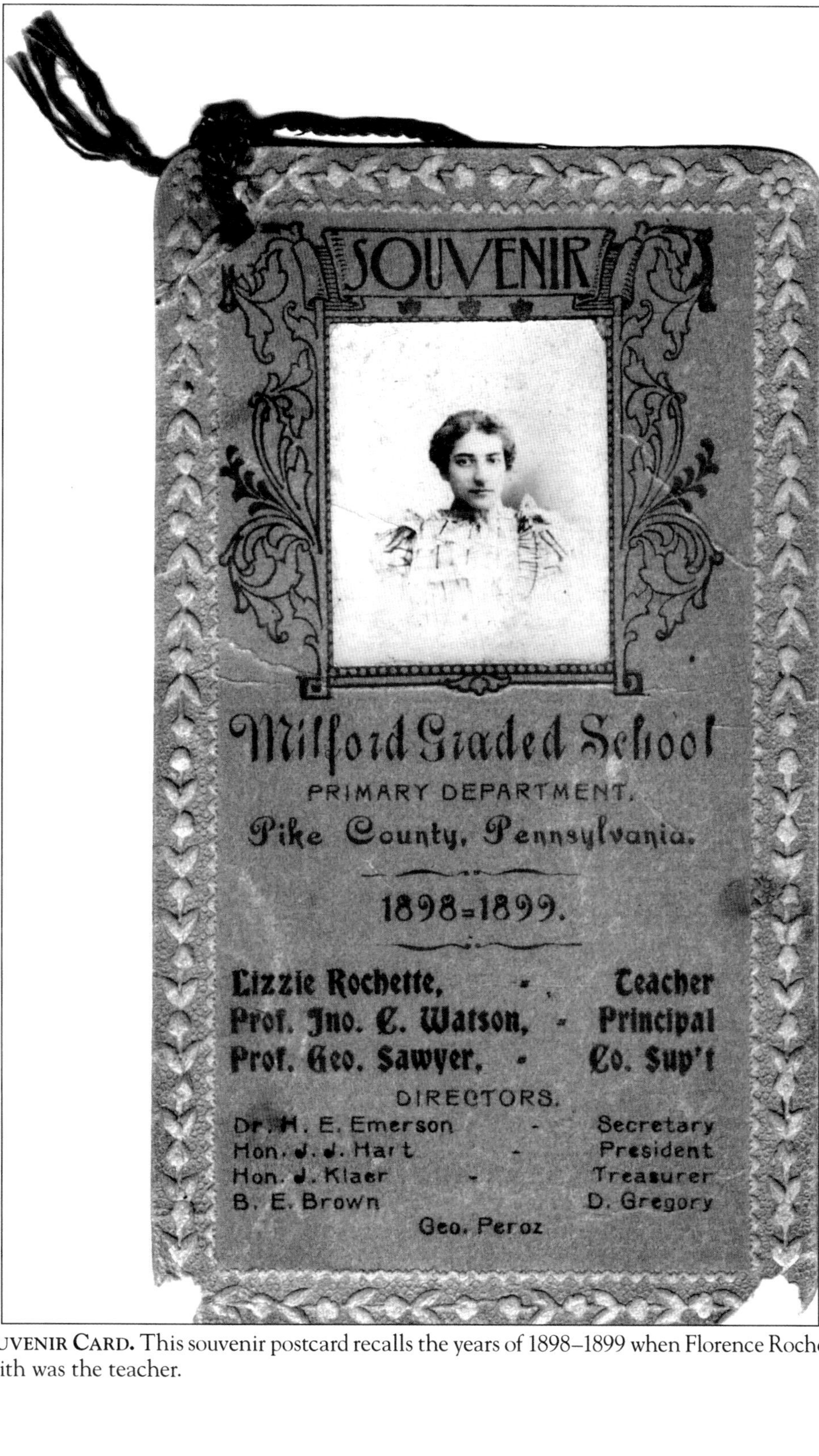

SOUVENIR CARD. This souvenir postcard recalls the years of 1898–1899 when Florence Rochette Smith was the teacher.

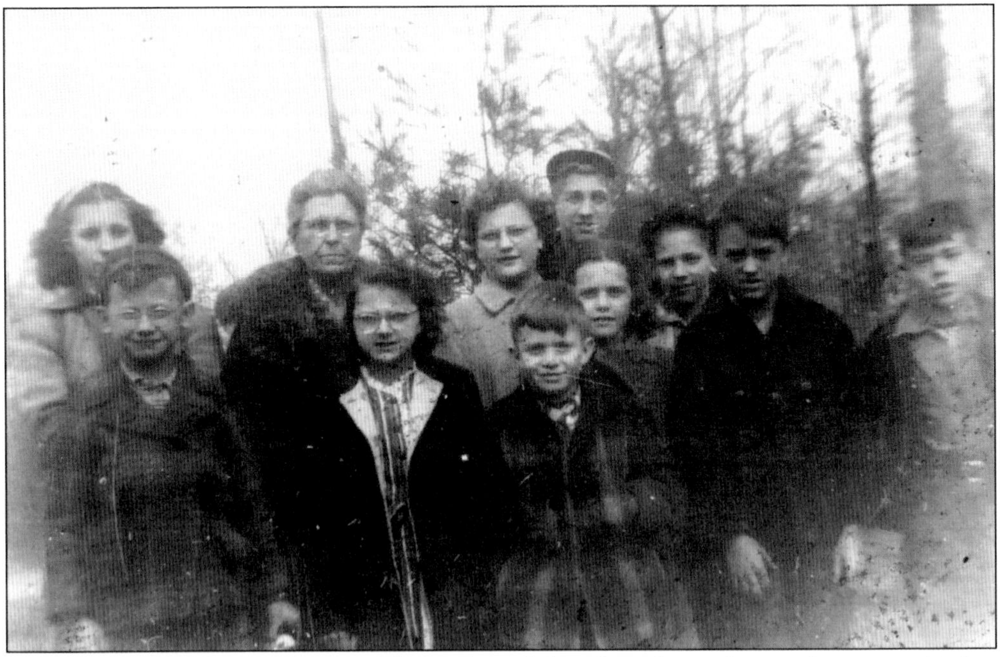

HUNTERS RANGE SCHOOL, 1940. The teacher of this class, Anna Courtright, poses with her pupils Jean Raith, Frances Fritz, Harry Ness, Richard Van Why, Donald Raith, and Gail and Robert ?.

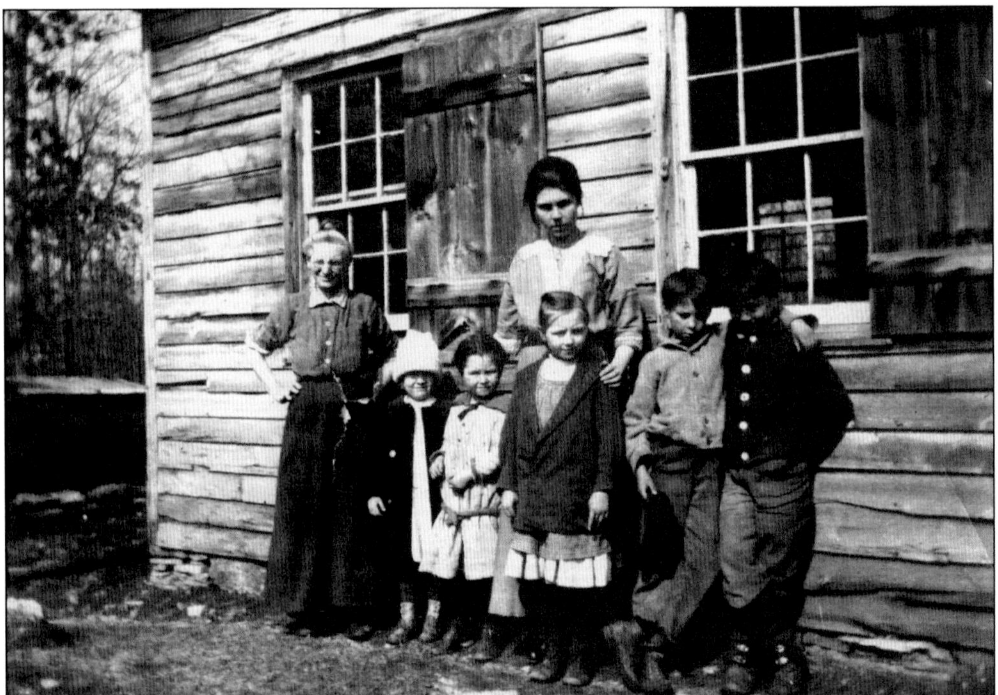

HUNTERS RANGE SCHOOL, PORTER TOWNSHIP, 1914. Margaret Courtright was the teacher, and she substituted for her sister Anna from time to time. The pupils pictured are Jeffrey Smith, Henry Miller, Ruth Miller, Mattie Miller, and Lina Van Why.

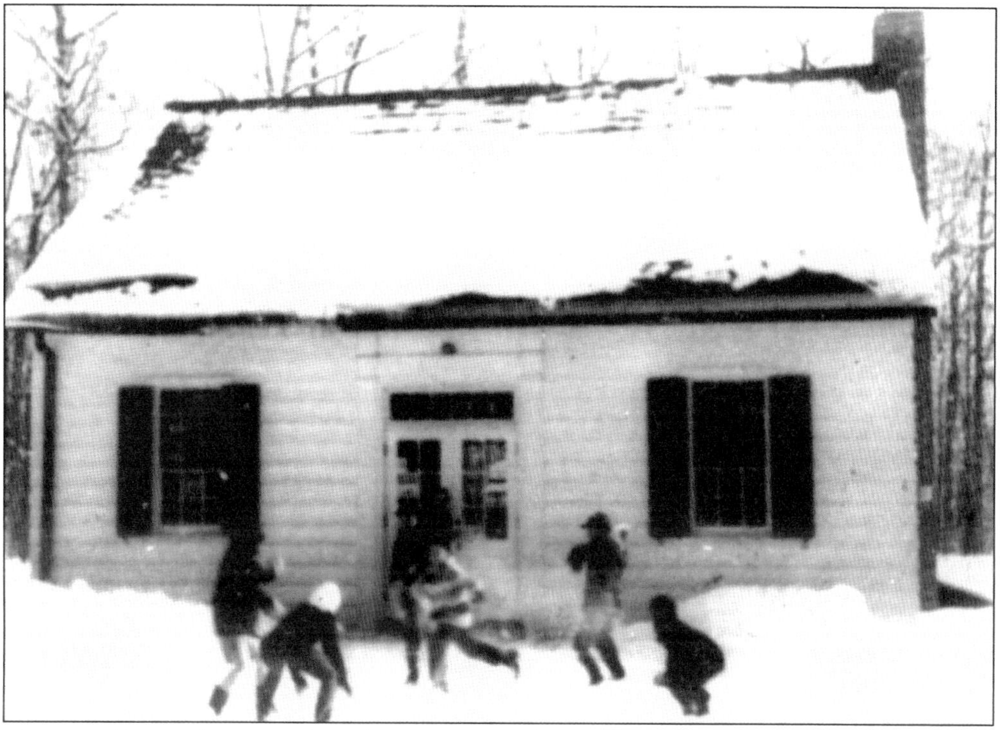

HUNTERS RANGE SCHOOL. The schoolhouse was also used for township meetings and elections. It closed in the 1940s.

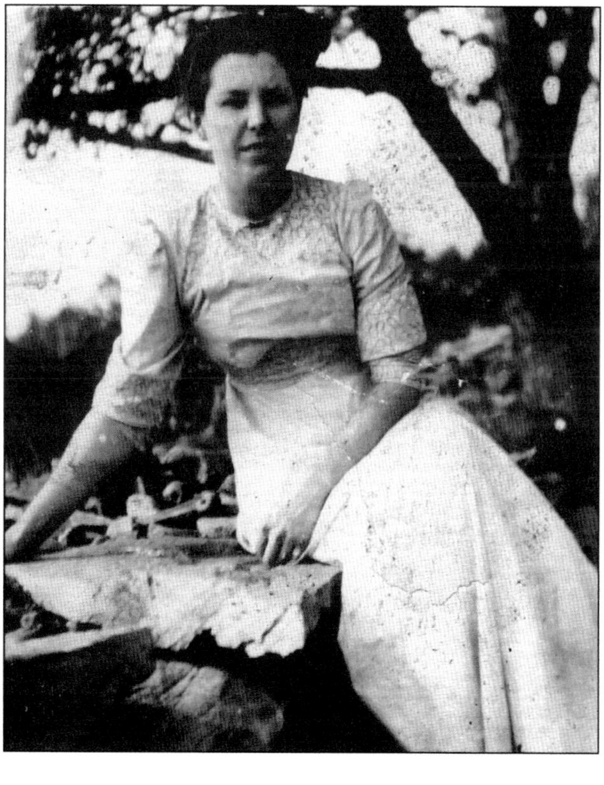

ANNA COURTRIGHT. Anna Courtright taught at the school for 20 years.

Consistent with our mission to preserve history on a local level, this book was printed in South Carolina on American-made paper and manufactured entirely in the United States. Products carrying the accredited Forest Stewardship Council (FSC) label are printed on 100 percent FSC-certified paper.

MADE IN THE USA